PUBLICATIONS OF THE BUREAU OF BUSINESS
AND ECONOMIC RESEARCH

Previously published in this series:

THE NATURE OF COMPETITION IN GASOLINE DISTRIBUTION
AT THE RETAIL LEVEL (1951)
by Ralph Cassady, Jr., and Wylie L. Jones

THE ROLE OF MERGERS IN THE GROWTH OF LARGE FIRMS (1953)
by J. Fred Weston

THE PACIFIC COAST MARITIME SHIPPING INDUSTRY
1930–1948
VOLUME I: AN ECONOMIC PROFILE (1952)
VOLUME II: AN ANALYSIS OF PERFORMANCE (1954)
by Wytze Gorter and George H. Hildebrand

(Published jointly with the Institute of Industrial Relations
Southern Division, University of California)

THE MEXICAN PETROLEUM INDUSTRY, 1938–1950

by J. Richard Powell

Publications of the
BUREAU OF BUSINESS AND ECONOMIC RESEARCH
University of California

The MEXICAN PETROLEUM INDUSTRY

1938
–
1950

1956
UNIVERSITY OF CALIFORNIA PRESS
Berkeley and Los Angeles

University of California Press, Berkeley and Los Angeles, California

Cambridge University Press, London, England

Copyright, 1956, by The Regents of the University of California

L. C. Catalog Card No. 56–5138

Printed in the United States of America
By the University of California Printing Department

This Book is Affectionately Dedicated to
HOPE and LARRY
Who Contributed with Work and Faith

Acknowledgments

I wish to express my thanks to the many individuals whose ideas and efforts have been incorporated in this volume. It is a difficult task to pick out individual names when one is indebted to so many, but my gratitude goes especially to Professor Warren C. Scoville for his incisive but kindly criticism and for the inspiration derived from a good many years' association with him. Professor Ralph Cassady, Jr., has given me much encouragement in this work. I want to thank Professors Dudley F. Pegrum, Robert Tannenbaum, and George H. Hildebrand, who read the manuscript in its various stages and offered beneficial criticisms and suggestions, and also Miss Pat Maass and Mrs. Dorothy Horn, who typed the manuscript, and Mrs. Grace Stimson, who carefully edited the study.

Almost inevitably an author's greatest debt is to his family, who suffer, challenge, aid, inspire, and admire his efforts. My gratitude and thanks go most to my wife, Hope Mortensen Powell, and to our son, Lawrence C. Powell.

J. R. P.

Contents

Tables

xiii

Chapter I

INTRODUCTION

On March 18, 1938, the Mexican government made the decision to expropriate the major part of the nation's petroleum industry and to operate it through a government agency. On that date, with shocking suddenness, it told between fifteen and twenty of the largest petroleum companies, including all those considered to represent pernicious "foreign economic imperialism," that all their property and equipment being used to exploit, transport, refine, or sell petroleum and its products had been expropriated. The shock did not arise because there had been no preliminary steps leading to the expropriation, or no handwriting on the wall; the shock for the oil companies lay in the fact that they little dreamed that Mexico would have the fortitude or audacity to attempt to operate the industry without the aid of foreigners.

Nearly forty years of oil activity in Mexico had instilled in the companies a sense of vested interest in the country, an acceptance of their status as the fountains of energy for prime movers, and, perhaps, a feeling that they were the torchbearers of civilization in a benighted land. At least from the time when the first great deposits of oil were discovered, the companies represented themselves as one of God's gifts to the Mexican people, and this was true in a sense. The Mexicans wished to convince the world and themselves that they constituted a sovereign nation with certain associated rights, privileges, and duties. If the righteousness of each party was not definitely established by the act of expropriation or in the subsequent polemics between the Mexican government and the oil companies, at least their positions became clarified in the bitter controversy.

Has the Mexican experiment in handling its own petroleum industry been successful? It is the purpose of this investigation to examine the petroleum problem of Mexico, to describe the organization and operation of the industry under Mexican management, and to indicate to what extent Mexico was successful in achieving the objectives of expropriation. The ramifications of the answer are deeply rooted in the history of the petroleum problem and in the history of the Mexican people.

Why is it desirable to investigate the Mexican petroleum industry and to attempt to answer this question? A great deal has been written on the industry, but much of the writing has been done in a spirit of heated controversy. Aside from satisfying curiosity, an impartial study is desirable because the question of success or failure is important to both Mexicans and Americans. From the standpoint of the availability of petroleum supplies, it is important that Americans know the prospects of Mexican sources of this strategic material. It is of concern to Mexicans to see how well they met their own rapidly rising consumption requirements, and how expropriation affected their international financial position and the dollar problem afflicting them.

The question is important from the standpoint of determining the future relationship between the Mexican government and other industries with heavy foreign investment, such as mining and electric utilities. The unqualified success of the nationalized petroleum industry would be an indication to Mexico that her period of financial and industrial infancy was over, and that the country would lose nothing by being weaned from foreign operation of other industries. There would be an incentive to regulate such industries more severely, and, perhaps, resort to outright expropriation at an opportune moment to satisfy the vociferous groups crying out against foreign economic imperialism. On the other hand, outright failure would tend to induce a more liberal policy toward industry dominated by foreign investors, which would again make the country attractive to capital that had become chary of investment in Mexico. Foreign capital might then have another heyday, but undoubtedly on a plane considerably below that enjoyed before the 'thirties.

The success of Mexico's experiment is important, too, from the standpoint of the example it sets for policy in other Latin American countries. These republics look upon Mexico as a leader in social reform. The experience of their northern sister is likely to have a strong influence upon their own attitudes toward foreign capital, particularly in the oil industry. In Colombia, although there is little likelihood of expropriation, the government has taken measures to assume control of portions of the industry as concessions expire. But, apparently unwilling to shut out completely the companies whose contracts are terminating, Colombia has granted new concessions. In Argentina the government has participated in the petroleum industry since its inception. Rising nationalism in the country has been accompanied by an increasing share in national production by the government agency, *Yacimientos Petrolíferos Fiscales.* In 1945 the government's share was more than two-thirds.[1] If Mexico should find the way to success, Argentina would probably find it easy to follow by taking over the industry completely. The degree of success in Mexico is also likely to influence tax and control policies in Venezuela.

Finally, Mexico's handling of her oil industry is significant as a laboratory study in government participation in business. To the Mexicans this is of particular importance, since one of the revolutionary aims was to introduce more planning and control in industry. From a broader viewpoint, however, the conclusions of this study cannot be applied as either approbation or condemnation of government ownership and operation. The study is significant in this respect only because it shows the results obtained by one government in a given situation with certain ethical standards, laws, customs, and objectives. The conclusions will have the value and limitations of all lessons taught by history in the broad uncontrolled laboratory of social relations.

At this point it is necessary to define the scope of this study. It is intended primarily to cover the accomplishments of *Petróleos Mexicanos,* commonly known as *Pemex,* the government agency set up in 1938 to manage and operate the expropriated oil industry. To understand the period after the expropriation and to determine the objectives and ideals sought through expropriation, it will be necessary to examine the history of the country and of the industry. An attempt will be made to evaluate the progress toward these goals by taking into consideration the organization and administration of the industry; activities and developments in exploration, production, transportation, refining, and marketing; labor policies and relations; financial policies; and the general social effects. It is not a primary concern of the study to evaluate expropriation objectives and ideals as desirable or undesirable, for to do this would be to evaluate the whole institutional organization and the social values of Mexico.

There will be no attempt to pass judgment on the act of expropriation, on the events leading to it, or on the subsequent negotiations for settlement with the expropriated companies, except insofar as the payments finally decided upon affect the finances of the

[1] For numbered notes to chap. i, see p. 241.

organization. For the purposes of this study such an evaluation is neither necessary nor desirable. In this controversy the attacks have been so bitter, the positions taken are so diametrically opposite, and the difficulty is so recent that it is well to let this bone of contention be buried, particularly at the present time when coöperation between Mexico and the United States is highly desirable. It is better to leave it to be unearthed by historians at a later date.

Since it is axiomatic that social studies cannot be neatly confined in mutually exclusive fields, points that are not strictly economic in character will not be shunned if they lead to a better understanding of developments in the petroleum industry. The primary aspect of the study is economic; and, basically, the project is a study of Pemex as a piece of economic machinery in the social life of the people. However, the achievements of Pemex are to be measured by the criteria of the aims of expropriation.

Now that the general nature and limitations of the problem have been described, it is necessary to define and analyze the problem by considering the broad historical background of Mexico and of its petroleum industry in order to determine the objectives and goals of expropriation.

Chapter II

THE HISTORICAL
BACKGROUND

Even a superficial analysis of the objectives of expropriation reveals that the aims were not entirely economic, nor were these
broader aims entirely compatible with the economic aims. It is
appropriate, in judging the achievements of expropriation, to consider the noneconomic objectives desired by Mexicans. For this
reason, one must have an understanding of the social milieu. Cultural differences between the United States and Mexico complicate
an American's problem in analyzing and judging the achievements
in the Mexican petroleum industry. Success from a Mexican's
viewpoint may differ materially from an American's concept. An
evaluation of the Mexican accomplishments in owning and operating the industry must take into consideration the situation faced
by the country when it expropriated the oil companies: the specific
problems that the Mexicans were trying to solve, the relevant institutions and traditions, and the long-run and short-run objectives of expropriation. An understanding of these factors will provide the basis for evaluating the Mexican efforts.

A review of some of the relevant features of Mexican history will
help provide a foundation for judgment.

Foreigners unfamiliar with Mexican history are apt to mis-
understand the petroleum reform, which was, in part, a delayed
reaction to the economic and social policies of Porfirio Díaz and
only one aspect of a general reform movement that affected other
facets of economic and social life. The seeds of this reform movement were sown in colonial Mexico long before independence.[1]
French Jacobins, fresh from freeing themselves from tyranny by
revolution and regicide, loosed their propaganda in America with
the idea of liberating the Spanish dominions and uniting them
with France. In spite of the Inquisition, revolutionary literature

---

[1] For numbered notes to chap. ii, see pp. 241–243.

5

circulated in Mexico. In the University of Mexico the philosophies of Descartes and Locke began to displace scholasticism. Intellectuals among the creoles and mestizos furtively read the works of Montesquieu, Voltaire, Rousseau, and others whose ideas caught their imagination.[2]

When Hidalgo led his Indians in the abortive uprising of September, 1810, he found that he was leading a social revolutionary movement of the lower classes directed against the feudalism imposed by the Spaniards after the conquest.[3] The few creoles in the movement had anticipated a military rebellion against the *gachupines* (the Spanish-born social hierarchy); but when their hand was forced prematurely, they discovered that nothing less than a social upheaval had been put in motion.

The leaders of the revolutionary movement failed because they undertook too much.[4] In fighting for the restoration of Indian lands, for racial equality, and for abolition of the privileges of the clergy and the army, the revolutionists alienated the landowners, the creole officials, the Church hierarchy, and the army, all of whom joined in the countermovement to suppress the revolution. After defeat in this primary stage, the creoles, long tired of the burdens of the Spanish government and of the privileges of the *gachupines*, finally felt strong enough to control the lower classes. They took up the cause of independence with the aid of the higher clergy and the conservatives, who had been alarmed by the radical revolution of 1820 in Spain.[5] These groups eliminated royalist strength from Mexico in a matter of months.[6]

The winning of independence, however, brought no relief to the oppressed lower classes, who had to wait until the War of the Reform for partial respite. Meanwhile, Mexico suffered more than thirty-five years of anarchy and civil war as the mestizos and creoles fought for control of the government, the army exploited any government it could, and the Church extended its power and wealth.[7]

In 1855, Santa Anna, who had dominated the political scene for a quarter-century, was overthrown by popular revolt. The progressive and conscientious Benito Juárez soon entered the stage to become the principal figure until he died in 1872. The *Ley Juárez* (Juárez Law) of 1855 abolished special law courts outside the state system, with the exception of the clerical and military courts, whose functions were closely restricted.[8] In 1856 the *Ley Lerdo* prohibited civil and religious corporations from owning any land except that used in the functions of the institution. The Constitution of 1857 dealt such a blow to special privilege that it brought on three years of civil war. During the war, Juárez struck at the legal position of the opposition by issuing his *Leyes de Reforma* (Laws of Reform) of 1859, which nationalized all remaining Church property, suppressed religious orders, and separated Church and state.[9] The defeated conservatives turned to Napoleon III, and French intervention followed the civil war chaos.

It was not until 1867, after Juárez had overthrown Maximilian and restored peace, that reform really began to take shape. The movement ended with the sudden death of Juárez in 1872,[10] and Díaz took over the presidency by revolution in 1876. The two principal objectives of the reform movement had been to promote democracy and stimulate economic development, but Díaz sacrificed the first in order to attain the second.[11] Through a period of thirty-five years, except for 1880–1884, Díaz remained at the head of the government and carried on a policy of buying or killing enemies in order to establish the peace necessary to the country's economic development.[12] He proposed to convert Mexico into a capitalistic country.[13] The cumulative errors in his methods of economic development brought his downfall and created attitudes continuing to the present time. To establish peace, he summarily executed unrepentant conspirators and subversive leaders; he appeased recalcitrant large landowners by opening the way for them to acquire greater land concentrations; he played off against one another dangerous elements in the political and military scene; he won over the clergy by ignoring the anticlerical laws of the reform period; he stifled active press opposition; and he picked a congress that would obey his orders.[14] Banditry and turbulence, except in a few desert areas and along the frontier, disappeared under zealous scourging by his magistrates and mounted police.

Díaz' ambition was to help Mexico economically by developing her resources in the pattern of the United States.[15] He invited foreign capital to the country on attractive terms which literally gave natural resources away and threatened popular resentment in the future.

Under Spanish rule the crown had enjoyed direct ownership of resources lying under the land surface. The surface owner might become the conditional possessor by special grant of the crown authorizing him to exploit the subsoil deposits and share in the fruits. However, the ownership of what remained in the subsoil was never separated from the crown, and the owner of the surface rights never acquired property rights in the unrecovered resources.[16] Díaz, in a series of laws, altered the concept of ownership in subsoil deposits. The Mining Law of 1884 made petroleum and other resources the exclusive property of the owner of the land.[17] The Mining Law of 1892, moving back toward the older concept of sub-soil rights, restricted the surface owner's right to exploit freely certain minerals, but permitted free exploitation of combustible minerals, including petroleum (which was not then commercially important in Mexico), without special concessions.[18] The Petroleum Law of 1901, concerned with concessions rather than titles, gave the federal executive the power to grant permits to explore certain lands and waters under federal jurisdiction.[19] The Mining Law of 1909 reaffirmed exclusive ownership of deposits of mineral fuels by the owner of the surface.[20]

Meanwhile, in 1893, Díaz turned government finances over to José Ives Limantour, who in later years dominated the dictatorship. With his entrance into the government came the rise of the *cientificos,* a group of young men of the postreform generation dominated by the philosophy of positivism.[21] They were materialists of great ability. Under their aegis railways, harbors, mines, and factories developed; public utilities grew; the valley of Mexico was drained; the country's income and the government's revenues soared. With the advent of the *cientificos* the dictatorship lost its Mexican characteristics and became progressively more the agent of foreign capital, for this group regarded the Mexican as backward, barbarous, and in need of the civilizing influence of foreign capital.[22] The government freely granted favors to foreign capital.

There was some exploration for oil before 1900, but the period of active exploration came after the turn of the century, when the American, Edward L. Doheny, began operations in Mexican territory.[23] The Petroleum Law of 1901 authorized Weetman Pearson, an Englishman, to operate on vacant and national lands.[24] In the same year the government offered special inducements to encourage petroleum companies to undertake oil development. It allowed them to export petroleum and petroleum products and to import certain materials and machinery for wells and refineries free of duties, and it exempted invested capital and capital goods from all federal duties, except the stamp tax, for ten years.[25] In 1901 the country produced about 10,000 barrels of petroleum, and production increased rapidly thereafter, reaching almost 4 million barrels in 1908 and more than 12 million in 1911.[26]

The United States exemplified the national economic organization that Díaz desired to emulate, but there were certain fatal flaws in his policy of adaptation. He ruthlessly submerged individual rights. At the same time, the existing feudalistic system of agriculture and land ownership was extended and became top-heavy. Estates of 6 and 7 million acres of land accumulated at the expense of peasant proprietors and Indians living in communal village organizations.[27] Holdings of land as large as 17 million acres were not unknown, and it is said that seventeen persons owned one-fifth of the total area of the republic.[28] This concentration of ownership of land developed and multiplied the evils of latifundia and debt peonage. The census of 1910 showed that nine or ten million Indians, that is, about three-fifths of the total population, were *peones de campo* (agricultural workers in debt service).[29] This feudalistic system entailed rigidities in the price and wage structure and an immobility of productive agents that could not long support a capitalistic system. In addition, the method of developing the country's resources not only violated tradition, but also made special concessions which in fact or in practical results discriminated against Mexicans in favor of foreigners.[30] Díaz, who had come to be regarded abroad as the champion of property rights, was not so highly esteemed as such at home, where he did not hesitate to confiscate property needed either by a favorite or for other purposes.[31]

Mexican capitalists did not fail to resent the favors redounding principally to the advantage of foreigners. Meanwhile, the growing body of industrial labor was getting new ideas. Frustrated and embittered by finding their strikes for higher wages suppressed by assassination and military action of the government,[32] the workers fell under the influence of migrants with radical solutions to their problem. There was a growing infiltration of socialist and anarchist doctrines after the turn of the century. A small group of theorists began to impress the masses with their ideas. This group included exiled anarchists from Spain,[33] Mexican workers who had returned from the United States, and Mexican intellectuals whose teachings of anarchosyndicalism reached responsive minds.[34] Lower classes deprived of their rights of landownership but bound to the soil by debt peonage awaited the propitious moment to regain what they had lost. In addition, a small minority, who by education and inclination demanded the chance to take an active part in politics, was growing restless.[35]

Almost ninety years after independence, the little change effected in the position of the lower classes was apparently for the worse, and the creoles had taken second place to foreigners. This potent, unstable, explosive mixture was ready for a spark.

Díaz provided the ignition himself in his famous interview with James Creelman. Creelman reported Díaz as saying that he believed Mexico was ready for democratic government and that he would welcome the emergence of an opposition party.[36] Díaz apparently intended this statement for ears in the United States, but it was heeded by vigilant Mexicans. An antireëlection group of young political idealists under the intellectual leadership of Francisco Madero responded to this "invitation," but they met an inhospitable official reception that resulted in Madero's being jailed in 1910.[37]

Escaping across the United States border after the "fixed" election of Díaz, Madero issued a proclamation of revolution on the principles of political reform and restoration of lands to the Indians.[38] The latter aim stirred up the deep economic and social discontent of the lower classes and brought Madero rapid and widespread support, which carried him to the presidency with practically no bloodshed. But Madero, absorbed in the political reforms which he felt would solve the nation's problems, did not understand the profound underlying sentiments of the masses, and so misinterpreted the spontaneous nature of the support which enabled him to overthrow Díaz.[39] His engrossment in political changes and his delay in bringing agrarian reform caused renewed unrest among the peasantry, even before the reactionary revolt of Huerta early in 1913.[40]

The thread of continuity in the turbulent period after Huerta's overthrow in July, 1914, by the combined forces of Carranza, Villa, and Zapata, is to be found not in the activities of any one of these leaders, but rather in the undercurrent of efforts by the masses to establish the revolutionary principles finally forced on Carranza and formally expressed in the Constitution of 1917. The superficial confusion of the Revolution, as seen in a study of these leaders individually, is due primarily to the fact that no one leader truly represented the whole mass movement throughout the entire period. Zapata was primarily interested in land reform; Villa was an exhibitionist who moved with the most turbulent political winds that blew; and Carranza was a rich landowner who did not at first understand, and was never to accept wholeheartedly, the social and economic motives of the lower classes. The body of revolutionary doctrine was to be molded by and crystallized out of the internecine conflicts among these three leaders.

During this struggle Carranza was driven to Vera Cruz by Zapata and Villa, and at the end of 1914 was forced to justify his position in order to get the general support he needed to defeat his enemies. To do this he issued a law of agrarian reform intended to restore land that had been illegally alienated from the Indians,[41] and made a pact with labor calling for a reform of labor laws in return for labor's active support.[42] His program of local government reform, general social legislation, and agrarian reform paralleled Zapata's and added measures to conciliate labor as well. This first comprehensive expression of the aims of the entire mass movement of the Revolution was the strategy that brought Carranza ultimate victory over Villa and Zapata.

From the mass of revolutionary literature and its interpretations, the principal aspirations of the Revolution may be summarized as follows:

1. To break down the large estates, destroy the system of peonage, and restore communal lands to villages.

2. To give workers greater participation in industry and a greater share in both its benefits and its responsibilities.

3. To overthrow the system of special privilege and industrial monopoly fostered by Díaz.

4. To restore the ownership of subsoil deposits to the state.

5. To control foreign economic influence in industry and agriculture.

6. To exercise controls in production, distribution, and prices.

7. To set up a genuinely national transportation system with less emphasis on export and import facilities.

8. To correct the social and political problems arising from the impingement of the two cultures of agricultural feudalism and industrial capitalism so as to form a modern nation-state with equality of rights.

9. To make effective the separation of Church and state and to destroy the Church's influence in economic life and in education.

These principles were incorporated in the constitution promulgated May 1, 1917. Despite betrayals and counterbetrayals of the faith of the populace by those in power, Mexico's struggle since 1917 has been a progressive, though somewhat faltering, movement to make effective the aims expressed in the new constitution. Articles 27 and 123 became of special consequence to the petroleum industry because of the provisions concerning the ownership of subsoil deposits and the status of labor, which was elevated, on paper at least, to a position nonexistent in any other country at the time. These articles were to give the oil companies and other property holders of foreign origin immediate and recurrent difficulties. Article 27 affirmed that the direct ownership of subsoil deposits belonged to the nation and that this right was "inalienable and im-

prescriptible." Only Mexicans or Mexican corporations might acquire land or concessions to exploit minerals. However, similar
rights might be extended to foreigners who agreed to consider
themselves nationals in the exercise of their rights, and not to in-
voke the protection of their governments under penalty of forfeit-
ing their properties.[43]

Villages and communities formerly owning land that had been
alienated by contravention of the land laws of 1856 were to have
their lands restored. Contracts and concessions made by state or
local governments since 1876, resulting in monopolization of land,
waters, or natural resources, could be revised or nullified in the
public interest.[44]

Expropriation was to be legal only if it served the public interest,
and only if private owners were indemnified.[45]

These clauses struck at the Anglo-Saxon concept of subsoil rights,
imported into Mexico under the Díaz regime to replace the older
Spanish concept. Whether or not the provisions concerning subsoil rights were to be retroactive was to be the focal point of a
recurring twenty-year struggle between the oil companies and the
Mexican government. The issue was also to be a central point of
controversy in the negotiations to determine the amount of indemnification to be paid the oil companies. The constitutional
provision regarding expropriation was also to raise questions concerning the constitutionality of the nationalization of the oil properties.

The immediate cause of the expropriation was to arise from the
attempts of labor to exercise the rights granted in Article 123. This
basic Mexican labor code provided for an eight-hour day and
limited night work; forbade the performance of dangerous, un-
healthy, or night work by women and children; and required at
least one day of rest for each six days of work. It set up the general
requisites for a minimum wage, which was to be determined by
commissions appointed in each municipality and subordinate to a
Central Board of Conciliation and Arbitration to be established
in each state. It exempted the minimum wage from attachments or
deductions; required equal pay for equal work, regardless of sex;
provided for profit sharing in a manner to be determined by special commissions in each municipality; forbade payment of wages
in scrip or merchandise or in anything but legal money; and required 100 per cent extra compensation for overtime. Under certain conditions employers were to provide low-cost housing, recrea-
tion centers, schools, and other municipal services. The right of

both employers and employees to organize was recognized. Legal strikes were defined as those that were intended to bring about a "balance between the various factors of production and to harmonize the rights of capital and labor"; strikes were illegal when the majority of workers resorted to acts of violence against persons or property. Lockouts were to be legal only "when the excess of production should render it necessary to shut down in order to maintain prices reasonably above the cost of production, subject to approval of the Board of Conciliation and Arbitration."

Special tribunals called Federal Boards of Conciliation and Arbitration (*Juntas Federales de Conciliación y Arbitraje*) were to serve in the settlement of labor-management controversies by imposing compulsory arbitration at the request of either party. Penalties were to be meted out to those who refused to observe the decisions of these tribunals. Certain types of labor contracts were outlawed, such as those calling for an "inhuman" day's work or for a wage considered unremunerative by the Federal Boards, or for renunciation of the legal rights of labor.

Other articles of the constitution[46] restated the measures designed in the reform period to control the influence of the Church. The prohibition against the holding of property by the Church, which Díaz had ignored, was reaffirmed, and even Church buildings became national property. The Church was denied the right to control elementary schools, organize political parties, or allow foreign priests to serve in the country. The constitution required the registration of priests and empowered each state legislature to limit the number of functioning priests within its borders.

The constitution was a composite declaration of aspirations that were impossible to realize immediately.[47] It would take years of education and of struggle against vested interests to consummate the ideals there expressed. Those articles affecting oil interests, for example, were to require more than twenty years to become a reality. The provisions concerning property rights in subsoil deposits and labor rights were to affect the petroleum industry most significantly.

Mexican oil production, exceeding 55 million barrels in 1917, was rising rapidly. Fabulous returns to the exploiting companies and the exigencies of war facing the United States government gave both parties especial interest in Mexican petroleum production. When his attempts to implement the constitutional provisions by law gave rise to strong feelings between Mexico and the United States, Carranza was moved to modify the laws in part.[48]

The overthrow and assassination of Carranza somewhat relieved the immediate tension between the two governments, but the United States refused to recognize the new Mexican government unless it would sign a treaty guaranteeing property rights of United States nationals acquired before May 1, 1917.[49] Obregón, the new president, refusing to sign a treaty under such conditions, proposed to set up a special commission to adjudicate claims that had developed from the revolution, whether they originated with United States or Mexican citizens.

The situation reached an impasse. Meanwhile, however, in a series of decisions known as the Texas Company Cases, the Mexican Supreme Court decided that Article 27 was not retroactive and did not affect rights legally acquired before May 1, 1917.[50] The court, avoiding a definition of legally acquired rights, specified that surface rights, in order to include rights to oil, must have been accompanied by "positive acts," that is, acts that showed the intention of the owner to exploit the oil.[51] Further clarification of the term "positive acts" was left until the time of the Bucareli Conferences in 1923. These conferences provided, among other things, a working agreement whereby the Mexican government recognized certain rights to subsoil deposits of surface owners who had performed positive acts toward the exploitation of those deposits before May 1, 1917.[52] Representatives of both governments agreed upon the specific procedures that constituted acceptable positive acts.[53]

Although the controversy appeared to have been settled, the Mexicans understood that oil rights consisted only of the right to explore for and produce petroleum in the subsoil deposits, but not to own the deposits themselves.[54] The companies understood that they owned the deposits. Consequently, a new law passed in 1925 seemed to impair oil property rights. This law required the oil companies to exchange their titles to oil lands for fifty-year concessions.[55] This was naturally objectionable to the companies because it constituted recognition of Mexico's earlier claim that all subsoil rights were vested in the nation and in effect made the constitutional provision retroactive. The United States government protested. Another Supreme Court decision in 1927 declared that the rights of the companies to explore for and produce oil could not be limited to fifty years.[56] Soon thereafter the Morrow-Calles agreement, recognizing the Supreme Court decision, ended the controversy. This aspect of the law was not raised again in the differences between the oil companies and the government until after expropriation.

Meanwhile, oil production in Mexico had reached a peak of

more than 193 million barrels in 1921. It then fell off continuously during the remainder of this controversy,[57] amounting to only 40 million barrels in 1930. The decline was ascribed to a number of factors. Producers attributed it to exhaustion of the old fields, uncertainty and restriction under Mexican laws concerning exploration for and exploitation of new fields, and high taxes.[58] Exhaustion of the old fields undoubtedly was a factor, and uncertainty in the law and the political situation probably also played a part. It is worthy of note that, although production increased continuously and rapidly during the most hectic days of the revolutionary period, legal and political uncertainty coupled with the growing strength of the Mexican government in the nineteen-twenties provided a basis for company fears. As for taxes, although they were higher than at earlier periods, their relatively low level hardly seems a real handicap. Another factor was undoubtedly that of chance in exploration. Exploratory activity apparently did not decrease following the peak year of production, and the rate of drilling of wells increased two and one-half times from 1921 to 1926.[59] The number of wells drilled in the four years 1924 through 1927 was more than five times greater than the number drilled in the whole period before 1921. Before 1921, less than 38 per cent of the wells were abandoned at the termination of drilling, compared to more than 55 per cent in the years 1921 to 1929, inclusive.

The Mexicans went along with some of the oil companies' arguments and added others.[60] They admitted that the companies had lost confidence in the country because of the petroleum laws, but they also attributed the decline in production to the liberality of the Mexican law, which allowed oil companies to hold vast tracts of land as idle reserves. The rate of drilling before 1927 seems to deny the effect of the latter contention, and the decline in drilling after 1926 can be explained, at least in part, by the rapid rate of discovery of rich oil deposits in Venezuela and the United States. These discoveries caused a relative increase in Mexican costs of production as compared with costs in other areas. In addition, according to the U. S. Bureau of Mines *Minerals Yearbook*, the wholesale price index for petroleum and petroleum products in the United States dropped more than 28 per cent between 1926 and 1927; and a continuing decline brought the 1931 index more than 60 per cent below that of 1926. Caught in the pinch of rising costs in Mexico and falling prices, the large oil companies focused their attention on Venezuela after 1927. However, even in 1930 they drilled 133 wells in Mexico. Although this was the lowest figure in a decade, it still exceeded by far the drilling in any year before 1921.

In the 'thirties, the oil controversy took a new turn. This time it was over the implementation of the basic labor principles expressed in the Constitution of 1917. The origin of this controversy lay in the developments in the labor movement from the beginning of the Revolution.

The overthrow of Díaz had freed the repressed labor movement but had left the incipient unions confused by their very freedom.[61] In 1912 the *Casa del Obrero Mundial* emerged as the dominant element in the labor movement. This organization provided coordination for the movement and a school for the early leaders. Extremists were very influential in the organization.[62] When Huerta came to power, he suppressed it. Carranza made no bid for the support of the working classes when he went to battle against Huerta, nor did he mention social reform until December, 1914, after Villa and Zapata had driven him to Vera Cruz.[63] Soon thereafter he made his pact with the *Casa del Obrero Mundial,* thus gaining the support of organized labor. After his victory, however, Carranza did not receive labor's demands for higher wages with sympathy, and great unrest developed in the labor movement in 1915 and 1916.[64] Although Carranza attempted to intimidate and suppress labor, the latter did not retaliate directly but awaited its chance. The opportunity came at the constitutional convention of 1917, where labor pushed through Article 123 over Carranza's objections.[65]

However, the federal government under Carranza did not act to put these constitutional provisions into effect. State governments that set up arbitration boards were denied authority to enforce their decisions by the federal Supreme Court.[66] At the same time Carranza moved to organize a subservient labor movement which he could use to displace the growing menace of an independent workers' organization.[67] In May, 1918, the *Confederación Regional Obrera Mexicana,* better known as the *CROM,* was organized through the influence of Carranza. However, the leaders were able to snatch control from the hands of Carranza and set up a small secret control group, whose basic philosophy combined practical trade unionism with an evolutionary movement to socialize the means of production.[68]

The controlling group, headed by Luis Morones, engaged actively in politics and in 1919 formed the Mexican Labor party, which aimed to socialize industry by political action.[69] With the aid of Morones, Obregón overthrew Carranza, and the *CROM* acquired a favored position from which it was able to suppress competing organizations. But Obregón, before the end of his term, alienated certain labor groups who felt that his method of handling strikes was undermining labor's power. Obregón did indeed shift his favor from labor to peasant groups toward the end of his administration, and Luis Morones shifted his support to Calles, who appointed Morones to a cabinet post after he came to the presidency.[70] There ensued a period of extreme corruption of labor leaders. Morones amassed a fortune by extortion from employers who were forced to buy industrial peace.

The backbone of the corrupt *CROM* was later broken by Calles and the machine he had built to perpetuate his control in the government. Growing conservatism on the part of Calles and fewer favors to labor's leaders alienated many groups in the *CROM*. Some favored renewing relations with Obregón, but this feeling was not unanimous and contributed to a loss of cohesion. The breakdown was precipitated by an issue raised at the ninth annual congress of the *CROM* in 1928.[71] The government had worked out a labor code to implement Article 123 and unify social legislation in the country. The leaders of the *CROM* feared the government would have too many controls over the activities of unions under this code, but many component unions of the organization saw in the law the realization of labor's revolutionary principles as expressed in the constitution. When leaders of the *CROM* withdrew their support from the government, many constituent unions left the central labor organization. The disintegration of this corrupt body was hastened by the succeeding president, Portes Gil, who supported revolutionary and communist groups independent of the *CROM* in order to destroy the latter's power. Once in control of labor, Portes Gil turned against the radical leaders, who were murdered or sent to penal colonies.[72]

A new power arising in political circles was partly responsible for these changes in the labor movement. A new generation, which had grown up under the Revolution and took its principles seriously, had begun to exert its influence. To this group the revolutionary ideals of the constitution were goals to be achieved and not merely rungs in the ladder for attaining political ambitions.[73] Its members had resented Calles' increasing laxity in carrying out constitutional provisions, his growing favor toward foreign capital, and his continued dominance of the government beyond his term of office. This left-wing group grew in strength within the councils of the National Revolutionary party formed by Calles to consolidate his control.[74]

In 1931 the government passed a Federal Labor Law implementing the basic labor principles of the constitution. Under this law, the federal government accepted the responsibility for uniformly carrying out the labor provisions of Article 123. The uncoordinated laws of the states passed out of the picture.

Calles, recognizing the growing strength of the leftist sentiment, set up defenses to ensure victory in the presidential election of 1934. His defense was concession to the younger leftist group in the party. He chose for his candidate Lázaro Cárdenas, whom he thought he could dominate, and started to formulate a national plan for development.[75] This was a program of expanding government control of industry, improvements in education, and agrarian development. It became known as Mexico's Six-Year Plan. The program eulogized labor and the nationalistic spirit; it stated labor's right to work and the state's responsibility in the exercise of that right; it favored compulsory union shops to promote collective bargaining.[76] The plan favored the establishment of a semi-official agency to aid in the development and regulation of the petroleum industry.[77] It stated further that production should be increased to a volume commensurate with what the reserves could "reasonably yield," that the concession system should be modified to serve better the national interests, and that measures should be taken to discourage the reimportation of Mexican oil processed abroad.[78]

Cárdenas was elected and, as it turned out, took his revolutionary views and the Six-Year Plan much too seriously for Calles, whom Cárdenas soon escorted to exile. During the next six years socialism and Marxism triumphed, and a strong sentiment of nationalism developed among labor groups. These growing factors broke the economic domination of the oil companies.

With Cárdenas' inauguration, labor-management strife increased rapidly. If there had been any question as to Cárdenas' attitude toward reform before he took office, within two years he had left little room for doubt. In a speech to workers and peasants in Monterrey, where considerable labor trouble had developed, he denied a charge by employers that Mexico was drifting into communism and anarchy, and he encouraged the organization of the laboring classes to combat their enemies and to achieve by legal procedures the gains (conquistas) compatible with the economic capacity of the enterprises in which they worked.[79] To the labor leaders, however, he counseled caution, telling them in a conference that he felt that labor was not yet prepared in experience, knowledge, or economic means to take over the financial and technical aspects of production.[80] In his annual message to Congress on September 1, 1936, Cárdenas said, speaking of the employers, "When they feel tired of the social struggle, they can turn their industries over to the workers or to the government."[81]

Meanwhile, a young intellectual and former university teacher, Vicente Lombardo Toledano, had set for himself the task of unifying labor. He had fought from within the *CROM* the corrupt leadership of Morones; and with the breakdown of that organization, he set about reconstructing the shattered labor movement. In 1932 he organized the General Confederation of Workers and Peasants (*Confederación General de Obreros y Campesinos*), which became the nucleus of the Confederation of Mexican Labor (*Confederación de Trabajadores Mexicanos*), formed by Toledano in February, 1936.[82] This organization, based on industrial unionism, rapidly became dominant in the labor movement under the favorable political climate provided by Cárdenas. The declaration of policy made shortly after its formation stated that the organization was not communist, that it did not propose to suppress private property, that it had no political aims, and that it would strive for the betterment of the Mexican working classes and for the defense of the economic, political, and cultural autonomy of the nation.[83] The Confederation of Mexican Labor was to play a very significant role in later developments in the oil industry.

In 1934 the oil workers formed unions on a company basis.[84] There was little direct contact among the company unions, and little uniformity in the contracts made by different companies with their unions. The petroleum workers and organized labor generally felt this was undesirable; and in December, 1935, the company unions, in order to bargain more effectively and write uniform contracts, joined together with the help of the Confederation of Mexican Labor and the encouragement of the government in an industry-wide union known as the Syndicate of Petroleum Workers of the Mexican Republic (*Sindicato de Trabajadores Petroleros de la República Mexicana*).[85]

The petroleum workers' syndicate did not delay long in making its influence felt. In July, 1936, it called a special convention to consider an industry-wide collective bargaining contract.[86] A contract was drawn up and presented to the employers, who, under their legal rights, united to defend themselves. They met with representatives of the syndicate but failed to come to an agreement. The principal demands of the syndicate related to the maxi-

mum number of confidential employees (those hired freely by the
management with no union control) allowed the companies; indemnification for layoff, death, or disability; the establishment of
the workweek, rest days, and vacations; provisions for savings funds
for workers, scholarships, training programs, housing, and disease
prevention programs; and increased wages.[87] Since no agreement
had been reached by the latter part of May, 1937, the syndicate
notified the companies of its intention to strike. The strike began
May 28, 1937. On June 7, the syndicate decided to enter a suit
before the Federal Board of Conciliation and Arbitration, Group
Number Seven, involving a "conflict of economic order,"[88] that is,
a "disequilibrium" in the returns to the factors of production.*
Eighteen companies were named in the suit.†

The Federal Board of Conciliation and Arbitration recognized
the dispute as a conflict of economic order and, as required by law,
appointed a commission to investigate wages and conditions in the
industry. The strike was then terminated pending the board's investigation and decision. The strike was generally viewed as more
than a fight for better wages and conditions by the leaders of organized labor, who saw it as a first step to protect national interests
and as a blow against foreign imperialism.[89]

The expert commission presented its report on wages and conditions in the petroleum industry to the Federal Board on August
3, 1937.[90] The report roundly condemned the principal oil companies. The commission displayed concern over the fact that the
largest companies were subsidiaries of British and American enterprises and had never become integrated with the country, and that
these companies had even displayed alien and sometimes opposing

---

* In labor-management disputes the labor code provides that, if management
claims economic inability to meet labor's proposed demands, either party can
initiate a suit before the Federal Board of Conciliation and Arbitration in a procedure known as a "conflict of economic order." The tribunal then appoints a commission of experts to investigate the organization's ability to meet the demands. The
board renders its decision on the basis of the report. Ley Federal de Trabajo, Título
IX, capítulo 7.

† These included the Compañía Mexicana de Petróleo "El Aguila," S.A.; Huasteca
Petroleum Company; Sinclair Pierce Oil Company; California Standard Oil Com-
pany of Mexico; Petróleos de México, S.A.; Compañía Petrolera el Agwi, S.A.; Penn
Mex Fuel Oil Company; Stanford y Compañía, Sucursales; Richmond Petroleum
Company of Mexico; Compañía Explotadora de Petróleo "La Imperial," S.A.;
Sabalo Transportation Company, S.A.; Compañía de Gas y Combustible "Imperio";
Mexican Gulf Oil Company; Mexican Sinclair Petroleum Company; Consolidated
Oil Company of Mexico; Compañía Naviera "San Cristóbal," S.A.; Compañía Naviera
"San Ricardo," S.A.; and Compañía Mexicana de Vapores "San Antonio," S.A. See
Mexico's Oil (México, D.F., 1940), p. 697.

interests to those of the country. It stated that the large oil companies exploited the rich subsoil, exported the oil, and left only wages and taxes in Mexico. Ignoring the function of profits and interest, the experts charged that the companies had reaped enormous profits that probably had more than recovered the investment of most of them ten years earlier. They claimed that the companies had also failed to coöperate in the social progress of Mexico, and that the larger interests had more than once influenced national, as well as international, political events.

The experts charged that production had fallen constantly for eleven years because of depletion of oil fields and because of an alarming failure to explore actively, and suggested that this was a considered policy of the companies. This, the commission feared, would lead to national shortages. There were signs of a trend toward increasing monopoly by the Compañía Mexicana de Petróleo "El Aguila." The commission said that real wages of oil workers were declining, as shown by the increasing cost of the workers' "basket of provisions," and that the majority of petroleum workers received lower real wages than those earned by workers in the mining industry or on the National Railroads of Mexico. It accused the oil companies of exporting Mexican oil to affiliated companies at prices below those in the world market in order to conceal their true profits. At the same time they sold petroleum products in Mexican markets at prices well above those charged abroad. This, the commission pointed out, was an obstacle to the economic development of the country. The commission's computations showed that annual profits of the defendant oil companies (with the exception of the Mexican Gulf Oil Company) in the period 1934–1936 amounted to 16.81 per cent on their invested capital. The commission concluded that the past earnings and future prospects of the oil companies warranted the employers' accession to the demands of the workers.

The oil companies presented an extensive and significant rebuttal at hearings before the Federal Board, August 27 to September 20, 1937 (see App. A-2). It is tempting to digress to evaluate the arguments presented by both sides. However, the purpose of this study is to determine the objectives of expropriation and to assess the Mexican achievement of those objectives. It would require extensive research to evaluate the contentions of both sides with complete justice; such an evaluation is a project for future probing. The obvious emphasis given here to the Mexican arguments is not to be construed as a defense of those arguments, nor is it implied that the Mexicans were right and the companies wrong in either a legal or a moral sense. From the standpoint of this study, the principal significance of the findings of the expert commission lies in the assessment of the oil problem and of the grievances against the oil companies. The judgment of the commission provides a clue to the objectives of expropriation.

On December 18, 1937, Group Number Seven of the Federal Board of Conciliation and Arbitration handed down its decision. The award cut into some demands of the syndicate and extended others. On the whole, it was highly favorable to the syndicate and can be considered a decisive victory (see chap. x). The Federal Board estimated that it would cost the companies about 26 million pesos more per year to meet the wages and other benefits provided for in the labor contract under consideration.[91]

On December 28, 1937, the oil companies presented a plea to the Supreme Court of Mexico for an injunction (*amparo*) on the grounds that Group Number Seven did not have jurisdiction; that the award went beyond the demands of labor; that the right of free contract was infringed; that the decision was void because of technical details; that the doctrine of financial capacity was wrong and not legally acceptable; that evidence had been ignored, misconstrued, and misrepresented; that the award would cost 41 million pesos rather than 26 million pesos; and that the Federal Labor Law was violated by the award.[92]

On March 1, 1938, the Mexican Supreme Court denied the injunction and upheld the decision of the Federal Board of Conciliation and Arbitration.[93] The oil companies resorted to delaying tactics while they attempted to improve their position by bargaining. However, this served only to give President Cárdenas time to consolidate public opinion so that, when he finally decided to expropriate, he was solidly backed by popular feeling.

As a result of the companies' delay in accepting the decision, the labor tribunal, at the request of the syndicate, on March 18 declared the existing contracts between the companies and the unions terminated.

The President was under great pressure from labor leaders and ultranationalists to take the far-reaching step of nationalization. Both groups had long clamored against the "economic imperialism" of capitalistic countries. In addition, the companies had antagonized public opinion by an attitude which seemed to Mexicans to defy the nation's sovereignty even within its own territorial limits. On the evening of March 18, the larger petroleum companies were shocked by the suddenness of President Cárdenas' message announcing the expropriation of their properties.

The presidential decree nationalizing the oil properties stated that, because (1) the decision of the labor tribunal had not been carried out and the contract had been terminated and (2) the petroleum industry was of so great public interest that paralysis by a work stoppage would cause extensive damage, the "machinery, installations, buildings, pipelines, refineries, storage tanks, means of communication, tank cars, distributing stations, embarkation installations, and all other goods, real estate, and property" were declared properties of the nation.[94]

The principal losers in the expropriation were the Royal Dutch-Shell group and the Standard Oil Company (New Jersey), which in 1936 together controlled more than 70 per cent of the total Mexican production.[95] The estimated producing capacity of the expropriated group was roughly 90 per cent.

These relevant features of Mexican history and of developments in the petroleum industry provide the basis for judging the achievements of Mexico in solving its oil problem. The aims of expropriation lie in this historical perspective. To point out these objectives is the next problem.

Chapter III

THE OBJECTIVES
OF EXPROPRIATION

The objectives of expropriation were never explicitly and completely stated by the government. Political factors probably explain this failure to provide a rationale of short-run and long-run aims. As pointed out in the preceding chapter, over the years Mexicans frequently criticized the petroleum industry. They complained about what the oil companies were doing and asserted what they thought the companies should do. Prior to expropriation Mexican emotions ran high as a consequence of events that stirred their wrath against the foreign corporations. The effervescent feelings and the sudden decision to expropriate were probably so surprising to Mexicans themselves that the leaders had no opportunity to formulate a complete statement of objectives. It is likely that government officials avoided too detailed a statement in order to prevent antagonisms among Mexicans because, although expropriation was popular, the aims of various groups were diverse and in some respects incompatible. It is the purpose of this chapter to ascertain the rational basis for the act; that is, to discover with the aid of hindsight the specific objectives that gave rise to this popular movement. To determine the objectives of expropriation one must examine, in the light of the Mexican historical background, statements of the President, of labor leaders, of the expert commission that investigated the oil industry, and of other influential Mexicans.

Until the announcement of expropriation, most of the official acts in the controversy appeared, on the surface at least, to be strong regulatory measures rather than steps to nationalization. However, the Revolution had revealed the deep-seated antagonisms of peasant and labor classes toward large landowners and foreign capitalists that foretold the almost inevitable result. In the favorable atmosphere that President Cárdenas created, labor brought great pressure on the oil companies. The companies resisted this pressure as they had always done, giving a little but maintaining their rights insofar as possible. However, in the controversy that developed in 1937 and 1938, the companies were forced into a resistance that appeared to challenge the sovereignty of Mexican law. This threat to Mexican sovereignty raised opposition from many who had little interest in the immediate causes of the conflict and little sympathy with revolutionary objectives, but who had the marked Mexican characteristic of intense patriotism.

Basically, the conflict leading to the expropriation was a flowering of the ideas of the revolutionary reform. Expropriation was a consummation of the reaction to the Porfirian free-for-all, open-door policy toward foreign capital.[1] The more immediate objectives of the expropriation were to assert once and for all the supreme authority of Mexican law and legal procedures, and to prevent catastrophic paralysis in the petroleum industry.

The rejection of the companies' plea for an injunction against the Federal Board's decision, and the interpretation of the companies' protests as a refusal to comply, led the board to declare that the action of the companies had terminated the existing labor contracts. The Syndicate of Petroleum Workers instructed the local sections to cease work at midnight on March 18, 1938. In a radio message at ten o'clock that evening, President Cárdenas announced the expropriation of the petroleum industry.

The message indicated that the immediate reasons for this step were both legal and economic. Cárdenas stated that the companies' refusal to comply with the decisions of the Federal Board forced the executive to prevent the companies from annulling or attempting to annul that decision by simply declaring themselves unable to pay, for this, of course, had been the point at issue in the judicial proceedings.[2] He expressed fears that both failure to act and any act short of expropriation would so curtail petroleum production as to endanger the economy and the government. Insofar as there was danger of a prolonged work stoppage, production facilities were also threatened, since shutdowns of producing wells could cause serious damage. After the expropriation, this sentiment was repeated in diplomatic notes expressing Mexican concern over the economic consequences of suspension of oil supplies.[3]

A more long-run cause of expropriation was the strong feeling among Mexicans that theirs was a semicolonial country, doomed to backwardness until it achieved economic independence and

---

[1] For numbered notes to chap. iii, see pp. 243–244.

freedom from economic imperialism. What the Mexicans meant by economic imperialism varied with the users of the term (see chap. xii). It was widely agreed, however, that the oil companies were among the most flagrant examples of foreign economic power and that they had invaded the country with no interest in it except to enrich themselves and depart.[4] Just before the expropriation, in a series of lectures to Mexican high school students sponsored by the Secretary of Public Education, several speakers had suggested that the country would be better off in the long run if it could achieve economic independence from the oil companies than if it continued to allow the country's resources to be drained away.[5] After the expropriation, the public schools taught that

> The expropriation . . . can signify the beginning of the economic independence of the country and liberation from exploitation by imperialistic companies, since it will result in coordination between production and consumption. . . .
> The act of expropriation also represents the beginning of an economic policy which will convert Mexico from a poor country to a rich and prosperous nation, losing the characteristics of a semi-colonial country in which its wealth never benefitted its own people, but only a few capitalistic companies, usually of foreign nationality.[6]

This desire for economic independence had long been felt and was pointedly expressed, even before Cárdenas' administration, in connection with the petroleum industry. At the time when the government was considering the establishment of *Petromex,* a semipublic corporation to engage in the petroleum industry, it was said that

> A nation jealous of its political independence must be careful . . . to insure its economic independence, and to this end it must not depend on foreign financial groups for the development of its vital industries except in a minimum amount. It is indispensable that the greater part of its necessary capital be found in the country.[7]

The writer implied that if private capital was insufficient, the government should lend aid in order to prevent the "infiltration" of foreign capital.

President Cárdenas more than once complained of the dependence of Mexico on powerful foreign economic interests. In addressing a group of senators just before expropriation, he used very direct words in support of the argument that the power of the large oil companies must be curbed "to bring to an end the economic dependence which has predominated in Mexico."[8] Again, in his message announcing the expropriation to the nation on March 18, 1938, he referred to the expropriation as an act of "essential economic liberation of Mexico."

Pamphleteers asserted that the companies had made enormous profits, carried huge amounts of wealth from the country, and evaded taxes by concealing profits.[9] The expert commission, investigating the oil companies involved in the labor dispute, reported serious discrepancies between the companies' reported profits and their real profits. The commission's financial analysis stated that for 1934 the companies (excluding the Mexican Gulf Oil Company) had reported profits of 20.5 million pesos, whereas their actual profits had been 51.5 million pesos; that for 1935 reported profits were 27.7 million pesos, and actual profits had been 62.0 million pesos; and that for 1936 reported profits were 20.5 million pesos, and actual profits had been 55.3 million pesos.[10] The analysis showed also that during the years 1934 to 1936 the average annual rate of return to the companies on their capital investment had been 16.81 per cent.[11]

The Mexicans also felt that the companies were a block to the economic and social advancement of the nation, for they carried wealth out of the country and kept real wages low.[12] The cost of living, according to the expert commission, was so high in the petroleum areas that the real wages of oil workers were lower than those of workers in either the mining or railroad industries. The commission found another block in the system of discriminatory prices maintained by the companies. The prices of important petroleum products were much higher in Mexico than in the foreign markets to which Mexican oil was exported.[13] Domestic consumption demands, the commission felt, were not being met. This, it was asserted later by a member of the commission, was a general characteristic of backward regions which developed under the pressure of great foreign enterprises—they frequently exported goods which did not constitute an "excess" above domestic "needs"* because the foreigners acted in conformity with their own interests and not with those of the country in which they operated.[14] The attitude was quite general that Mexico had an inherent right to the benefits accruing from her own resources, that hers was a first claim, and that it was her privilege to keep down the cost of fuel so

---

* Jesús Silva Herzog used the terms "excess" and "needs," but did not define them. By "needs" he apparently meant wants or desires, not demand in the economic sense of desire backed by purchasing power. By "excess" he apparently meant goods over and above wants. By this definition, a society never has an excess of an *economic* good.

that its price would not be a deterrent to the development of domestic industry. This attitude, of course, ignored the function of price and its relationship to the most economic allocation of resources.

Another stated objective was the rebuilding of the oil industry, which the companies had allowed to deteriorate. The expert commission reported that the decline in production was due to the depletion of existing reserves and to the failure of the companies to carry on adequate exploration and drilling programs. This, it thought, might have been due to a definite policy of restriction.[15] The Mexican government directed this indictment particularly at the American companies.[16] The official attitude was that the American companies had carried on a policy of amortizing their capital by limiting their activities merely to production from wells already in operation, and had completely neglected exploration and progressively reduced their operations in surface installations.

The decline of the industry was an undeniable fact. For a number of reasons (see pp. 14 to 16) the oil companies were turning their attention to Venezuela and other areas where production was increasing.[17] The decline of the Mexican industry was a serious threat to the economy because of the importance of oil for home consumption and for export. In 1934 petroleum products had accounted for almost 25 per cent of the total value of Mexican exports, but they had dropped to less than 20 per cent by 1937.[18] The progressive decline in the relative importance of petroleum among exports gave little comfort in view of the exchange problems facing Mexico.

Some writers asserted that the companies enjoyed uncontrolled monopoly power which should be destroyed. The government had attempted to combat such monopoly powers by passing maximum price laws and by setting up various public or semipublic agencies to compete with the oil companies and to guarantee the government sufficient supplies of petroleum for its own uses. These agencies apparently failed to produce enough even to meet government needs. The report of the expert commission warned of a growing tendency to monopoly in the industry and of price discrimination unfavorable to the domestic market.[19]

The economic power of the companies had indeed been felt within the petroleum industry and also in a much wider sphere of the economy. According to President Cárdenas, in a speech to the First General Ordinary Congress of the Confederation of Mexican Labor in February, 1938, the companies had exerted this influence to create doubt and fear in the country by suddenly withdrawing deposits from the banks and by conducting a newspaper campaign to spread alarm among businessmen.[20]

Probably first among the legal and political objectives of expropriation were those of enforcing the observance of Mexican law and legal procedures and of establishing beyond doubt the sovereignty of Mexico. It had been the custom of the major oil companies to observe Mexican law, at least on the surface, but by various stratagems they had been able so to influence the law that they seldom found themselves in a legal corner from which the only escape was to break the law or make significant sacrifices. They had usually managed to compromise on major issues, either by exerting their own influence or by calling in their home governments.

In his message announcing the expropriation, President Cárdenas stated that the government had a clear-cut case; it was compelled to expropriate in order to make the oil companies obedient and submissive to the law. This point was reiterated in the exchange of diplomatic notes:

. . . The ground of public interest that directly led to the action taken [expropriation], was in this case established by the contumacy of the oil companies in refusing to abide by a final and absolute judgment rendered by the highest court in the republic.[21]

Labor leaders widely publicized the attitude of the large oil companies toward the Supreme Court and the Federal Board award as an infringement on Mexico's political sovereignty. One official of the Confederation of Mexican Labor, speaking in the United States, said that the disregard of the decision of the Supreme Court defied "the law of the land, making naught of the country's sovereignty and dignity."[22] He went on to say that the oil conflict was not simply a conflict between labor and capital, but between the oil companies and the Mexican people and their government, and that "we would not tolerate our country's subordination to Standard Oil and the Royal Dutch Shell." Justice Xavier Icaza, in a speech before the Supreme Court on March 1, 1938, referred to the conflict as a political battle between the companies and Mexico.[23]

However, the political and legal stakes were not merely respect for the labor code and for legal procedures. Involved also was the long-standing dispute over Article 27 of the constitution, concerning ownership of the subsoil deposits. The Bucareli Agreements had apparently supported the companies in their refusal to recognize the nation's ownership of the subsoil deposits acquired by

private interests before May 1, 1917. These agreements were regarded by some Mexicans as a dishonorable compromise of the
nation's sovereignty.[24] The objective of making Article 27 the controlling element in subsoil ownership was expressed in the Six-
Year Plan, which called for effectuating the nationalization of the
subsoil and for modifying the system of concessions so as to harmonize with national interest.[25]

Mexicans resented the interference of the major oil companies
in the country's internal politics. The report of the expert commission in the petroleum controversy stated that the exploitation
of petroleum in Mexico had long been accompanied by internal
and even international disturbances, and charged this to the "rebellious attitude of the oil companies in their dealings with the
authorities emanating from the Revolution, and in opposition to
the principles and provisions enacted by them in pursuit of a
just recovery of national wealth."[26] President Cárdenas, from his
long experience in government service, knew of the interest and activities of the oil companies in domestic affairs. In his announcement of expropriation, he accused them of intervening during the
revolutionary years and of encouraging the ambitions of dissident
and rebellious elements in later periods whenever the oil interests
were adversely affected by the government in power. One writer
of this period expressed a feeling widespread among Mexicans when
he said that the expropriation "shows the world that Mexico has
now entered a political state of maturity and national consciousness that will not again permit the humiliating introduction of
imperialistic capitalism into the internal affairs of Mexico."[27]

Marett, a British businessman in Mexico, asserted that the expropriation was aimed at advancing the ambitions of a political
clique led by Lombardo Toledano, the leader of the Confederation
of Mexican Labor.[28] He said that President Cárdenas, in his devotion to the lower classes, had become Lombardo Toledano's tool.
Certain labor leaders within the oil industry probably did press for
expropriation in order to advance their own ambitions for power
and political influence. In the light of subsequent events this seems
a distinct possibility (see chap. x). However, it is a mistake to say
Cárdenas was Lombardo Toledano's pawn. He had already demonstrated his strength and singleness of purpose, and the act of expropriation was quite consistent with his expressed aims and with
the objectives of the National Revolutionary party.

The expropriation was also a step toward the revolutionary objective of improving social conditions for the lower classes. As has already been pointed out (see pp. 18–19), President Cárdenas' policy from early in his term of office was highly sympathetic with the labor and peasant elements. Less than a month before the expropriation, in addressing the Confederation of Mexican Labor, he said:

I wish . . . to reaffirm to the people of Mexico that the social policy of the government will continue to be to safeguard definitely the economic achievements of the producing classes, with a view to improving their standard of living and obtaining a greater satisfaction of their needs through full compensation for their efforts.[29]

He went on to say that the policies of his government were respect for life, protection of the individual, freedom in politics, cancellation of privileges, and a fairer distribution of public wealth. He referred to the large petroleum companies and the petroleum controversy when he said:

In order that the progress of the Revolution continue without delaying the execution of the work necessary to its constructive action, it is necessary that we be prepared to resist, even at great economic sacrifice, the attacks of those who do not understand the justice of Mexico's position and who insist on destroying our cause by creating conditions of uncertainty and alarm.[30]

The expert commission had stated that, despite the increasing profits of the companies in the period 1934 to 1936, real wages of workers had fallen and were lower than those in either the mining or the railroad industries.[31] President Cárdenas, announcing the expropriation, objected to the exploitation of the oil workers and to the failure of the companies to protect the general welfare of workers in isolated oil zones. Many influential Mexicans with leanings toward theoretical Marxism agreed with Jesús Silva Herzog, who attributed the decline in real wages to the irreconcilable conflict of interest between employer and worker, a conflict that he believed would be resolved by government administration.[32]

Expropriation was to be a means of raising the standard of living of the masses to the level in other countries.[33] The major oil companies were foreign; their only interest in the country was the profit they could take out. The state, it was felt, could with proper management of this important basic industry elevate the whole nation.

The objectives of expropriation can be briefly summarized. The economic aims included avoidance of a work stoppage as a result of the termination of the petroleum workers' contract. The government feared that a suspension of oil production would result in paralysis in the economy and damage to wells. Many Mexicans felt that elimination of the large oil companies was a key step in achieving economic independence for Mexico and in resisting foreign economic imperialism. Many thought that expropriation would advance the nation economically and socially by diverting oil and oil profits from foreign interests to the benefit of the nation itself. The expert commission pointed to the declining interest of the oil companies in Mexico. Some Mexicans felt that the only way to rebuild the industry and to realize the rate of production of the early 'twenties was to enlist a new producing agent without possible ulterior motives for restricting production. They believed that the size and power of the oil companies gave them a privileged, monopolistic position through which they periodically created uncertainty and alarm that upset the economic and social life of the nation.

Political and legal objectives were very important. Mexicans wanted to force powerful foreign economic units to respect and observe Mexican laws and legal procedures. Those individuals steeped in the revolutionary tradition resented the Bucareli and Morrow-Calles agreements. They wanted to abrogate those portions of the agreements that effectively barred the claim of the nation to ownership of the subsoil deposits, as asserted in Article 27 of the constitution. The Mexicans wanted to establish beyond doubt the political independence and sovereignty of the country by ending the interference of powerful foreign companies in internal political affairs.

The general social aims of the Revolution were significant motives in expropriation. Cárdenas and many other leaders who had had direct contact with the Revolution hoped that expropriation would elevate the lower classes and secure a fairer distribution of wealth and income in Mexico by putting the tremendous earning power of the companies at the disposal of the nation. Labor groups and industrialists resented the privileges granted by Díaz to foreigners, and demanded their cancellation. These Mexicans wanted to reëstablish the Mexican nationality as the basis of the economic life of the country.

Against this setting, how did Mexico go about solving the problem of its oil industry? The manner in which Mexico attacked the problem and the degree to which the objectives were achieved are the next concerns.

Chapter IV

THE ORGANIZATION
AND ADMINISTRATION
OF THE INDUSTRY

The first effect of expropriation was to end private administration of the largest oil properties and to place the Mexican government in charge of about 90 per cent of the productive capacity of the industry. A number of the objectives of expropriation were achieved immediately by the act itself. The attainment of others or, at least, the permanence of their achievement remained in doubt, since immediately after expropriation there was some possibility that the properties would be returned to the companies. The Mexicans were afraid that the veneer of the Good Neighbor policy might be thin and that, consequently, much pressure might be brought to bear from Washington for restoration of the oil properties. Other objectives were only gradually achieved by the hard work of the management under conditions that at times must have seemed very disheartening.

The act of expropriation prevented the economic paralysis threatening the country. The government's action also destroyed the dominant position of the large British and American oil companies in the industry, confirmed the supremacy of Mexican law and legal processes, and canceled the privileges of the companies. Although the act did not definitely establish state ownership of subsoil deposits, it gave the government control over them. The companies were to carry on a campaign to force the Mexican government to pay for the subsoil rights they claimed.

The threat of economic paralysis in the country on March 18, 1938, was serious. The Federal Board of Conciliation and Arbitration had on that day declared the existing contracts terminated. The syndicate headquarters instructed the locals to stop work on March 18.[1] It was almost a miracle that expropriation did avoid a

---

[1] For numbered notes to chap. iv, see pp. 244–245.

complete stoppage in the petroleum industry. Upon expropriation the strike orders were canceled. Although there was a marked slowdown, the dire predictions of the expropriated companies never came true. Petroleum production, falling off somewhat after expropriation, continued without interruption despite the fact that the change in administration literally came overnight (see table 1).

TABLE 1

THE RELATIVE PRODUCTION OF CRUDE OIL, REFINERY OUTPUT, AND CONSUMPTION OF
GASOLINE IN MEXICO, BY MONTHS, JANUARY TO SEPTEMBER, 1938
(January, 1938 = 100)

Month	Production of crude oil	Refinery production	Consumption of domestically produced gasoline
January.............................	100	100	100
February...........................	97	122	92
March..............................	96	106	136
April...............................	51	63	109
May................................	60	72	112
June................................	62	72	109
July.................................	69	94	103
August..............................	78	98	108
September.........................	82	92	102

SOURCE: Basic data from *Boletín de minas y petróleo*, October, 1939–June, 1941.

On March 19, no non-Mexican officer of any expropriated company was allowed to enter his office.

The government, though facing a host of new problems, met them with determination and purpose. The Mexicans were not completely unprepared for their task, and they were able to carry on for a number of reasons. First, the government had as a matter of policy long required the oil companies to train Mexican personnel in the industry; second, the government had actively participated in the industry; and third, the labor syndicate and Mexicans in general received the announcement of the expropriation with such enthusiasm and support as to contribute to success.

It had been a government policy to require the training of Mexicans for administrative and technical positions.[2] The Labor Law of 1931 had specified that at least 90 per cent of the workers in any establishment should be Mexicans. An immigration ruling of 1933 required individual contracts for importing foreign technicians. Permits were not to be granted if competent Mexicans were available, and enterprisers were required to train Mexicans to replace imported technicians on the termination of their contracts.

As early as 1913 and again in 1916, during revolutionary disturbances, the Mexicans had temporarily operated the Doheny oil properties after Americans had evacuated the region.[3] Since that time a new generation of geologists, engineers, and other technicians had been trained in Mexico and in foreign schools. In 1925 the government had set up the National Petroleum Administration (*Control de la Administración de Petróleo Nacional*), a government agency which engaged in production and refining in competition with private capital and also regulated the domestic prices of petroleum products.[4] The functions of this organization were taken over in 1934 by a semiprivate agency, *Petróleo de México, S.A.*, more commonly known as Petromex.[5] The purposes of this company were to regulate the internal market for petroleum and petroleum products, to assure a supply of petroleum for the country and especially for the needs of the railroads and the government,* and to train Mexican personnel. In organizing this agency the government provided that the capitalization be not less than 10 million pesos, and that the government own 50 per cent of the stock and have 40 per cent of the control. Foreigners were barred from stock ownership. Petromex was given power to explore for oil deposits; exploit them; build pipelines, navigation lines, and storage facilities; and encourage the investment of Mexican capital in the oil industry.

In 1937, apparently feeling a need for more effective control of the petroleum industry, the government created a corporation as a direct dependency of the executive department.[6] This organization, known as the General Administration of National Petroleum (*Administración General de Petróleo Nacional*), was authorized to take over the properties of Petromex and to perform essentially the same functions. Although this organization owned only three wells in March, 1938, it had a reported production of 16,000 barrels a day.[7] Mexicans trained in these organizations and in the expropriated companies themselves, together with a few independent American drillers, formed the small nucleus for continuing operations in the industry on the morning of March 19.

The industry to which Mexico fell heir by expropriation was pretty much a hodgepodge that needed extensive reorganization to form a rational national system. The administrative structure

---

* According to the *Revista industrial* of the Secretaría de Economía Nacional for February, 1934, the national railroads and the government were consuming 40 per cent of all petroleum products sold in the domestic market.

included somewhat less than a score of more or less parallel, independent organizations that had been built on a competitive basis. These parallel structures represented too much duplication of efforts and offices to fit into a coördinated and unified plan. The production aspects of the industry were, however, highly favorable. In 1939 average daily production per well in Mexico was approximately 137 barrels, compared to 41 barrels in California,[8] whose wells are among the most prolific producers in the United States. The refining facilities acquired by Mexico were in questionable physical condition. The companies, apparently anticipating expropriation at some time, had made their investments with appropriate circumspection. The refining and transport facilities were mainly geared to export requirements. Marketing arrangements were already largely in the hands of Mexican enterprisers who operated on a contractual basis.

The administrative problem facing the Mexican government was met provisionally on the local level by the establishment of boards (*Consejos de Administración*) by sections of the labor syndicate,[9] which was organized locally on a company basis. On a national scale, the government set up an administrative council of nine members, two representing the Secretary of the Treasury, three the Secretary of National Economy, three the Syndicate of Petroleum Workers, and one the already existing government agency, General Administration of National Petroleum.[10] This council was to supervise the general operation of the industry and to formulate plans for permanent organization. In the early stages, the relationship between the control council and the local boards was coöperative, with the local boards retaining almost complete autonomy. The groups coöperated well at first, but the local boards quickly built up a tradition of independent action which presaged ill for future centralized control.

On June 7, 1938, the basic plan for permanent organization of the industry was enacted.[11] A demand by the Syndicate of Petroleum Workers to take over complete control of the industry, as had just been done with the railroads, was rejected by President Cárdenas in favor of joint control by government and labor, with the government retaining the major voice in the management. The law of June 7[12] set up two public agencies. *Petróleos Mexicanos* (Pemex) was organized to carry on exploration, production, refining, and all other processes up to marketing; and the *Distribuidora de Petróleos Mexicanos* was formed to handle marketing at home and abroad.

Pemex was organized as a public corporation (*institución pública
. . . con personalidad jurídica*) and was placed under the management of a board of directors composed of nine members, two representing the Secretary of the Treasury, three the Secretary of National Economy, one the General Administration of National Petroleum, and three the Syndicate of Petroleum Workers. The
president, vice-president, and secretary of the board of directors
were to be appointed by the president of the republic. The federal
executive and the syndicate were free to remove their respective
appointees at any time. The board was given power to appoint the
general manager (*Gerente General*) of Pemex and such other
managers and officeholders (*empleados*) as were needed. The salaries of the managers and officeholders were to be fixed in the annual budget. The members of the board of directors were to receive 50 pesos for each meeting attended, but no other compensation. The law provided that the annual budget was to be approved
by the board of directors and by the president of the republic.
Profits were to be placed at the disposition of the Treasury Department.

The *Distribuidora de Petróleos Mexicanos,* also set up as a
public corporation, was charged with the marketing of petroleum
and its derivatives, whether produced by Pemex, by the General
Administration of National Petroleum, or by others. This corporation was to have a general manager and a board of five directors,
including two representatives appointed by the Secretary of the
Treasury, one by the Secretary of National Economy, one by the
General Administration of National Petroleum, and one by the
Pemex board of directors. To initiate the activities of the *Distribuidora de Petróleos Mexicanos,* a fund of 200,000 pesos was to
be set up by equal contributions from Pemex and the General Administration of National Petroleum. With regard to price policies
the law was vague, providing only that the Distribuidora should
pay to those for whom it acted as marketing agency the amount
received for the sales, less the expenses of marketing and "an
amount per unit of production for services rendered," in accordance with agreements between the producers and the Distribuidora.

The Mexican concept of a public corporation, as exemplified in
Pemex, appears to be similar to the American concept. The Distribuidora was disbanded in 1940, but Pemex had much the same
privileges and responsibilities (and, perhaps, some of the same confusions) as public corporations in the United States have. There
was much uncertainty as to whether or not Pemex should be op-

erated as a business concern, but the courts ruled that the institution was to pay taxes as does a private business.

The law specified that the corporation was a legal entity with all the powers necessary to carry out its aims. The principal aim was declared to be not profit, but the achievement of "social" rather than of "speculative" ends.[13] However, the administrators generally felt that the organization should maintain itself on an independent financial basis. One of the most "collective-minded" of the administrators, Jesús Silva Herzog, an economist of Marxian leanings, expected the organization to realize earnings that would cover costs and leave a surplus to pay for schools and hospitals for workers, to meet the developmental costs of the industry, and to make a profit for the government as "unquestionable owner of the subsoil."[14] The administrator after 1946, Antonio Bermúdez, regarded Pemex as a corporation based on the same operating principles that govern private business. "Petróleos Mexicanos," he said, "ought to increase its capital and profits. . . ."[15] However, price policies were not directed toward maximizing profits. In fact, although Pemex was an autonomous government agency, the executive department of the government exercised price control from the very beginning (see chap. viii).

On the other hand, the leaders of the syndicate in general did not regard the organization as a commercial enterprise, and were little concerned about the necessity of making expenses and income meet. Their excessive demands for larger portions of Pemex' revenues (see chap. x) raised protests even from the leaders of the Confederation of Mexican Labor. The syndicate resented the attitude of the administrators, who considered that Pemex was much "like private enterprise."[16] Many labor leaders, apparently unmindful of any need for an accounting system, and either ignoring or denying the function of money in allocating resources, looked upon the organization as an opening wedge to economic planning.

Pemex, as a government corporation in the eyes of the law, was an independent agency of the government;* as such it had to pay taxes, as did private corporations. When the federal government, through its port authorities, demanded that Pemex pay certain shipping penalties in 1941, Pemex applied for a court injunction to exempt it as a government agency. The Supreme Court denied this plea on the ground that the only organizations not subject

---

* However, the independence of Pemex was not infrequently violated by the intervention of the federal executive during the first years of its existence. The organization's business principles appear to have been frequently compromised for political ends. See chap. x.

to the fiscal laws were those directly dependent on the government, but that the exemption did not extend to autonomous public corporations unless expressly provided by the legislature.[17] However, Pemex appeared to be exempt from import duties on materials other than petroleum by default of action by the Secretary of the Treasury.[18]

An amendment to the basic law of June 7, 1938, adopted on August 9, 1940, provided that Pemex could issue credit instruments in accordance with the Law of Deeds and Credit Transactions.[19] The law also allowed the institution to sell assets to carry out its authorized functions, except that the sale of real estate required the approval of the president of Mexico through the secretaries of the Treasury and of National Economy, and that petroleum deposits might not be sold nor the right to exploit them alienated. The act also provided that the government receive 3 per cent interest on its investment (to be charged as an operating expense) plus royalties to be fixed each year by the Secretary of National Economy at a figure between 10 and 35 per cent of the production of Pemex. After these charges and other costs of production had been met, earnings in liquid form (*rendimientos líquidos*) were to be distributed as follows: 20 per cent for a reserve fund, 60 per cent for the federal government, and 20 per cent for labor. The law also provided that the government, acting through the executive, might turn its interest or royalties back into the organization to increase the capital investment.

The administrative organization as first set up was highly unsatisfactory. There were three principal difficulties: (1) Great duplication of effort and expense resulted from retaining the parallel organization of the expropriated companies, and also from continuing the General Administration of National Petroleum. (2) The inability of management to establish effective control by the local labor boards, because of the power and prestige of labor groups, resulted in a lack of coördination and made it impossible to control expenses. (3) The provision for a separate organization to handle marketing arrangements was unsatisfactory.

Before expropriation, labor had been organized along company lines. After March 18, the locals organized the administrative boards that controlled operations within the framework of the private companies. The eighteen different administrative systems involved a great deal of duplication in distribution, sales, accounting, and technical services. At the same time, the local boards were practically outside the control of the central administrative organization, both in the coördination of operations and in the hiring of personnel. Although the board of directors had power to appoint officers, its attempts to bring local activities under control were met by the firm opposition of local labor leaders, who were enjoying a period of unsurpassed prestige and power and were rapidly building vested interests in local control.

The central administration faced, on the one hand, mounting expenses because of duplication of effort, poor coördination, and excessive hiring by the locals, and on the other hand, reduced revenues because of the lost export markets. To meet the threat, the management tried to centralize accounting, legal, medical, engineering, and sales services by setting up unified departments.[20] At the same time, Pemex attempted to absorb the General Administration of National Petroleum. Fearing displacement of personnel, labor objected strenuously to both these proposals. By February, 1939, however, despite labor opposition, the management was able to force through the unification of the accounting, legal, medical, and engineering services.[21] It was estimated that these reforms would result in saving 3 million pesos annually.[22]

As a consequence of more ardent labor opposition, the management did not so easily eliminate duplication and centralize control in the domestic marketing organization. The oil companies had not directly operated gasoline stations, but had put them in the hands of independent businessmen on a fixed commission basis.[23] The Distribuidora preserved this contractual method of handling retailing, but the flow of products to the market outlets was rather firmly controlled by local labor leaders. This raised problems of coördinating production and sales as well as of eliminating the duplication of distributive outlets. The central administration naturally wanted to bring all these matters under its control, and planned, among other things, to eliminate the Distribuidora. The long, bitter battle that ensued between labor leaders and management removed the last vestiges of the coöperative spirit that had characterized their early relations. It was not until December, 1939, that the centralization of retail agencies in each large city was completed, and the centralizing of the bulk distributing plants took even longer.[24] The strength of labor was such that displaced personnel were not discharged, but were used to establish new agencies, especially on the frontier. These border agencies could compete with distributors of United States products, who were allowed to operate in that region because of their proximity and because of the difficulty and expense of transporting Mexican products to outlying regions.[25] Attempts to fuse the Distribuidora with Pemex at this time were unsuccessful.

In November, 1939, there were rumors that the General Administration of National Petroleum would be absorbed by Pemex;[26] but, apparently as a result of protests by those labor sections whose interests were threatened, fusion was delayed for some months.

By January, 1940, the industry was in such dire straits, both from financial difficulties and from lack of adequate central control, that reorganization was fast becoming an absolute necessity to avoid complete collapse. However, bitter controversy developed between management and labor over the steps to be taken in reorganization and over the nature of the economies to be effected. As a consequence, no progress was realized until August 8, after the bitterness of the dispute had induced President Cárdenas to intervene. At this time the General Administration of National Petroleum and the Distribuidora were abolished and their assets and functions transferred to Pemex.[27]

The same law effecting this reform gave the federal executive power to appoint the general manager and the assistant general manager of Pemex. As a concession to the syndicate, the representative on the board of directors formerly appointed by the now defunct General Administration of National Petroleum was to be replaced by another representative of the syndicate, thus giving labor four representatives to government's five. The repeated request of the syndicate to have the petroleum industry placed under union management was opposed both by President Cárdenas and by public opinion, which had been impressed by the failure of union management of the railroads.*

The management established effective control over the local administrative councils only after long controversy with labor. Before expropriation, the companies had maintained administrative control through nonorganized employees who were appointed by the management and over whom the syndicate had no power. The holders of these managerial and supervisory positions were known as "confidential employees" (*empleados de confianza*). With the expropriation, all confidential employees were ousted except those few who held the confidence of labor, and the positions were filled by syndicate personnel.[28] When friction began to develop between

---

* At the end of 1940 the deterioration of the railroad lines and the impairment of their efficiency induced the government to set up a new administration with limited worker representation, but with a majority of representatives appointed by the president of the republic. See George Wythe, *Industry in Latin America* (New York, 1945), p. 288.

labor and management, labor discovered that the sympathy of the incumbents in these positions of management and supervision was a powerful weapon. The administrators found themselves in the embarrassing position of being unable to control the organization. Consequently, they began to replace these individuals as rapidly as possible with others who enjoyed the confidence of the administration. As might be expected, this policy brought strong protest from the syndicate, and the issue became a major one in relations between management and labor (see chap. x).

The issue also belatedly aroused the government to pass another law on April 7, 1942,[29] to establish and enforce the powers of the board of directors as set down in the basic law. The new law declared that these powers had gone unrespected as a consequence of the decision of the Federal Board of Conciliation and Arbitration in the conflict of economic order of 1940, and authorized the board of directors to appoint certain key officers.* The board also received specific powers to approve certain operations with the concurrence of three of the federal government representatives, and these powers could not be delegated.† Effective control was not definitely clinched until the first collective contract was signed in May, 1942; but, in fact, the management appears gradually to have extended its control after the reorganization award of the Federal Board of Conciliation and Arbitration in November, 1940 (see chap. x).

Another administrative change in December, 1946, provided that the chief officers of Pemex were to be a general director (*Director General*) and three subdirectors in charge of production, administration and legal affairs, and business affairs (*Subdirector Técnico de Producción, Subdirector Técnico Administrativo y de Asuntos Jurídicos,* and *Subdirector Técnico Comercial*).[30] The law also put the directors on a fixed monthly salary of 500 pesos with no other payments, in place of the former allowance of 50 pesos per meeting. With this change, the management modified the internal administrative framework. Before December, 1946, the chain of administration was from the general manager through the assistant

---

* The appointees included the general manager, the assistant general manager, department managers, assistant department managers, the general purchasing agent, the general auditor, the general accountant, and the treasurer.

† These powers included approval of the general operations program, the budget, contracts for construction of refineries and pipelines, the annual balance sheet and the distribution of profits, export sales, sale of real estate, acquisition of real estate valued at more than 20,000 pesos, purchase or sale of ships, leases or use of refineries abroad, loans of more than 100,000 pesos for more than thirty days, and authorization of credits in excess of 100,000 pesos for more than ninety days.

general manager, below whom were seven operating departments of exploration, production, refining, domestic sales, export sales, finances, and social welfare (personnel and administrative services).[31] The general manager was aided by two special assistants, one in charge of coördination of departments and the second in charge of technical matters. The assistant general manager also had a technical assistant.

The administrative reform of December, 1946, more closely coördinated the various related activities in the company before they

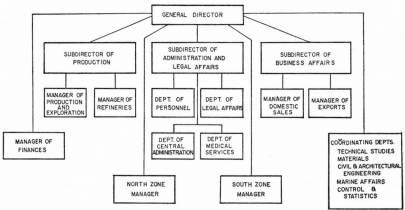

Fig. 1. Administrative organization of Pemex.

reached the level of the general director. It placed exploration, production, and refinement under the subdirector of production. The subdirector of business affairs was charged with domestic and export sales. The subdirector of administrative and legal affairs took over personnel, worker welfare, medical, and legal matters. A coördinator, a manager of finances (in charge of funds, accounting, credit, and the budget), and two zone managers, of the north zone (Tampico, Golden Lane, and Poza Rica fields) and the south zone (Isthmus fields), were placed directly under the general director (see fig. 1).

Information concerning internal administration is difficult to obtain. Pemex, suffering from internal frictions until 1947, was unwilling to publicize its problems. Matters became so critical in the late 'forties that Pemex called in an American company to study its internal management. No report was published.

The concession system, which gave rights to the subsoil, had long been a thorn in the flesh of many Mexicans. By expropriation and the settlement of indemnification, the Mexican government was able to establish definitively its direct dominion over the subsoil.* The controversy, which had recurrently broken out during twenty years and was incapable of a solution satisfactory to Mexicans so long as the large oil companies remained, was unequivocally settled. In 1939 the Mexican Congress passed legislation to implement the constitutional provisions. Article 27 had provided that all minerals or substances found in veins, deposits, or pools—including fuels, petroleum, and all hydrocarbons in any form—belonged to the nation and that this property right of the nation was "inalienable and imprescriptible." Concessions (*concesiones*) might not be granted for the exploitation of petroleum and hydrocarbons. The article specified that supplementary legislation should indicate the methods by which the nation would carry on exploitation of these substances.

Congress passed the basic legislation on December 30, 1939, and amended it on May 2, 1941.[32] As provided by Congress, a presidential order of December 16, 1941, specified the detailed regulations of the petroleum industry.[33]

The basic law, as amended, asserted the "inalienable and imprescriptible" ownership rights of the state over petroleum deposits and all forms of hydrocarbons, whatever their physical state. The petroleum industry was subject to exclusive federal jurisdiction, and only the federal government might set up regulations governing it or might levy taxes on it. Operations in the petroleum industry required authorization from the executive department in accordance with provisions of the law.

The law declared the petroleum industry a "public utility," by virtue of which it was to enjoy a preference in the use of the surface of the land. Land needed in the industry might be expropriated with proper indemnification to the owners, who were to receive no other payment for the petroleum that might be recovered from the subsoil.

The law provided for exploration for and production of oil by three types of agencies: (1) direct dependencies of the government, (2) government corporations created by law for that purpose, and (3) private interests on a contractual basis under certain circum-

---

* There may have remained slight technical ground for doubt as to the nation's absolute dominion over the subsoil, since a few small, foreign oil companies still operated in Mexico for a number of years after expropriation. For all practical purposes any claims of these or of private Mexican companies to the subsoil could have been counted out. It is significant, however, that as late as 1948 a contract between the Mexican government and the Cities Service Company specified that the latter relinquish its claims to confirmatory concessions based on Mexican law before 1917. See *World Oil*, International Section, May, 1948, p. 282.

stances. Exploitation and production by government corporations were to be carried out under land "assignments" (*asignaciones*) made by the Secretary of National Economy (later called Secretary of Economy) upon petition from the government corporation. Such assignments were to become incorporated into the assets of the petitioner for exploratory and production purposes. Exploration and production by private interests were to be carried on under contracts calling for cash payment for such operations, or for an agreed percentage of production if the operations turned out successfully. Contracts were to be authorized only after an investigation had established the convenience and necessity of such operations, and only with those who offered the most favorable terms. Such contracts were limited to a period of not more than thirty years, were nontransferable, and might be made only with (1) individuals of Mexican nationality, (2) companies of Mexican nationals, or (3) companies of "mixed capital" (*economía mixta*) in which the federal government held a majority of the controlling stock. The presidential order of December 16, 1941, limited concessions to any single individual for exploration and production to 30,000 hectares (74,130 acres). In no case were the companies to issue stock with freely transferable shares.

The government did not require contract authorization for superficial surface exploration on government lands, but permission was to be obtained from the owners of private property that might be explored. If the owner refused, the Secretary of Economy might, after hearings, grant the permission, provided that bond was established for any damages the owner might sustain.

To ensure petroleum supplies to the nation, the federal executive might, after study of oil-bearing lands, set aside as national reserves one-half of such lands discovered by government corporations or by private individuals or corporations under contract, and he might open reserves by presidential order. The federal executive department was to establish police regulations and technical standards to which production must conform.

The Secretary of Economy was empowered to authorize concessions for the transportation, storage, and refining of petroleum, and the distribution, capture, and manufacture of gas. Such concessions were subject to the following restrictions: (1) they were to be authorized for a period not exceeding fifty years, and at the time of expiration the installations were to revert to the government without compensation; (2) they were to be granted only to individuals or companies of Mexican nationality, or companies of "mixed capital" in which the government held the majority of the controlling stock; (3) the government was to have the right at any time to use up to 20 per cent of the capacity of the systems, plants, or installations governed by the concession; and (4) the recipient of the concession was obliged to carry on regular operations in accordance with the supplementary regulations issued by the executive department in the enforcement of the law. The presidential order of December 16, 1941, provided that recipients of concessions for the construction of transportation facilities must handle the oil of any individual or company requesting service, although concessionaires, if producers also, might reserve 50 per cent of their capacity for their own use. The construction of storage tanks of a capacity of less than 150 cubic meters, or of those intended by producers for their own private use, was not to require concessions, but only permits from the Secretary of Economy. Those receiving concessions for storage tanks must make them available to anyone requesting storage facilities, except that such concessionaires, if producers also, might reserve 50 per cent of their capacity for their own use.

The transportation, storage, and refining of petroleum and the manufacture and distribution of gas were declared public services, and such concessions were to be regarded as public utilities. The Secretary of Economy, after hearings, was to authorize the tariffs to be charged for their services.

Concessions might be revoked by the Secretary of Economy for (1) failure to carry on regular operations, (2) transfer of the concession to unqualified persons, and (3) failure to pay federal taxes. For less serious infractions of the law, the Secretary of Economy might levy fines in amounts ranging from 100 pesos to 20,000 pesos, as might seem fitting in his judgment.

The law had some ambiguous provisions concerning royalty payments to holders of concessions granted under earlier laws. The gist of these seems to be that royalty payments were to be made to those holding confirmatory concessions under the Petroleum Law of 1925, but not to those holding ordinary concessions. However, it appears that Pemex did not pay royalties to private parties. In 1946 a large group of persons who had been denied such payments formed a "Committee of Defense of Royalties."[34] They seem to have had little success, but the government did announce in 1947 that it would begin to liquidate a backlog of accumulated royalty payments amounting to 30 million pesos.[35] How much of this was paid off is unknown.

The presidential order of December 16, 1941, to carry out the provisions of the basic law, stipulated that government corporations, upon authorization of the Secretary of Economy, had the power to construct and operate facilities for the transportation, storage, and refining of petroleum, and for the recovery, manufacture, and distribution of gas as governed by the regulations covering petroleum operations. When contracts to private individuals or companies, or authorizations to public corporations, involved overlapping claims over a single pool the parties were required to develop such pools on a unit basis to avoid reservoir losses. The government might require that all or part of the production of any organization be sold to the government at prevailing world prices.

The law gave the Secretary of Economy authority to supervise the petroleum industry and carry out regular and unscheduled inspections. The Office of Mines and Petroleum was directed to maintain a public register of petroleum property and to record concessions, assignments of land, contracts, and reserves designated by the executive department.

After March, 1938, the government gradually extended its domination of the industry. It did not employ such spectacular methods as expropriation, but resorted to purchase and various pressures and incentives. After expropriation there were about forty independent producers, most of them Mexican nationals, in the Tampico region.[36] The Secretary of Economy continually reviewed old concessions, annulling those which had been allowed to lapse,[37] and purchased some small companies. In 1947 Pemex completed arrangements to buy four subsidiaries* of the Cities Service Corporation, leaving only one United States firm, the Mexican Gulf Oil Company.[38] An added inducement to reduce outstanding concessions came on January 19, 1943, when an amendment to the petroleum laws[39] provided that tax debts arising from confirmatory concessions were to be canceled upon relinquishment of the concessions. Through annulment and relinquishment of rights granted under the Petroleum Laws of 1925, the government reduced the number of concessions from 1,628, covering 6.3 million hectares, in 1940 to 1,348, covering 4.1 million hectares, in 1947.[40] However, even those who retained concessions lost the power to dispose of them as they wished. In a test case, an individual who tried to turn

---

* The Mexico-Texas Petroleum and Asphalt Company, the Sabino-Gordo Petroleum Corporation, the Mexican Eastern Oil Company, and the Compañía de Terrenos Petrolíferos Imperio.

certain concessions over to Pemex was denied this right by a federal court on the grounds that ownership of the subsoil was vested in the government, which alone could make concessions.[41] Mexicans appear to have been at least as unsuccessful as the expropriated companies in establishing claims to ownership of subsoil oil.

After World War II, Mexico was under tremendous pressure to modify its policy toward foreign participation in the oil industry. Since the country lacked capital and equipment for carrying on exploratory drilling,* the government decided that private capital should be encouraged to enter the industry. Mexico turned first to its own sources, but efforts to interest private Mexican capital in the petroleum industry proved unsuccessful. In 1946 the government asked Mexican nationals to apply for exploration and development rights on a tract of 30,000 hectares in Sinaloa.[42] The contract was to allow 87.5 per cent of any recovered oil to the contractor and reserve 12.5 per cent for the government. One-half of any oil-bearing zones were to go to government reserves. This was the first new property offered for private development after expropriation.[43] A Mexican national received the contract but allowed it to lapse, apparently because he was unable to obtain drilling equipment.

In looking farther afield for the necessary capital and equipment, the Mexican government had to tread carefully to avoid arousing the highly nationalistic labor movement, which jealously guarded against anything smacking of foreign economic imperialism. Any action of the government which suggested a possible compromise of public domination of oil deposits immediately raised a great hue and cry from organized labor. Pemex opened negotiations with certain small American oil companies, but it was difficult to negotiate with them under any conditions because of labor opposition. In September, 1947, however, Pemex did finally succeed in making a contract with a company to which labor could hardly object.[44] It was a small, practically unknown enterprise that had not previously engaged in Mexican oil production. In fact, the company's principal virtue, from the viewpoint of Mexican labor, was the cause of its downfall: it was so lacking in potential economic imperialism and economic power and had so little influence in the United States that it was unable to get the necessary drilling equipment to carry out its contract. The contract became a dead letter.

In April, 1948, Pemex signed a contract with the Cities Service

---

* The inability to obtain equipment appears to have been due in large part to the continued hostility of the large oil companies, which brought pressure to bear on supply concerns.

Company, whose four Mexican subsidiaries had behaved so circumspectly that they had not been expropriated in 1938.[45] This contract, to be consistent with Mexican law, was put in the form of an agreement whereby Pemex was to be in charge of drilling (although it might hire independent drilling contractors),* and the company was to provide the technical and administrative staff and to aid in acquiring necessary equipment. Other terms of the contract included the right of Cities Service to purchase 50 per cent of any newly discovered oil at an agreed price, presumably 16 to 18 cents per barrel below the Gulf Coast price.

The next step came in March, 1949, when Pemex signed a contract with an American group (consisting of the American Independent Oil Company, the Signal Oil and Gas Company, and Edwin W. Pauley) which set up a Mexican subsidiary for exploration and drilling.[46] The details of this agreement are not known, but it was asserted that the subsidiary would have wide latitude in its conduct of operations.

The difficulty of attracting private enterprise, and the interest of certain groups in the United States government, led Pemex to turn next to Washington as a source of capital for the long-run development of the Mexican petroleum industry. In March and April, 1949, the general director conferred with various government officials in Washington in an effort to negotiate a loan of about 500 million dollars from the Export-Import Bank.[47] However, the negotiations were unsuccessful. A study of the opposing forces in the parleys would be an interesting chapter in American domestic, as well as international, affairs. It appears that the Department of Defense favored a loan in order to develop petroleum resources close to home, and that the State Department supported the military because development of Mexican petroleum would help Mexico toward stability and prosperity. On the other hand, large American oil companies opposed the loan, preferring that oil development be undertaken by private capital. Moreover, the Export-Import Bank followed a fairly well-established lending policy of avoiding competition with or displacement of private capital. Pressures in Washington sufficed at this time to maintain the bank's principle. The American negotiators urged Mexico to open the oil industry to foreign private capital before the United States made any loan commitment. Mexican negotiators, realizing that such action would mean political suicide, officially broke off the talks.[48]

---

* This clause seems to have been, in part at least, a subterfuge to pacify labor, for Pemex awarded the drilling contract to Cities Service. See *Oil and Gas Journal*, Mar. 17, 1949, p. 59.

In summary, expropriation threw the organization and administration of about 90 per cent of the petroleum industry into the hands of the Mexican government. The government met the immediate problem by depending heavily upon the Syndicate of Petroleum Workers. This policy prevented the paralysis that might possibly have resulted from a strike. The preliminary structure of the expropriated industry, paralleling that of the private companies, was characterized by much duplication and wasted effort. At the same time, the necessary dependence upon the syndicate raised serious problems later, when management tried to centralize control and eliminate the costly organizational structure. Management integrated control only after several years of struggle.

The government attacked the problem of control by establishing a government corporation, Pemex. Labor received a voice in the management of the corporation, but the government retained voting control. The dominance of the nationalized portion of the industry was extended by purchase and by termination of concessions.

Although Pemex was set up as a public service corporation, its chief officers and the presidents of Mexico generally regarded it as a business enterprise that should be run on sound financial principles and be self-supporting. This attitude was certainly in harmony with the basic conditions in the petroleum industry, which in earlier times had been one of the richest industries in the country. However, the syndicate tended to disagree with management on the business character of Pemex. The nature and policy implications of this disagreement will be considered further in chapters x and xii.

The laws regulating petroleum development after expropriation were heavily influenced by highly nationalistic groups. Uncertainty in the law and hostility among labor groups created serious obstacles to participation in the industry by foreign capital. The law limited the ownership of petroleum deposits to the nation itself, and exploration for and exploitation of oil deposits were hedged around with many restrictions which laid a haze of illegality over foreign participation in oil development. Labor groups sought to maintain the nebulous legality because they opposed anything even remotely resembling foreign economic imperialism. It is likely that domestic capital, at least tacitly, supported labor in this hostility because Mexican capitalists opposed foreign competition. (The existence and implications of this feeling will be more extensively explored in chap. xii.)

Expropriation did much to break down the long-disliked concession system, and Mexico, in its need for foreign aid, attempted to attract foreign capital by other devices more agreeable to nationalistic groups. Pemex induced a few American companies to do exploratory work on a contractual basis, without benefit of concessions that allowed claims to subsoil deposits. Attempts after the war to raise an intergovernmental loan in Washington for oil development were not successful.

By 1950 Mexico had established without significant qualification its claim to subsoil deposits. It had quite effectively unified the structure of the industry. On the surface, the problems of internal management appeared to have been solved. A more complete understanding of the problems of management and of their solution must await a description of Pemex' operational problems, which are considered in the succeeding chapters.

Chapter V

EXPLORATION
AND PRODUCTION

Among the ills that Mexico hoped to rectify by expropriation were the declining trend in oil production and an alleged lack of interest in exploration by the oil companies. Did Mexico solve these problems by expropriation? Was the trend of production reversed? Did interest in exploration increase? The answers to these questions are the concern of this chapter.

Production of petroleum on a commercial scale in Mexico began in 1901.[1] The story of the succeeding twenty years is a saga of fabulous oil strikes that resulted in theretofore unheard of yields escaping with such speed and violence as to be uncontrollable. One unexpected oil gusher ran uncontrolled for six months, overflowed hastily constructed earthen reservoirs of more than 3 million barrels capacity, followed the Tuxpam River thirty-four miles to the sea, ruined fishing banks and oyster beds in the vicinity, and created a threat of fire which jeopardized the entire area.[2] The nation's output skyrocketed so that, by 1918, Mexico stood second in the world with a production of almost 64 million barrels. This position was held until 1928, when Venezuelan production of almost 106 million barrels surpassed Mexico's 50 million barrels for the year. Mexico's record year was 1921, when the subsoil yielded 193 million barrels (about one-fourth of the world's total) of the black flowing wealth that was enhancing the country's reputation for boundless natural riches. Thereafter, however, the decline in production was almost as breath-taking as the initial rise. In the ten years preceding 1921, the rate of increase in production averaged about 32 per cent per year, but in the seven years following, the rate of decrease averaged about 21 per cent per year. Production dropped to less than 33 million barrels in 1932, when Mexico stood seventh in world production. (See fig. 2.)

---

[1] For numbered notes to chap. v, see pp. 245–246.

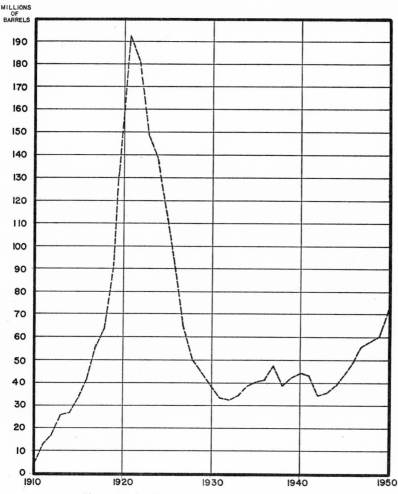

Fig. 2. Crude oil production in Mexico, 1910–1950.

In the years after 1932, annual production increased slowly but steadily until the year of expropriation. The year 1938 brought a drop of more than 8 million barrels, or about 18 per cent. Output slowly picked up in the next two years, faltered in 1941, and dropped sharply in 1942 to less than 35 million barrels, the lowest figure in nine years. Production increased very slowly until the end of the war, and then it strengthened considerably, reaching a twenty-four-year high in 1950, with more than 72 million barrels. After World War II, production averaged about 58 million barrels a year. Mexico accounted for less than 2 per cent of the world pro-

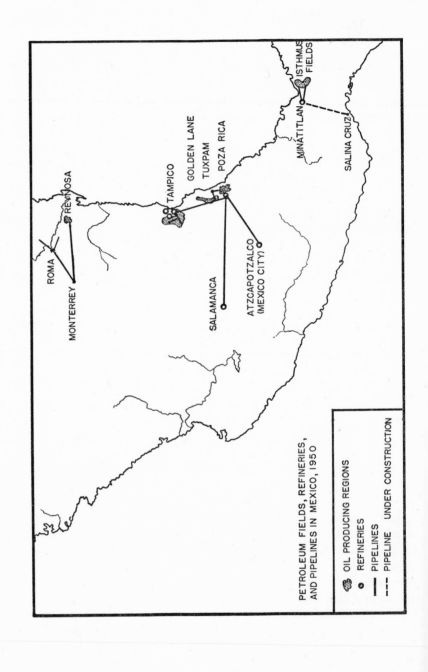

PETROLEUM FIELDS, REFINERIES, AND PIPELINES IN MEXICO, 1950

OIL PRODUCING REGIONS

o REFINERIES

— PIPELINES

--- PIPELINE UNDER CONSTRUCTION

ISTHMUS FIELDS

MINATITLAN

SALINA CRUZ

GOLDEN LANE

TUXPAM

POZA RICA

TAMPICO

REYNOSA

ROMA

MONTERREY

SALAMANCA

ATZCAPOTZALCO
(MEXICO CITY)

duction of crude petroleum from 1938 to 1950 and usually stood in sixth place, although in 1944 and 1945 it stood fifth because production in Rumania and the Dutch Indies declined.[3] The drop in 1938 and the comparatively slow rise in the first three years of operation by Pemex reflected the world boycott imposed on Mexican oil by the expropriated companies. The faltering during the war period 1942–1945 was due principally to the loss of foreign markets resulting from inadequate shipping facilities and from Germany's submarine campaign and to the inability to get necessary refining equipment because of material shortages and the continued hostility of large influential companies in the United States. The freeing of export markets and the increasing availability of necessary materials for exploration, production, and refining accounted for the postwar recovery in annual production.

The expropriated companies made many dire forecasts of the Mexican government's inability to operate the industry successfully. However, in 1938 the field of production offered fairly bright prospects; and, in fact, one of the principal problems during the first years was the surfeit of oil threatened by the boycott engineered by the expropriated companies. The chief difficulty faced by the production department was how to shut in wells without damaging them.* This particular problem was complicated by a shortage of petroleum engineers. The production department was said to have only five in the period after expropriation.[4]

The four principal petroleum-producing regions in Mexico were all situated in the eastern coastal region, in the states of Vera Cruz, Tabasco, Chiapas, San Luis Potosí, and Tamaulipas. They were (1) the Pánuco-Ebano region west of Tampico, (2) the Golden Lane region south of Tampico, (3) the rich Poza Rica field about thirty-five miles south of the Golden Lane, and (4) the southern fields in the region of Coatzacoalcos at the Isthmus of Tehuantepec.

The most important of these fields was Poza Rica, which at the time of expropriation was the second largest pool in the world.[5] It was discovered in 1930 by the *Compañía Mexicana de Petróleo "El Aguila,"* a subsidiary of Royal Dutch-Shell that was known as "El Aguila." Development was slow because of a dispute over land-holdings with the government company, General Administration of National Petroleum. However, by 1937 production was well over 18 million barrels, amounting to 40 per cent of the national output (see table 2). In February, 1938, there were only nineteen wells in

---

* Data from Pemex indicates that in January, 1943, of 1,211 wells in the country, 591 were shut in and 620 were in operation.

in the Poza Rica field, but their daily production was almost 52 per cent of the country's total.[6] By 1947 the yield was more than double that of 1938 and amounted to about 57 per cent of the national production (see table 3). This field produced the best of all Mexican crude. It was a light, paraffin-base oil of about 30° A.P.I. gravity.[7] In 1947, Poza Rica, the most important field on the basis of both current production and proved reserves, contained about three-fourths of Mexico's known deposits. It was in the stage

TABLE 2

ANNUAL PRODUCTION OF CRUDE OIL IN THE POZA RICA
FIELD FOR SELECTED YEARS, 1931–1950
(In thousands of barrels)

Year	Production of crude oil
1931	13
1933	811
1935	9,485
1937	18,694
1939	26,361
1941	25,449
1943	20,719
1945	22,946
1947	31,953
1948	34,406
1949	36,839
1950	46,716

SOURCES: Years 1931–1941 from Noriega, *Influencia de los hidrocarburos*, p. 45. Years 1941–1947 from Pemex. Year 1948 from Secretaría de Economía Nacional, *Memoria, 1948–1949*. Years 1949–1950, *World Oil*, July 15, 1951, p. 160.

of flush production, whereas the other major regions were in various stages of depletion.

The Pánuco-Ebano region was the area of the first oil strikes. The first commercial production in Mexico was in Ebano, about forty miles west of Tampico, and the Pánuco field was opened in 1910.[8] The oil of this area was of heavy asphalt base, running about 12° A.P.I.[9] and possessing a high percentage of sulfur. In 1947 the heavy crude of this region accounted for about 18 per cent of the country's production. Probably a little less than 15 per cent of the proved reserves of Mexico were in this field.

The second oil area in the historical development of the industry was the southern region at the Isthmus of Tehuantepec. It was opened in 1904. At the time of expropriation four of the five Isthmus fields were in a state of decline, and the fifth was shut down for lack of oil transportation facilities.[10] It was not until 1942 that Pemex produced appreciable quantities from the fifth field. The Isthmus fields were gradually decreasing in importance, producing about 11 per cent of the country's total in 1947 as compared to about 25 per cent in 1937.[11] The crude produced there was on the whole a light oil, but varied in gravity over a considerable range

TABLE 3

PERCENTAGE[a] OF TOTAL PRODUCTION BY THE VARIOUS OIL REGIONS
OF MEXICO, BY YEARS, 1940–1949

Region	1940	1941	1942	1943	1944	1945	1946	1947	1948	1949
Poza Rica....	65	59	63	60	55	53	53	57	59	59
Pánuco-Ebano.....	14	14	11	9	10	12	18	18	18	17
Golden Lane.	9	13	11	18	22	23	17	14	13	13
Isthmus.....	13	14	15	14	14	12	12	11	10	11
Northeast (Reynosa).	..	..	..	..	..	..	..	..	b	b

a Figures may not total 100 per cent because of rounding.
b Less than 1 per cent.
SOURCE: Basic data from Pemex.

from 22° to 36° A.P.I.[12] Somewhat less than 10 per cent of Mexico's proved reserves were in the Isthmus.

The fields that gave Mexico its fabulous reputation between 1908 and 1925 were those situated in the *Faja de Oro,* or the Golden Lane, a series of pools about seventy miles south of Tampico extending approximately thirty miles from Dos Bocas to El Chapapote on the Tuxpam River. Of declining importance after the 'twenties, these fields accounted for only 14 per cent of the total product in 1947. The oil was of paraffin base and relatively light, running about 20° A.P.I. About 15 per cent of Mexico's reserves were in the Golden Lane.[13]

In August, 1948, a new pool was reported in Reynosa, near the Texas border.[14] Although believed to be a major pool, the field did not achieve great importance in production. After the discovery of additional pools, production in the northeast area reached 624,000 barrels in 1950.[15]

The cumulative total production of crude oil through 1950, in millions of barrels, for each of the Mexican producing areas, is given below:[16]

Region	Cumulative Production
Golden Lane	1,103
Pánuco-Ebano	821
Poza Rica	412
Isthmus	169
Northeast	1
Total	2,506

After expropriation the principal producer of petroleum in Mexico was, of course, Pemex, which accounted for about 98 per cent of the total. The independent producers operated principally in the heavy-crude-oil regions of Tampico. None had entered either Poza Rica or the Isthmus region. Their total annual production ran between 1 and 2 million barrels (see table 4), with about 80 per cent classed as heavy crude. These producers were small operators, the largest of whom produced less than 600,000 barrels in 1940; only four of them produced more than 100,000 barrels in that year.[17] The relative importance of independent production appeared to be declining.

Pemex managed additional privately owned wells in the north Tampico area. In 1946 production from these wells was 1.6 million barrels, or about 3 per cent of the total output.

Although independent operators appeared to have relative freedom of activity in 1950, the early years of expropriation were difficult ones for them. They faced labor troubles and the same marketing problems as Pemex, for the boycott of Mexican oil in world markets did not discriminate among different producers. Before expropriation, in January, 1938, their reported average daily production had amounted to 13,328 barrels; it dropped to only 3,770 barrels in January, 1939.[18] To protect their wells, the independents produced slowly and stored the oil. Among the factors favorable to continued operation of the small-scale independents were their relatively insignificant size, the Mexican nationality of most of them, and the need for oil after 1945.

A more detailed analysis of production changes after expropriation shows that a number of disruptive and limiting factors complicated production after 1938. Until early in 1945, production difficulties limited output less than complications arising after recovery of the oil. In later years, the exhaustion of known reserves became increasingly significant as the limiting factor in production. The first factor to force curtailment of production was the loss of export markets. After expropriation, the oil companies boycotted Mexican oil in a vigorous campaign[19] and virtually excluded it from many former markets. Pressure was brought to induce buyers in the United States to refuse Mexican oil. According to reports, the companies requested the United States government to take steps to

TABLE 4

ANNUAL PRODUCTION OF CRUDE OIL BY PEMEX AND BY INDEPENDENTS
IN MEXICO, 1938–1950
(In millions of barrels)

Year	Pemex	Independents	Total
1938	36.6[a]	1.9	38.5
1939	41.8	1.1	42.9
1940	42.1	1.9	44.0
1941	41.5	1.6	43.1
1942	33.3	1.5	34.8
1943	34.2	1.0	35.2
1944	37.0	1.2	38.2
1945	42.1	1.4	43.5
1946	47.9	1.3	49.2
1947	54.8	1.5	56.3
1948	56.5	2.0	58.5
1949	59.3	1.6	60.9
1950	70.7	1.7	72.4

[a] The 1938 figure includes production of expropriated companies.
SOURCES: 1938–1939, Pemex. 1940–1950, Secretaría de Economía Nacional, *Memoria, 1940–1951*.

prevent the export and sale of oil obtained from the expropriated properties; and although there is no direct evidence of response by the government, the boycott may have influenced some government agencies.[20] There was litigation in both French and American courts to prevent the sale of Mexican petroleum on grounds that the expropriation was invalid and the sale of the petroleum illegal.[21]

In the year before expropriation, Mexico exported about 25.0 million barrels, or 53 per cent of its total petroleum production, whereas in 1938 exports amounted to only 14.7 million barrels, or about 38 per cent of the national output.[22] This precipitous decline of 10.3 million barrels resulted from reduced sales of all major exports except crude gasoline and light crude oil.[23] Table 5 shows in greater detail the dramatic suddenness of the break in exports. In 1937 the monthly average of petroleum exports had been 2.1 million barrels; in 1938 it was 1.2 million barrels. The decline in production after expropriation was not due to any drop in the domestic market; the decline in domestic consumption was negligible in 1938, and the increase was rapid thereafter.[24]

The effectiveness of the boycott is shown by the drop, between 1937 and 1938, of about 7 million barrels, or about 61 per cent, in exports to the United States and to Holland and its possessions.[25] Sales to the British Empire fell by about 800,000 barrels, or ap-

TABLE 5

Exports of Petroleum and Its Derivatives from
Mexico, by Months, 1938
(In thousands of barrels)

Month	Exports
January	1,650
February	2,011
March 1–18	936
March 18–31	95
April	311
May	1,147
June	865
July	1,039
August	1,373
September	1,171
October	1,460
November	1,319
December	1,360

Source: *Boletín de minas y petróleo*, October, 1939–June, 1941.

proximately 12 per cent, and exports to Latin America dropped by slightly less than 1 million barrels, or 71 per cent, because most of the necessary shipping was owned by the large expropriated oil companies. By 1939 the effectiveness of the boycott was breaking down, except in the Dutch Antilles. In addition to disintegration of the boycott, a good market for crude oil was found in Italy, but war was to close this outlet the following year. In 1940, the vigorous efforts of the Distribuidora split the boycott in the United States wide open, and the physical volume of sales soared to more than double that in 1937. The entrance of the United States into the war cut short this hard-earned respite, and the scarcity of shipping closed in on the industry for the duration of the conflict. Pemex had to curtail production drastically in 1942. Although exports continued to fall, reaching a low of slightly less than 5 million barrels in 1944, increasing domestic consumption made it possible to increase production after 1942.

The oil companies did not limit their boycott to the closing of export markets, but attacked Mexico with a campaign to stop supplies of oil-well equipment. In the period immediately after expropriation, this caused serious difficulties only in the Isthmus region. There, one of the five fields, a new one, had its five wells shut down because the Richmond Petroleum Company, owner of the field at the time of expropriation, had not yet built pipelines as production outlets.[26] Other fields in the region were relatively old, and their problems arose from failures in the worn equipment. In other regions this phase of the boycott does not seem to have affected production significantly.

Labor and organizational problems affected the efficiency of the industry. Although in the early years they did not impinge so seriously on production as on other aspects of the industry, differences as to whether labor or the government should have the controlling voice undoubtedly contributed to production losses (see chap. x). Statistics on worker productivity do not altogether reflect these confusions of administration, but it is significant that the annual output per worker in production dropped from 5,800 barrels in 1937 to 5,300 in 1938 and to 4,700 in 1939, a decline of 19 per cent from 1937 to 1939 (see table 25). This decline was largely due to the central administration's loss of control over hiring, and probably in some degree to the decline in well productivity accompanying depletion of the fields. The coördination of production activities was almost impossible under the local administrative boards, which were virtually independent of the central administration. Action depended upon coöperation, which in turn depended upon the administration's remaining in the good graces of the union; and harmonious relations did not last long. The management did not solve the problem of labor discipline until December, 1946, when President Alemán took office. Then wildcat and illegal strikes were virtually eliminated (see chap. x).

It is likely that a sizable portion of the products normally sold in the foreign market could have been sold in the domestic market, which showed a remarkable absorptive capacity, if Mexico's refining facilities had been adequate. But three of the completed refineries obtained by expropriation were in bad physical condition.[27] The company policy of making only necessary replacements just before expropriation had left the refineries under the constant threat of breakdowns. The difficulties of Pemex were multiplied by its inability to obtain parts under the materials boycott. In addition, the necessity of adjusting end products to new market conditions created problems. Refining schedules had to be modified because of the loss of export outlets for former surplus products. As a rule, considerable flexibility in the end products of refinement is possible with proper equipment and technically trained men, but the adjustment may be expensive and complex. A shortage of competent technicians in refining added to the difficulties.[28] Although the problem was not acute, unfamiliarity with equipment slowed refinery processes. The first three annual reports of the general manager indicate the gravity of refinement problems (see chap. vi).

A closely allied problem was that of storage space at refineries.[29] The seriousness of the frequent breakdowns in some of the refineries would have been alleviated by more adequate storage space. As it was, trouble in a refinery was likely to disrupt the whole productive chain, from oil field to market.

As a consequence of these difficulties, the quantity of refined products fell off sharply with expropriation, and the downward trend continued slowly for about two years.[30] The inadequacies of refining and storage facilities continued to plague the industry even after 1944, when world markets began to open up and the urgency of labor and administrative problems began to diminish. Then other factors, such as the condition and amount of petroleum reserves, the number of producing wells, and the engineering techniques used, arose to limit production.

The expert commission studying the petroleum industry in 1937 accepted an estimate that petroleum reserves amounted to 650 million barrels, 500 million in Poza Rica and 150 million in the other three regions.[31] In his annual message to Congress on September 1, 1945, President Avila Camacho estimated reserves at 870 million barrels.* The general director of Pemex placed them at 1,058 million barrels as of the end of 1946, and at 1,424 million as of the end of 1951.[32] Between 1938 and 1947 no new deposits were discovered. The increase was due to upward adjustments of the estimates on existing fields.

Despite the increase in estimated reserves, the depletion of the

---

* Early in 1944 the Petroleum Administration for War of the United States estimated Mexico's proved reserves at the much lower figure of 600 million barrels, distributed as follows: Poza Rica, 425 million; Isthmus region, 50 million; north and south Tampico regions, slightly less than 75 million each. See L. J. Logan, "Pemex Plans Vigorous Exploration Program," *Oil Weekly*, International Section, Nov. 5, 1945, p. 44.

fields put production under pressure. In order to meet the demands for oil after 1944, Pemex pushed production at Poza Rica field to the point where some engineers felt that it crowded, if it did not exceed, the maximum efficient production rate.[33] Certain pessimistic observers believed that the fast rate of production was endangering the Poza Rica field, because the pool was in a stratum of porous limestone over salt water, which threatened to rise and trap oil in gaps between wells.[34] That Poza Rica was being pushed beyond the production rate most desirable from the standpoint of maximum recovery is probably true, judging from the available fragmentary evidence on well production, but this threat seems to have been met in part by increasing the number of wells and operating all wells at lower rates.* However, there is no doubt that Pemex could have increased maximum recovery at Poza Rica by changing the technique of exploitation. A gas-reinjection system, utilizing the prolific gas production to maintain reservoir pressure, would have been beneficial. In 1942 two American engineers, called in for consultation, estimated that reinjection of 75 per cent of the gas would have increased recovery at Poza Rica by 112 million barrels.[35] Pemex was unable to do this because it could not afford the large expense of installing compressors. Consequently the gas has gone to waste.†

In 1946 gas reinjection was utilized only in the Isthmus region, where 147 wells were on gas lift.[36] It was suggested that it might be financially feasible to combine a gas-reinjection system with a desulfurization plant, since the Poza Rica gas contained from 3.2 to 3.4 per cent hydrogen sulfide gas.[37] However, Pemex was not financially able to carry out even this project before 1950. Without a pressure-maintenance system, less oil could be recovered by utilizing reservoir energy, and pumping would have to be resorted to sooner. There is little doubt that, if Pemex could have raised the funds, a system of gas reinjection would have more than paid for itself in the long run.

In addition, the lack of a gas-reinjection system necessitated more wells to maximize recovery. Pemex' problem was to apportion its limited drilling equipment between developmental drilling and exploratory work. Developmental drilling was carried on at the expense of much-needed wildcatting, especially after 1945.

---

* Data from Pemex show that between 1941 and 1946 the number of producing wells in Poza Rica was increased from 35 to 65, whereas the mean annual production per well was reduced from 116,000 barrels to 64,000. By 1950 Pemex had 119 wells at Poza Rica. See World Oil, July 15, 1951, p. 160.

† From 1939 to 1945, about 23 billion cubic feet (660 million cubic meters) of gas were burned each year as waste. Most of it was burned in the atmosphere at Poza Rica.

Despite the limitations of the Poza Rica field and the upward trend of consumption, which presaged serious shortages of petroleum, exploratory work lagged far behind. Immediately after expropriation, the richness of the existing fields and the disappearance of export outlets seemed to minimize the need for exploration, and during the war it was practically impossible to obtain well-drilling equipment. Consequently, in the first six years of Mexican control Pemex drilled only 126 new wells,* of which 123 were developmental and only three were exploratory. This figure compares unfavorably with the 480 wells drilled in the six-year period before expropriation (1932–1937), and with the 2,665 drilled in 1920–1925, the heyday of Mexican production (see appendix table 2).

After 1943, with the increasing availability of materials and equipment and the threat of petroleum shortages, drilling for exploration and development increased. The hope of redeveloping petroleum export markets became an important incentive. In the three years 1944 to 1946, Pemex reported 132 wells drilled, of which 23 were exploratory.† The annual reports of Pemex indicate that 50 exploratory wells were drilled in 1947 and 1948.‡ Although Pemex stepped up total drilling in 1949 and 1950, exploratory drilling lagged. In those two years Pemex drilled 375 wells, compared to only 327 in the eleven preceding years. But only 20 of the wells drilled in 1949–1950 were exploratory, compared to 61 in the period 1938–1948 (see appendix table 2). Of the 763 wells drilled in 1938–1950, only 81, or about 11 per cent, were exploratory, and it was not until 1948 that Pemex made any significant discovery of new pools. The company lagged in exploratory drilling apparently because it was unwilling to risk its scarce capital. Of the 780 wells drilled in 1938–1950, 458 were successful and 322 were abandoned. Drilling in the El Plan field in 1943 and 1945 located two new oil horizons, which kept production in the Isthmus zone on a paying basis.[38] Although 10 of the 81 exploratory wells drilled in 1938–1950 were oil producers,[39] exploratory efforts resulted in no significant achievements until the summer of 1948. Up to that time, the drilling program had simply augmented the number of producing

* Independent companies drilled thirty-two wells during the same period, according to data of Pemex. (This figure does not check with that given by the Secretaría de Economía in *Compendio estadístico, 1948*. See appendix table 2.)

† Data from Pemex indicate that from 1944 to 1946 independents drilled only three wells.

‡ This differs from the figure of thirty-five exploratory wells reported for 1947 and 1948 by *World Oil*, July 15, 1949, p. 89. However, the difficulty of classifying developmental and exploratory drilling in the vicinity of existing fields makes possible honest differences of opinion.

wells in already developed areas, and had made possible upward revision of the estimates of known reserves, but it had discovered few new deposits.

Pemex carried out preliminary geological exploration on a much reduced scale in the years immediately after expropriation, when most of the technicians left the country. In 1938 there were no geological exploration parties. Two were organized in 1939, and the number increased gradually, reaching thirty-four in Septem-

TABLE 6

EXPENDITURES IN EXPLORATORY ACTIVITY BY PEMEX, 1938–1948

(In thousands of pesos)

Year	Exploration parties	Drilling	Other expenses	Total[a]
1938	341	687	539	1,567
1939	951	293	2,428	3,672
1940	1,424	548	2,072	4,044
1941	1,369	952	1,622	3,943
1942	1,574	1,138	64	2,776
1943	2,807	2,482	23	5,612
1944	5,411	4,397	31	10,162
1945	8,001	7,910	67	16,608
1946	9,520	10,547	44	20,693
1947	11,175	21,931	497	36,158
1948	22,555	26,284	500	49,340[b]

[a] There are some unexplained discrepancies in the original data between total expenditures and the sum of the component items.
[b] Estimate.
SOURCE: Pemex.

ber, 1948.[40] The principal areas explored were the northeast frontier region, almost the entire east coast to and including the north side of the Isthmus of Tehuantepec, the Yucatán peninsula, and the central part of Lower California. In 1950 there was exploratory offshore drilling in the Gulf of Mexico.

The expenditures for exploration reveal an inadequate program of search for new fields. Pitifully small initially, they amounted to only about 1.5 million pesos in 1938. Even the expenditure of an estimated 50 million pesos in 1948 was incapable of maintaining reserves and of meeting rapidly growing consumption. Early in 1948, the subdirector in charge of exploration estimated, on the basis of American drilling experience, that Mexico needed seventy-five exploratory wells annually at an approximate cost of 800,000 pesos each.[41] Even this modest estimate required an expenditure of 60 million pesos a year for drilling alone, whereas only about 26 million pesos were spent in 1948. Pemex classified as exploratory only thirty-eight of the eighty wells drilled. (*World Oil* classified only seventeen as exploratory.[42] See appendix table 4.)

The dearth of exploration was due largely to the inability to import drilling rigs, pipe, and other necessary equipment from the United States because of wartime shortages and, more recently, to a lack of capital to finance such purchases. In 1947 Pemex possessed only twenty-nine sets of drilling equipment and, as pointed out earlier, opened negotiations for drilling with several companies in the United States. A contract made in the latter part of the year with a small Louisiana oil company to drill one hundred test wells[43] lapsed because the company was unable to get equipment. Meanwhile, the Cities Service Company contracted to lend Pemex 1 million dollars annually for ten years for exploration and development in northeastern Mexico, where Cities Service held unexpropriated concessions. Cities Service agreed to relinquish all claims to the concessions, furnish technical advice, and aid Pemex in getting equipment. The Mexicans agreed to do the drilling (or contract for it), to repay principal plus 3 per cent interest on the loan in ten annual installments starting in 1952, and, if oil were discovered, to give Cities Service the right to purchase 50 per cent of it at well below the market price.[44] The agreement, to be reviewed annually, could be continued by mutual consent. The fifty-eight drilling rigs operating in Mexico in 1948 drilled forty-five developmental and thirty-eight exploratory wells.

Pemex made additional contracts for exploratory drilling. The general director asserted that expenditures for exploration amounted to 129 million pesos in 1951. Nevertheless, exploratory drilling remained below the minimum estimated as necessary to maintain Mexican reserves at a level appropriate to the growing requirements of the nation. In Illinois, whose oil production was comparable to Mexico's, 2,033 wells were completed in 1947, and 521 of them were exploratory.[45]

One cannot completely ignore the influence of conservation upon production, though it is impossible to estimate its extent with accuracy. In part, government efforts to obviate wasteful practices took the form of regulations governing production techniques. Until 1944, however, conservation policies did not seriously limit production. After that time, increasing output made conservation more necessary, and the Mexicans had to choose between lower rates of production with maximum recovery and higher rates of production with less recovery. Their principal concern in conservation was not to maximize social well-being over time (that is, to preserve oil deposits for future generations*), but rather to minimize waste insofar as this was consistent with consumption needs and production costs. Exactly what compromise was effected between these differing aims is difficult to say in objective terms. As pointed out earlier, some American engineers felt that production in some fields, especially Poza Rica, was being pushed beyond the maximum efficiency rate, though such estimates may not have been based on accurate current data. (It need hardly be said that such estimates were at best only informed guesses, and that current data, difficult to obtain for the Mexican industry, are a prerequisite to accuracy, since conclusions depend upon knowledge of cost and price factors as well as of engineering techniques.)

It is likely that, in the early years of government control, insufficient engineering knowledge was a handicap to conservation, but after the war the Mexicans had the advantage of young engineers trained at home and abroad, and of foreign specialists called in for counseling. Fragmentary data on well production in Poza Rica suggest that, within the limits of available capital, sound engineering practices were being observed. But lack of capital and wartime shortages prevented utilization of the latest engineering techniques (gas-reinjection systems, for example) that would have reduced waste. Data from Pemex indicate that, between 1939 and 1945, about 17 billion of approximately 34 billion cubic feet of wet gas produced annually were delivered to absorption plants and that only slightly more than half a billion cubic feet were returned to the pools, whereas 16 billion cubic feet were burned in the atmosphere, and the remainder was lost or consumed in operation. Almost half the dry gas coming from the absorption plants was burned in the atmosphere, less than 3 billion cubic feet were returned to the pools, and 6 billion cubic feet were lost or consumed in operation. The Poza Rica field in particular needed facilities for drying gas and returning it to the subsoil to maintain pool pressure. Pemex was in an enviable position in the development of the Poza Rica field, since exclusive ownership and control of this rich deposit made unitary operation possible and prevented competitive exploitation. Pemex could not blame its failure to make the most of

---

* The Mexicans possessed a strongly optimistic feeling that this would not be a serious problem in the foreseeable future, because they believed that there were vast undiscovered oil deposits in the country. This optimism was not unfounded. Geologists generally felt that Mexico had much undiscovered oil (see John J. Slattery, "Mexican Oil in Danger," *Mexican American Review*, Aug., 1947, p. 10), and oil companies showed a strong inclination to return to the country.

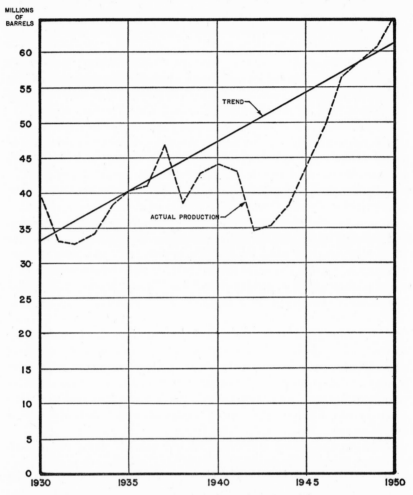

Fig. 3. Trend of annual production of petroleum in Mexico, 1930–1950
(based on 1930–1937 experience).

its unimpaired property rights and of the tremendous reservoir
energy entirely on external conditions beyond its control. Pemex'
failure to raise capital was a serious indictment of its financial
management and of influential groups directly or indirectly connected with the industry.

The problem of judging the extent of petroleum production in
Mexico had expropriation not taken place is, of course, insur-
mountable. It is impossible to say how oil production would have
been affected under private exploitation by such intangibles as the

war, the attitude of the Mexican government toward private operators, and the willingness of the United States government to supply the material needs of the Mexican industry during the war years. It is certainly arguable that the United States would have favored Venezuelan oil development even if Mexican production had remained in private hands. Costs of production were lower in Venezuela, and its oil enjoyed a strategically superior location.

Observation of the production trend from 1930 to 1937 suggests that production during 1938–1947 would have been greater under private exploitation than it actually was under government operation (see fig. 3). However, the acceleration in the rate of production in the earlier period is partly attributable to recovery from the depression years; production might have leveled off considerably had the private companies remained. Moreover, production in 1948 and 1949 was only slightly under the projected trend for 1930–1937, and in 1950 exceeded the trend. Even under private exploitation, the war would probably have affected the industry adversely, despite the possibility that the United States government might have allowed greater exports of materials and supplies to Mexico. Shipment of petroleum to the United States was impracticable except by tanker, and until 1944 at least the German submarine campaign was so effective that the petroleum output would probably not have been appreciably higher even under private exploitation. Arguments as to what trend production would have followed without government operation are largely futile in an industry so uncertain as oil production. Any speculation must be inconclusive.

More to the point from the Mexican view were the results achieved. As will be shown in detail later, the domestic consumption of petroleum products increased under the pressure of lost foreign markets, but until 1949 production did not limit consumption. On the other hand, immediately after the war Mexico could not fully exploit the lucrative export markets in petroleum because of limited production, and faced imminent domestic shortages because of insufficient exploration. Oil for export would have been a desirable corrective of Mexico's seriously adverse balance of trade after 1943; the rising domestic consumption threatened to accentuate the difficulty in the future. But the postwar attitude of the United States toward imports and heavy production of oil by British and American companies in the Near East raised doubts as to what extent oil for export could have helped Mexico's balance of trade.

Final judgment of the accomplishments of Pemex must be tempered by the acknowledgment that serious obstacles barred the way to success. The boycott, the war, the scarcity of capital, and the attitude of recalcitrant elements in the population were difficult hurdles. The war left its mark on the industry, and the other difficulties continued in greater or less degree. Financial management improved after 1946, for the general director, a successful businessman, faced existing problems more realistically than had any of his predecessors. His methods gave promise of bringing order out of the financial chaos.

By 1950 the industry had established its ability to survive. However, it still had to meet the challenge of maintaining the nation's self-sufficiency in oil through increased production, and perhaps also of helping to alleviate the dollar shortage. Mexico also had to keep costs down so as to enjoy a comparative advantage in oil production and thus enhance its economic well-being. The problems of monetary and economic cost will be considered further in chapters xi and xii.

Chapter VI

REFINING

The proponents of expropriation were much concerned about Mexico's economic development. The "colonial status" of the country irritated and alarmed them. They saw the failure of the oil companies to build numerous large, modern refineries turning out many highly refined and valuable products. This, they thought, was economic neglect of a country so richly endowed with oil as Mexico, which should be processing the oil and exporting the valuable refinery products rather than the cheaper crude oil. They objected to Mexico's importation of refined products as evidence of economic backwardness. The extent to which Mexico solved the refining problem is the subject of this chapter.

The earliest refineries in Mexico were crudely fashioned stills constructed by the natives to refine seeping petroleum, which they bottled and sold for medicinal purposes.[1] In 1920 there were twelve refineries with a total daily capacity of about 250,000 barrels, about three-fourths of which was in topping plants and one-fourth in complete refineries.[2]

Official data of the petroleum division of the Department of National Economy indicate that just before expropriation there were twenty-two refineries of all types with a combined crude input capacity of 124,000 barrels a day.[3] However, eleven of these were only gas-drying plants with a combined capacity of 2,000 barrels of gasoline a day, and one was a tiny experimental plant with a capacity of six barrels a day. The ten refineries that were significant as individual plants (see appendix table 5) had a combined capacity of 124,400 barrels of crude oil a day. Four were complete refineries with a daily input capacity of 114,330 barrels, or about 92 per cent of the total, and six were topping plants with a daily input capacity of 10,070 barrels, or about 8 per cent of the total. The capacity of the four complete refineries ranged from 10,330 to 50,000 barrels a day. The six topping plants ranged in capacity from 60 to 7,500

---

[1] For numbered notes to chap. vi, see pp. 246–247.

71

barrels a day, but only two plants exceeded 200 barrels of daily input. From the records available, it is not possible to determine precisely the cracking capacity of the plants, but the charge ran between 11,500 and 13,000 barrels a day.[4]

Before expropriation the Mexican government owned but one refinery, a small topping plant at Bella Vista in the vicinity of Tampico. This plant had a daily input capacity of 2,000 barrels, or 1.6 per cent of the total refinery capacity of Mexico. Expropriation brought under government operation the five largest operating refineries of the country and one large topping plant then under construction at Poza Rica by "El Aguila." The five expropriated operating refineries included the four complete refineries with a capacity of 114,330 barrels of crude oil a day, and one topping plant of 7,500 barrels daily capacity. Since these plants together represented 97.9 per cent of Mexico's refinery capacity, the government monopoly was virtually complete.

The expropriated refineries included the following:

1. The Ciudad Madero refinery of "El Aguila" (Royal Dutch-Shell interests) at Tampico. This plant was the largest, with an input capacity of 50,000 barrels a day. It was a complete refinery coupled with a Gyro cracking unit of 5,700 barrels capacity and an alkylation plant with a capacity of 1,600 barrels.

2. The Minatitlán refinery of "El Aguila" at the Isthmus of Tehuantepec. This was a complete refinery with a daily input capacity of 30,000 barrels. It had a Dubbs cracking unit producing 2,500 barrels of gasoline daily.

3. The Mata Redonda refinery of Huasteca at Tampico. This was a complete refinery of 24,000 barrels per day input capacity. It was combined with a Kellog cracking unit of 3,500 barrels input capacity. The cracking plant, six years old, was the most modern in Mexico.

4. The Arbol Grande refinery of the Sinclair Pierce Oil Company at Tampico. This complete refinery had an input capacity of 10,330 barrels a day. It had no cracking facilities.

5. The Atzcapotzalco refinery of "El Aguila" near Mexico City. This was a topping plant of 7,500 barrels daily input capacity. It had no cracking facilities.

6. The Poza Rica refinery of "El Aguila." This half-finished topping plant, under construction in the Poza Rica field, was designed to have a capacity of 8,000 barrels a day.

These plants, except for those at Atzcapotzalco and Poza Rica, were not only close to the source of crude oil, but also oriented toward the export markets. Of the outwardly oriented refineries, three were near the port of Tampico, and one was near tidewater at the Isthmus of Tehuantepec. In neither of these locations was there a significant local market; although they might have been desirable spots for coastal shipping, the principal locational factor was the export market. On the other hand, the companies had not overlooked the domestic market. The Atzcapotzalco plant, whose principal objective was to serve Mexican consumption, was located in the heavily populated and industrialized plateau area on the outskirts of Mexico City. The Poza Rica topping plant was especially designed to supply either the Atzcapotzalco refinery for the domestic market or the port of Tuxpam for shipment abroad.

Expropriation, revolutionizing the market for Mexican petroleum, necessitated the complete reorientation of refinement and transportation. In refining, the pull of the market is a strong locational factor because it costs more to transport refined products than crude oil. The influence of the market was more and more evident with the unfolding plans of Pemex. The preëxpropriation orientation of the industry to tidewater left its mark on refining, and the adjustment was complicated by factors similar to those affecting production, as pointed out in the previous chapter. After 1938, however, the primary objective of plans for the modification and expansion of refining was an about-face in favor of the domestic market.

In general, the refining equipment inherited by Pemex through expropriation was old, badly worn, inefficient, and obsolescent. The few cracking units in the country were antiquated, the most modern being a six-year-old Kellog unit of 7,000 barrels charging capacity at the Mata Redonda refinery. In one respect, the obsolescence of refinery equipment might have been fortunate, for it relieved Mexico of the necessity of disinvestment in a refinery system unsuited to its needs and aspirations. It was important, too, because the value of the refineries helped to determine the amount of expropriation compensation. In most respects, however, the bad condition of the refineries seriously handicapped the industry, especially since the materials boycott and wartime blockades and shortages prevented significant new construction or replacements in the first five or six years. In those difficult years, Mexico could have put even badly located equipment to good use; and, indeed, Pemex sent some crude oil by sea to be refined in the United States. Although apparently intended for export to Europe, some of the products were returned to Mexico for consumption.[5] The extent to which output was impaired by the deterioration of refining equipment cannot be exactly determined, but it is perhaps significant that the official estimate of refining capacity as of October 31, 1939, was only 98,000 barrels per day as compared to the preëxpropriation estimate of 124,400 barrels.

Aside from the condition of the plants, it was no small task for Pemex to coördinate and unify the odd assortment of refining facilities independently built up by the several companies with little thought for domestic consumption. The shortage of technical men

TABLE 7

RELATIVE VOLUME OF REFINERY OUTPUT IN MEXICO, BY
MONTHS, JANUARY–SEPTEMBER, 1938
(January = 100)

Month	Index
January.	100
February.	122
March.	106
April.	63
May.	72
June.	72
July.	94
August.	98
September.	92

SOURCE: *Boletín de minas y petróleo*, October, 1939–June, 1941.

in refining, although not so acute as in production, complicated the task.[6] Pemex was reported to have had 74 refinery technicians in 1939, compared to 104 formerly employed by the expropriated companies. The contraction of foreign markets forced Mexico to plan refining carefully and to absorb the surfeit of oil at home; this entailed a much more rapid development of the domestic market than was envisioned by those who favored expropriation as a means of keeping in Mexico the fruits of her own soil.

Monthly figures of refinery output in the critical period after expropriation reflect these difficulties. Refinery production in April, 1938, was 37 per cent below that of January and almost 50 per cent below that of February (see table 7).

Immediately after expropriation, because of the boycott threat, a refinery program for domestic consumption only seemed essential, but within a few weeks this proved unnecessary.[7] By 1940, conditions in the European export markets resulting from the war, and the heavy stocks on hand in refineries again forced Pemex to limit refined products to domestic needs,[8] but an easing in the American market brought partial relief that lasted until 1942. Nevertheless, refinery programs called for careful planning and frequently for extensive modification. Although the demand for high-grade gasoline was good and easily absorbed refinery output, it was necessary in 1938–1940 to cut down the total products of refinement, as shown in table 8, since surpluses could not be exported as before.[9] Pemex

TABLE 8

INDEX OF THE ANNUAL PHYSICAL VOLUME OF REFINERY
OUTPUT IN MEXICO, 1937 TO 1950
(1937 = 100)

Year	Index
1937	100.0
1938	78.4
1939	74.0
1940	69.5
1941	81.2
1942	76.7
1943	79.1
1944	83.5
1945	91.2
1946	102.3
1947	107.9
1948	110.6
1949	123.0
1950	125.9

SOURCES: Basic data from *Anuario estadístico* (1937), records of Pemex (1938–1946), and *Informe anual* (1947–1950).

absorbed these surpluses by various expedients. For example, it used accumulating stocks of gas oil to develop a lower viscosity type of locomotive and industrial fuel oil and to substitute for diesel oil and refinery fuel.[10] Experiments with residues uncovered new ways of combining surplus products as charging stocks in cracking plants.

The industry faced the problem of excessive stocks of low-grade gasoline. By law, gasoline had to be maintained at 57-octane or above. The boycott by the Standard Oil group included a refusal to sell ethyl fluid to the Mexicans. Ethyl was necessary to bring substandard gasoline up to the legal requirements. At first Pemex blended straight-run gasoline from Atzcapotzalco with high-octane gasoline derived from cracking plants in Tampico.[11] Then, to supply the deficiency, an ethyl plant was built in 1940, but fire destroyed it the same year. However, Standard raised the ethyl boycott shortly thereafter. Although the reorientation of refinery production to domestic needs was forced on the industry at an early date, the necessary alterations and expansion to meet new conditions had to be postponed, first, until foreign resentment over expropriation had died down, so that the boycott on Mexican oil and on Mexican purchases of petroleum equipment could be lifted, and, later, until material shortages arising from the war had eased. In fact, the industry was hard-pressed, under these circumstances, to make even necessary repairs and alterations to existing equipment in order to handle the volume of crude oil produced and to meet current market conditions. Some of the efforts in adapting used materials and producing homemade substitutes were close to heroic.[12]

The three bright spots in the refinery sky were the Atzcapotzalco and the Arbol Grande plants, both in good condition, and the Bella Vista plant of the General Administration of National Petroleum, which was able to get needed spare parts because it was paying royalties on its small Dubbs plant.[13] In their dire need, the Mexicans turned to Germany to obtain refineries under a barter arrangement, but the war dashed these hopes by blockading in Genoa the German-built primary plant intended for Bella Vista.[14] Improvements that increased the capacity of the Ciudad Madero refinery and gave it more adaptability in end products included the adaptation of an old gasoline-treating plant for cracking heavy products to get high-octane gasoline.[15] Pemex completed the unfinished auxiliary topping plant at Poza Rica and put it into operation in 1939.[16] Despite these improvements, Pemex was under pressure, at least until 1942, to boost output enough to meet domestic demands with its limited capacity.[17]

Even before the termination of the war, Pemex began to plan long-run programs for refinery construction to meet the rapidly growing domestic needs. The United States Petroleum Reserve Corporation coöperated in a twenty-year project to expand the Mexican petroleum industry as a step toward coping with expected shortages of oil after the war.[18] The Mexican plans, primarily concerned with the domestic market, provided for new refineries on the central plateau near the large consuming areas.

In 1944, the Export-Import Bank authorized a 10-million-dollar credit for the construction at Atzcapotzalco of a high-octane gasoline refinery with a designed capacity of 36,000 barrels daily output. The United States government classified this as a war project to provide Mexico with aviation gasoline for hemispheric defense. The plant was completed in the latter part of 1946 at a reported cost of about 32 million dollars (155 million pesos).[19] The plant, as reconstructed and expanded, included three primary distillation units of 37,000 barrels per day capacity, a straight-run fractionating unit of 2,870 barrels per day capacity, a thermal cracking unit taking a charge of 11,070 barrels per day, an isomerization unit of 350 barrels per day, and an alkylation unit taking a charge of 1,415 barrels per day.[20] With the expanded facilities the gasoline capacity of this refinery more than doubled, and Mexico was able to produce its first high-octane aviation gasoline. However, the production of aviation gasoline, amounting to about 1,060 barrels per day,[21] was low relative to the volume of crude input. This was because of the scarcity of materials at the time of construction. The plant made it possible to produce kerosene, stove oil, and bottled gas in large quantities to meet rising consumption needs on the populous central plateau. In 1947, the production of various fuel oils was about 20 per cent greater than in 1946 (see appendix table 6). This increase was possible largely because of the increase in capacity at Atzcapotzalco. The plant also relieved the shortages of gasoline and other products suffered periodically in the Mexico City region because of transportation difficulties. Facilities for the production of lubricants and wax were badly needed, but were not built into the plant because of materials shortages; however, provision was made for the later addition of these facilities.[22]

In 1948, Pemex had seven refineries operating on a commercial scale and had started construction on another large refinery of 30,000 barrels daily capacity at Salamanca, in the state of Guanajuato, to supply the populous section of the plateau north of Mexico City.[23] This refinery was intended to serve particularly the cities of Guadalajara, Querétaro, Morelia, and San Luis Potosí, and the adjacent territories. The plant, the most modern in Latin America at that time, was designed to produce 1,500 barrels of lubricants and 65 tons of paraffin daily, thus eliminating the large imports of these costly products.[24] The estimated cost of the refinery during construction was 75 million dollars. In 1950 Pemex also built a small refinery in Reynosa of 4,000 barrels per day capacity. This was the distillation plant designed to handle oil produced in the northeast.

The long-run refinery program visualized further adjustments to the increasing domestic consumption. The plans called for the addition of a cracking plant to the Ciudad Madero refinery to increase the production of high-octane gasoline and an addition to the Atzcapotzalco refinery for the production of lubricating oils and paraffin.[25] The discovery of oil in northeast Mexico gave impetus to the construction of a new refinery at Monterrey, and plans for the more distant future called for refineries at Guadalajara, on the plateau, and at Guaymas and Salina Cruz on the Pacific side to ease the long-standing problem of serving the western littoral.[26]

In 1946, the largest of the seven refineries operating on a commercial scale was that at Ciudad Madero, which produced nearly two-fifths of the total refined products. Of all Mexican refineries, it was the greatest producer of raw gasoline and had the widest variety of products. Next in size was the Atzcapotzalco refinery, which ac-

TABLE 9

RELATIVE PHYSICAL OUTPUTS OF REFINERIES OF PEMEX,
1938 AND 1946

Refinery	Percentage of output	
	1938	1946
Ciudad Madero	38	38
Atzcapotzalco	16	19
Minatitlán	24	16
Arbol Grande	10	14
Mata Redonda	10	8
Poza Rica	..	3
Bella Vista	2	2
Total	100	100

SOURCE: Basic data from Pemex.

counted for almost one-fifth of the total and was the largest producer of refined gasoline and sole producer of aviation gasoline. Third largest was the refinery at Minatitlán, which produced about one-sixth of the total refinery products and was especially important in producing the components of most of the Mexican lubricating oils.[27] Minatitlán was followed closely in volume of products by the Arbol Grande refinery, which produced about one-seventh of the total. The small Bella Vista refinery was dismantled. Production at independent refineries was very small. Figures are not available, but it was estimated that between 1938 and 1948 their products amounted to much less than 1 per cent of those of Pemex. Independent producers sold most of their oil to Pemex or sent it abroad without refinement. According to Pemex records, there was only one independent refinery in Mexico in 1948, a small plant in Ciudad Juárez, refining about 20 barrels of crude oil a day.

There is considerable variation in figures for total refining capacity in 1950. With the completion of the Salamanca refinery, capacity was brought up to slightly more than 200,000 barrels of crude oil a day,* with cracking capacity of about 28,000 barrels a day (see appendix table 7).

The figures for the relative physical output of the various refineries (see table 9) reflect both the shift in emphasis to home consumption and the changing sources of crudes. Between 1938 and

TABLE 10

MEXICAN PETROLEUM AND DERIVATIVES CONSUMED AT HOME AND EXPORTED ANNUALLY, AND THEIR TOTAL COMPARED TO ANNUAL PRODUCTION OF PETROLEUM AND TO THE ANNUAL OUTPUT OF REFINERIES OF PEMEX, AS GIVEN BY THE LATTER, 1938–1948

(In millions of barrels)

Year	Home consumption	Exports	Total	Refinery production	Crude-oil production
1938	19.7	14.8	34.5	33.7	38.5
1939	21.6	19.2	40.8	31.8	42.9
1940	23.9	20.8	44.7	29.9	44.0
1941	28.4	16.5	44.9	34.9	43.1
1942	28.6	6.5	35.1	33.0	34.8
1943	33.1	5.7	38.8	34.4	35.2
1944	35.3	5.0	40.3	35.9	38.2
1945	38.0	8.3	46.3	39.2	43.5
1946	40.7	10.0	50.7	44.0	49.2
1947	42.1	15.3	57.4	46.4	56.3
1948	45.5	13.2	58.7	47.5	58.5
Total	356.9	135.3	492.2	410.7	484.2

SOURCES: (1) Home consumption, exports, and crude-oil production from Secretaría de Economía, *Memoria*. (2) Refinery production from records of Pemex and from *Informe anual*.

1946, the output of all Pemex refineries, except that at Minatitlán, increased in absolute amount, and the output at Atzcapotzalco and Arbol Grande increased in relative amount. At the same time, the output at Minatitlán declined both relatively and absolutely because of the decline in the Isthmus fields and the growing importance of domestic consumption of refined products as compared to exports. Although the Mata Redonda plant increased its output slightly in 1946 compared to 1938, its relative significance declined.

For crude oil, the refineries, of course, relied heavily on fields in their vicinity, but crudes from more distant places were frequently

---

* According to *World Oil*, July 15, 1951, p. 162, Mexican refineries had a total crude charging capacity of 224,000 barrels a day. The figures in *World Oil* indicate that Ciudad Madero's crude charging capacity was 75,000 barrels a day.

used to get more desirable charging stocks. In 1948, 50 per cent or more of the crude used by the refineries at Ciudad Madero, Arbol Grande, and Mata Redonda was the light oil of Poza Rica, the proportions of the mixture depending upon the end products desired.[28] Minatitlán, which in 1938 relied entirely on local Isthmus fields for its crude supplies, was later hampered by declining crude-oil production in the Isthmus and began to depend in part on tanker shipments from northern fields. Atzcapotzalco used almost entirely synthetic charging stocks from Poza Rica.

More detailed analysis of the products of refinement and of the trends of physical output of specific products and classes reveals some highly significant features of the refining industry. First, however, some general comments on the nature of the data are in order.

The official figures for total output of Mexican refineries, as published by the Mexican government in the *Memoria* and the *Anuario estadístico* of the Secretary of Economy, differ markedly from those in the office records of Pemex and from those in the *Annual Report* of the general director of Pemex (see appendix table 8). The government figures are consistently much higher. For 1948, the government placed output at more than 16 million barrels, or 35 per cent higher than the output as given by Pemex. Independent refineries did not account for the difference, for their output was negligible, according to Pemex records. Pemex data appear to be more reliable than government data. If we add the annual domestic consumption of Mexican oil (as given in the *Memoria* of the Secretary of Economy) to the annual export of petroleum, we arrive at a figure so close to that offered by Pemex as to cast serious doubt upon the government figures.

The conclusion that the Pemex figures are more reliable is bolstered by the fact that Mexican crude-oil production was also reasonably close to the total refinery output, as given by Pemex, plus crude-oil exports. Crude-oil production in the years 1938 to 1948 totaled approximately 484 million barrels, and refinery output, according to Pemex, amounted to 411 million barrels. During this period, 64 million barrels of unprocessed crude oil were exported.[29] This, added to the refinery output, amounts to 475 million barrels. The remaining 9 million barrels (1.9 per cent) can reasonably be accounted for as losses in refinery operations and storage. Furthermore, the data from Pemex are more in harmony with an index of refined products published by the Secretary of Economy[30] than are the data on physical quantitites emanating from the same source. Since there is thus good reason to believe that the government figures have been "doctored" or mislabeled, Pemex data will be used in discussing the general changes in total refinery output.

The impact of expropriation was strongly evidenced by the figures for total refinement. In 1938 refined products fell 9.3 million barrels, or about 22 per cent, below the 1937 figure (see table 8). The movement continued downward for two additional years, so that in 1940 refined products amounted to less than 30 million barrels, which was 30 per cent under the 1937 figure. The refining industry recovered slowly in succeeding years, but did not exceed the 1937 level until 1946, when the output stood at 2 per cent more, or 44 million barrels for the year. In 1948 refinery output was well over 47 million barrels. However, this rise of about 11 per cent was insignificant compared to an increase of about 115 per cent in domestic consumption.[31] In 1950 refinery output amounted to 52 million barrels, 26 per cent above that of 1937.

The changes in specific refinery products and their relationships to each other are significant to the study of the petroleum industry. In this investigation the limitations of the available data must be recognized. An accurate breakdown of total refinery output by specific products is not available. The study of these tendencies depends on the official figures of the Secretary of Economy, and there is reason to suppose that the relative amount of physical output attributable to each product does reflect their actual relationships fairly accurately.

Accepting the official figures with these limitations in mind, one can deal with the various products as percentages of each year's total refinery output (see appendix tables 6 and 17). The outstanding development in refining, as revealed by these percentages, is that the more highly refined products declined relative to the less highly refined products (see table 11). In 1936, refined gasoline, refined kerosene, refined paraffin, and lubricants together constituted 21.5 per cent, and in 1937, 20.3 per cent of the total refined products for the year. Expropriation brought a significant decline in these more highly refined products, and the figures for 1938 and 1939 were 14.5 per cent and 11.9 per cent, respectively. The relative amount of more highly refined products later rose, and by 1950 had reached 20.2 per cent, almost as high as in 1937. Especially significant was the decline in the relative position of refined gasoline, from 16.9 per cent in 1937 to 10.8 per cent in 1940. The figure remained low until 1948 and climbed to a high of 15.9 per cent in 1950. The physical quantity of refined gasoline did not reach its preëxpropriation level at least until 1947, and there is some doubt that the 1947 figure actually was greater than that of 1937. The highly refined lubricants also declined significantly, both percentagewise and in physical quantity. The percentage drop from 1937 to 1948 was from 1.2 to 0.6 per cent, which represented a physical decline as well. In the group of more highly refined products, only refined kerosene in-

TABLE 11

MEXICAN REFINERY OUTPUT: COMPARISON OF RELATIVE PORTIONS OF MORE
HIGHLY REFINED PRODUCTS AND OF LESS HIGHLY REFINED PRODUCTS, 1936–1950

Year	More highly refined products[a]	Less highly refined products[b]	Miscellaneous	Total
	per cent	per cent	per cent	per cent
1936	21.5	74.7	3.7	99.9
1937	20.3	78.2	1.6	100.1
1938	14.5	84.6	0.9	100.0
1939	13.9	85.4	0.7	100.0
1940	13.3	86.1	0.7	100.0
1941	12.2	86.6	1.1	99.9
1942	13.4	85.9	0.6	99.9
1943	14.5	84.7	0.8	100.0
1944	14.4	84.9	0.7	100.0
1945	15.3	84.0	0.7	100.0
1946	15.2	84.2	0.7	100.1
1947	16.7	82.5	0.9	100.1
1948	18.8	79.4	1.9	100.1
1949	19.4	78.8	1.8	100.0
1950	20.2	77.8	1.9	99.9

[a] Includes refined gasoline, refined kerosene, refined paraffin, and lubricants.
[b] Includes fuel oils, gas oil, raw gasoline, raw kerosene, raw paraffin, and asphalt.
SOURCES: 1936–1942, basic data from *Anuario estadístico, 1942.* 1943–1950, basic data from Secretaría de Economía Nacional, *Memoria, 1943–1950.*

creased relatively; this, of course, reflected a rise in the absolute production of kerosene.

On the other hand, the less highly refined products, including fuel oil, gas oil, raw gasoline, raw kerosene, raw paraffin, and asphalt, increased notably. In 1936 and 1937 these products constituted 75 per cent and 78 per cent of total refinery output, whereas in the postexpropriation period they consistently varied between 84 per cent and 86 per cent, until 1947 when they dropped to 82.5 per cent. In 1950 they dropped further to 78 per cent, but the absolute amount was much more than before expropriation. The most marked increased was in the production of raw gasoline, which jumped from 11 per cent in 1937 to more than 25 per cent in 1938, and stood at nearly 16 per cent in 1950. The relative movement of

raw gasoline upward and of refined gasoline downward is significant in view of the rapid increase in the rate of gasoline consumption. Between 1937 and 1946, consumption of gasoline rose more
than 150 per cent, or from 3.2 million barrels to 8.1 million barrels.[32] In order to meet the domestic demand it was necessary to increase imports of gasoline from 270,000 barrels in 1938 to 1,956,000
barrels in 1947, according to Pemex records. However, as noted
earlier, refinery construction at Atzcapotzalco made it possible after
1946 to produce aviation gasoline for the first time.

Other important tendencies can be traced from the official figures
of output of specific products. After 1939, when refining was at its
lowest point, kerosene was the product that showed the most significant relative increase. Pemex implemented the desire of the
government to substitute petroleum fuels for charcoal in domestic
use, in order to conserve the timber of the central plateau. To this
end, production of both kerosene and liquefied gases was increased.

Especially notable also was the relative and absolute decline in
output of lubricants, as noted above. Although there was some increase after the low of 1941, even the government figure for production in 1948 was far below the preëxpropriation figure. The refinement of lubricants is an intricate process, and the downward tendency in Mexico was attributable to the lack of adequate facilities
for producing high-grade lubricants and to a decided Mexican preference for lubricants of United States origin, which increased imports. Plans for refinery expansion called for equipment to produce
these much-needed items.

The fall in asphalt production, both relatively and absolutely,
primarily reflected the loss of export markets. After the low of 1942,
production increased significantly until 1947, reflecting both more
Mexican consumption and more exports after wartime shipping
problems were relieved. In 1948 asphalt production fell off drastically.

These relationships between the more highly refined products
and those less highly refined suggest that refining was not keeping
pace with the increasing rate of consumption of the more valuable
cuts of crude petroleum.* This conclusion is substantiated by an
investigation of Mexico's trade in petroleum products. The country
was becoming more and more dependent on foreign sources, principally the United States, for the more highly refined products
(see chap. ix).

---

* For example, gasoline constituted less than 33⅓ per cent of crude-oil runs to
refineries, compared to more than 40 per cent in the United States. See *United States
Petroleum Refining, War and Postwar,* U.S. Department of Commerce (Washington, 1947), p. 8.

In evaluating Mexican refining, it must be pointed out that the serious problem of finance was even more of an obstacle in refining than in production. Mexico was favored by no such windfall in refining as in production, i.e., the existence of the rich Poza Rica pool. Investment in refineries is expensive, and the rate of obsolescence is high. Of course, these were factors against Mexico. New construction was limited to expansion at Atzcapotzalco and the new plant at Salamanca. Even this advance had been long delayed, and to keep

TABLE 12
ANNUAL REFINERY OUTPUT PER REFINERY WORKER,
1938–1946
(In barrels)

Year	Output per refinery worker
1938	4,144
1939	3,165
1940	3,204
1941	3,672
1942	3,530
1943	3,667
1944	3,633
1945	3,376
1946	3,919

SOURCE: Basic data from Pemex.

abreast of the rising domestic demand for petroleum products, the country needed refineries at Monterrey and Guadalajara and on the west coast, whose supply had always been a serious problem. Investment in additional cracking facilities was also needed. Despite the growing importance of catalytic cracking as a refinery technique after the 'thirties, the Mexican refineries employed only thermal cracking, and cracking capacity relative to crude-oil distillation capacity remained low, amounting to less than 15 per cent.

The seriousness of the scarcity of capital was stressed by the general director of Pemex in his statement before the Federal Board of Arbitration and Conciliation in the "conflict of economic order" of December, 1946. Asking for a readjustment of the existing labor contract, he pointed to the necessity of economizing in order to finance refining and other facilities. In 1949, when the general director came to the United States seeking a government loan, he wanted capital partly for refinery expansion, so that Mexico could save some of the 109 million pesos spent in 1948 for imported petroleum products.

Labor problems, also, critically affected refineries. In 1934, refinery output per refinery worker was 5,271 barrels.* In 1938, the figure dropped to 4,144 barrels and in 1939 to 3,165 barrels (see table 12). The drop in 1939 resulted principally from the management's loss of control over hiring, but partly, perhaps, from depreciation of the refineries. By 1946, conditions in the refineries were much improved, and management had more control over hiring. Refinery output per refinery worker consequently reached 3,919 barrels. The loss in productivity between 1938 and 1946 was evidence of the labor syndicate's strength in guiding hiring policies and in shortening hours of work, and also of the industry's failure to make technological advances in refining that would have offset the concessions to labor.

In evaluating Mexican achievements in refining, one must keep in mind the goals of expropriation. The Mexicans did wrest control from the large oil companies, which they regarded with heavy suspicion. Within the limits of refinery capacity and technology, the nation was able to produce and consume those products that it most wanted. Expropriation increased the freedom of the country to engage in central planning of petroleum development. Mexico was able and, in fact, forced to shift its emphasis from production for export to production for the home market. On the other hand, there was much doubt whether these developments improved either Mexico's over-all economic well-being or the prospects for general economic development.

Expansion of refinery facilities was not impressive until 1948, when construction began on the Salamanca plant. Granted that Pemex successfully tackled a big problem in reorienting refinery facilities to domestic market needs, there still remained the question of whether the country was better off in consuming larger portions of its own production. Against this must be weighed the loss of income that might have been derived from export sales. If Mexico hoped to emerge from its "colonial status," it might have achieved this aim with less economic cost by closer regulation of the privately owned industry. The government might have required the construction of refineries, limited the export of unrefined products, set export quotas, fixed prices, etc. However, it probably could not have carried regulation very far because there were indications even

---

* In 1934 there were 7,081 persons in refinery work (Miguel Manterola, *La industria del petróleo en México* [México, D.F., 1938], p. 70), and refinery output amounted to 5,934,000 cubic meters, or 37,325,000 barrels. (*Anuario estadístico, 1942*, p. 944.)

before expropriation that the oil companies were losing interest in Mexico. Extensive regulation might have caused large emigration of capital. Other aspects of economic colonialism will be discussed in chapter xii, but first the extent to which Mexico met its domestic needs and the extent to which it relied on foreign sources must be considered.

Under private ownership, the refining industry would almost certainly have escaped some of the heavy pressure from labor that so drastically reduced average labor productivity after expropriation. Or the former owners, with their great capital resources, might at least have offset the concessions to labor by technological advances in refining. Under government control, labor exerted great political and other pressure on management's hiring policies. This adversely affected productivity. Management had neither the capital nor, in the period before 1946, a strong incentive to offset the decline in productivity.

Chapter VII

TRANSPORTATION AND STORAGE

After expropriation, transportation was one of the harassing problems of the petroleum industry. The transportation network available for oil movements was directed mainly to tidewater for export. Since one objective of expropriation was to retain more natural resources for home consumption, a reorientation of the transportation network was necessary.

Lack of equipment and malfunctioning of the railroad network were perpetual obstacles to the smooth operation of the industry. Pemex' failure to meet the country's need for petroleum products (especially gasoline), so frequently criticized up to 1946, can be traced in large part to faulty transportation facilities. The difficulty of maintaining exports at a high level after expropriation was also due, as already noted, to a lack of tank ships; and this lack caused most of the initial decline in exports.

Even before 1938, the domestic transportation system faced serious difficulties. Between 1937 and 1946, the total length of railways in Mexico increased less than 1 per cent, whereas freight traffic measured in metric ton-kilometers increased more than 50 per cent and the number of passenger-kilometers increased 75 per cent,[1] placing the railroads under heavy pressure. The change of emphasis in the petroleum industry, from export markets to domestic markets, aggravated transportation problems. Pemex attempted to find a solution in increasing reliance on pipeline and tanker.

Official government sources indicate that in mid-1939 there were 1,165 kilometers of oil trunk lines.[2] The small amount of construction in the preceding year[3] suggests that 1,150 kilometers of oil pipeline is a reasonable estimate as of the time of expropriation. This figure is substantiated by the 1937 report of the expert commission, which showed 1,200 kilometers of oil trunk lines as of December 31, 1936.[4] Figures for the carrying capacity of these lines

[1] For numbered notes to chap. vii, see pp. 247–248.

are unreliable.* In 1939, in addition to the oil lines, there were 308 kilometers of gas lines with a daily carrying capacity of 1.6 million cubic meters.[5]

The oil lines comprised six principal systems. The Pánuco basin system moved crude oil from the fields in the vicinity of Tampico to the refineries and export points along the Pánuco River. The Golden Lane–Tampico system carried crude from the various fields of the Golden Lane north to the terminals along the Pánuco River. A minor system moved crude from the Golden Lane to Tuxpam for export shipment without refinement. The fourth system took the crude of Poza Rica field north to Tuxpam where exising connections could carry the oil farther up the coast to the terminals in the Tampico area. The fifth system carried the Poza Rica oil to the Atzcapotzalco refinery for the domestic market on the plateau. The pipelines of the Isthmus region were used principally to move crude oil from the fields to the Minatitlán refinery, the most important line extending from Tonalá west to the refinery. Another line carried natural gasoline from the fields to an export point near Puerto México.

The location of the pipelines and terminals indicated the heavy emphasis on export. About three-fourths of the tanker shipments moved from Tampico, about one-fourth left the depots along the Coatzacoalcos River at the Isthmus, and minor quantities were shipped from Tuxpam.[6] About 45 per cent of the exports were carried in British ships, 20 per cent in American ships, and 35 per cent in ships of various registry, mostly European.

The domestic market for petroleum products was served principally by rail transportation. The completion of the Poza Rica–Atzcapotzalco pipeline in 1932 temporarily relieved the pressure on the railway network.[7] In 1935, of the petroleum products shipped by rail, fuel oil constituted slightly less than half, and gasoline, gas oil, and kerosene together made up about one-fourth of the total. Crude oil was unimportant, amounting to only about 6 per cent.[8] The rail shipments went mainly from the refineries at Atzcapotzalco and Tampico to domestic markets within their area. Mexico City was the shipping point for about 38 per cent of the petroleum products moving by rail. Tampico was the origin of an equal percentage.[9] The port of Vera Cruz received a large amount of oil in coastwise ships, and originated about 7 per cent of the rail shipments to the

---

* The daily carrying capacity of the oil lines in Mexico as of December 31, 1936, was 703,000 barrels, according to the expert commission. See *Mexico's Oil* (México, D.F., 1940), p. 157.

interior. These products were widely distributed. The principal cities on the receiving end included Mexico City, with about 39 per cent of the total, and Tampico, Puebla, Torreón, San Luis Potosí, and Monterrey, with less than 5 per cent each.

In 1935 coastwise shipping, amounting to 537,000 metric tons, was a little more than half the tonnage of rail shipments.[10] For the most part it carried refined products for domestic markets, and only an insignificant amount of crude oil. More than 50 per cent of the coastwise shipping tonnage was fuel oil, and about 25 per cent was gas oil. Lubricants and gasoline accounted for about 5 per cent each. The chief shipping ports were Puerto México and Tampico, where about 99 per cent of all coastwise shipments originated. About two-thirds of these shipments went to Vera Cruz. Tuxpam and Tampico also received large amounts. Consumers on the Yucatán peninsula, isolated by land, had to depend on coastwise shipments through the port of Progreso. Appreciable quantities also went to Pacific Coast ports.

Immediately after expropriation, the basic transportation needs were inverted. The loss of export markets and the increase in domestic consumption threw a heavy burden on rail and coastal facilities, which were the principal means of transporting refined products to the home market. However, when the companies withdrew from Mexico, they took their tanker fleets with them, leaving the country with few facilities for coastwise shipments. The load thus fell on the railroads, which were incapable of handling it. Pemex exerted itself to expand the pipeline network and to build a fleet of tankers.

To this end, Pemex started work in 1939 to increase the capacity of the Poza Rica–Atzcapotzalco line. By straightening the line and installing pumps of greater displacement, the company increased the daily capacity, during 1941, from 15,000 to 22,500 barrels.[11] A parallel branch line was run from Poza Rica to Tuxpam, where additional submarine loading lines were installed. A new line was built from Poza Rica to the Golden Lane as an extension of the Golden Lane–Tampico system. This made it possible to supply the Tampico refineries with Poza Rica crude without pumping through the terminal at Tuxpam, which originally had been designed as an embarkation point. These improvements gave the system more flexibility by permitting the transportation of larger amounts of oil either to Tuxpam for water carriage or to the refineries at Tampico. In his annual report for 1942 the general director stated that the total daily capacity of various pipelines had been increased by about 135,000 barrels, and government sources indicated that additions to trunk lines amounted to a little more than 100 kilometers by August, 1940.[12]

However, extensive additions to the network were planned.[13] Pemex wanted to lay lines to plateau market centers to avoid dependence upon the railroads, and to span the Isthmus of Tehuantepec with a pipeline to eliminate the long haul by tanker through the Panama Canal to west coast markets. But little could be accomplished toward these objectives while the war tied up the necessary pipe and steel.

In 1946, Pemex began construction of a crude-oil line from Poza Rica to Salamanca in the state of Guanajuato to supply the proposed new refinery. In 1947, the company started a 240-kilometer line to bring fuel gas from Poza Rica to industrial users in Mexico City. This line, completed early in 1949, had a daily capacity of 50 million cubic feet. In his annual report of March 18, 1949, the general director stated that construction had begun on the long-desired 260-kilometer pipeline across the Isthmus of Tehuantepec. Although this line was initially designed to carry refined products to the port of Salina Cruz for supplying west coast markets, Pemex planned instead to build a refinery at the port and use the line to supply crude oil from fields on the Gulf Coast. Long-run plans called for additional pipelines to Guadalajara and Monterrey, when proposed refineries there were begun. This program, however, required more capital than was then available to Pemex. Even construction on the Poza Rica–Salamanca pipe was slowed down by lack of funds.[14] Independent companies began construction of additional gas lines to connect various northern cities with gas fields at Misión and Reynosa.[15]

The Mexican pipeline network, after ten years of government control, showed only a slight net improvement. According to its records, in 1947 Pemex owned 1,191 kilometers of trunk lines for oil, with a carrying capacity of 312,000 barrels a day. Although the total length of oil lines had by this time increased less than 50 kilometers, there had been significant shifts in the location of lines. Some lines were removed from the fields north of Tampico and additional ones installed in the Golden Lane and Poza Rica. There were no important changes in the Isthmus zone, except for the construction of a short line to give the isolated field of Cuichapa an outlet. However, the completion of the Poza Rica–Salamanca line and other improvements brought total trunk lines in 1950 to about 1,625 kilometers, with a capacity of about 574,000 barrels a day.[16]

The figures of Pemex indicated that both the length and capacity of gas pipelines had declined by 1947, when there were 277 kilometers. These lines, owned by independents, brought gas from northeastern fields to the industrial center of Monterrey. The completion of the Poza Rica–Mexico City line in 1949, together with other improvements by independents, increased the length of gas lines to 513 kilometers and their capacity to 160 million cubic feet a day.[17]

In 1938 the newly nationalized petroleum industry faced a difficult water-transport problem. At the time of expropriation, the Mexicans possessed but one seagoing tanker, the *18 de Marzo,* with a capacity of 60,000 barrels. Before the end of the first year, a small 28,000-barrel tanker the *Cuauhtémoc,* had been acquired.*[18]

Had it not been for the lack of home-owned tankers, Mexican exports probably would have declined relatively little after expropriation. The oil companies' boycott, withdrawing tanker services as it did, closed to Mexico the potential markets of Latin America and other parts of the world.[19] The difficulty was increased not only because Mexico lacked shipyards to build tankers, but also because the international exchanges were so tight after expropriation that she was unable to buy ships. The lack of shipping hampered access to foreign markets and also created a serious problem at home, for rail service to the west coast was inadequate and ships were the most desirable method of supplying those areas. The expropriated companies had met the needs of the North and West by having petroleum products sent down from California, but this source was cut off by the boycott.[20] In 1939, Pemex' two tankers were put into service on the west-coast run from Gulf ports through the Canal.

With direct aid from the government, several tankers were chartered in 1938 and 1939, and vigorous efforts were made to meet the requirements for both overseas and coastal transport. In 1940, a third ship, the *Juan Casiano,* was purchased, and two more, of 65,000-barrel capacity each, were bought from Norway.[21] Three additional 10,000-ton tankers were ordered for construction in Italy, to be paid for on an oil-barter basis, but the war kept Italy from fulfilling the contract. However, Italy was unfortunate enough to have had nine tankers in Mexican ports at the time she went to war. The Mexican government interned them, and in May, 1941, happily for the petroleum industry, turned them over to Pemex. This windfall raised the tanker capacity of the organization by 540,000

---

* In 1939 the entire Pemex fleet consisted of 2 seagoing tankers, 3 seagoing tugs, 1 motorboat, 1 stationary dredge, 3 river tugs, 46 motor launches, 79 barges, 3 lifeboats, 1 motor barge, 1 crane barge, and 1 floating dry dock.

barrels.[22] In the same year three more ships were acquired, which brought the total seagoing carrying capacity up to 1,068,000 barrels in March, 1942, according to the annual report of the general manager. However, Axis submarines sent six tankers to the bottom, reducing the total by about one-third. These losses were offset in part by the acquisition of two more ships in 1942 and 1945 with a combined capacity of 115,000 barrels. In August, 1948, Pemex had thirteen seagoing tankers with an aggregate capacity of 858,000 barrels.*

The expansion of the tanker fleet was a significant and expensive accomplishment, necessitated by the heavy pressure on the industry to get its oil to market. The growing ocean transport facilities enabled Pemex to meet contractual obligations, assumed shortly after expropriation, to independent firms in the United States, and also to seek other markets that would have been inaccessible even with foreign carriers.[23] Not having to rely upon the costly and often delayed rail transportation, Pemex found it easier to supply the domestic market.[24] The first tanker shipment from the Tampico refineries to the west coast was made in August, 1938.[25] This was so successful that rail shipments to that area were practically eliminated, and plans were laid for constructing an embarcation port on the Pacific side of the Isthmus at Salina Cruz, to be supplied by rail from Minatitlán. By this means, the overtaxed railway systems of central Mexico would be relieved and the long haul through the Canal would be avoided. As mentioned earlier, construction was started on an Isthmian pipeline to supplement or replace the rail hauls.

---

* Records in the maritime office of Pemex list the tankers and their carrying capacity as follows:

Poza Rica	90,000 barrels
Potrero de Llano II	80,000 barrels
Vera Cruz	80,000 barrels
Cacalilao	75,000 barrels
Ebano	72,000 barrels
Minatitlán	71,000 barrels
Pánuco	70,000 barrels
Totec	68,000 barrels
Tampico	65,000 barrels
Cerro Azul	64,000 barrels
18 de Marzo	60,000 barrels
Azteca	35,000 barrels
Cuauhtémoc	28,000 barrels
Total	858,000 barrels

The remaining water facilities were 10 tugs, 1 dredge, 1 floating dry dock, and 143 lighters and launches.

Pemex reported that its water-borne traffic had increased from the humble beginnings described above to 3.3 million barrels transported on the high seas and 6.3 million barrels in cabotage traffic during 1945.[26] In that year, Mexico stood third among Latin American countries in registered dead-weight tonnage of tank ships.[27]

Railway transportation remained the weakest link in the oil transportation system. The Mexican railroads had a history of unreliable service, irregular schedules, and accidents.* The additional load thrown on them after expropriation did not reduce the prevailing confusion. It was said that shipments were sometimes delayed as long as fifteen days in traveling the 323 miles from Tampico to Monterrey.[28] Administrative conflicts between the railroads and the petroleum industry were periodic occurrences.

In March, 1938, Pemex had the use of 771 tank cars. The number increased to 1,476 by 1944 and to 1,822 by 1951.[29] From 1938 to 1944, rail shipments of petroleum products, measured in metric ton-kilometers, increased about 40 per cent, whereas general traffic increased 47 per cent,[30] and the unsatisfactory handling of petroleum transportation brought on an open conflict between the general manager of the National Railroads of Mexico (also a government agency) and the general manager of Pemex. Shortages of petroleum products in various parts of the country aroused public clamor. In the ensuing argument as to where the responsibility lay, the railway chief complained of serious delays in loading tank cars at refinery sidings and of irregular supplies of locomotive fuel. The head of the petroleum industry countered by saying that empty cars were not delivered to the refineries and that full ones were not taken away. The President of the republic intervened with a face-saving agreement for both parties,[31] but the issues were not resolved. In 1945, the general manager of Pemex announced the purchase of 17 locomotives in the United States to be operated by the National Railroads of Mexico for the exclusive purpose of hauling petroleum products.[32] In 1948, the general manager of the National Railroads charged that 239 tank cars were empty and idle because of negligence by Pemex.[33] Wherever the responsibility lay, it is evident that poor coördination hurt the petroleum industry, adversely affected public opinion, and forced Pemex to develop alternative means of transportation. In 1950 it did not appear likely that the number of tank cars would be increased. Between 1938 and 1947, the rail movement of gasoline and fuel oil increased from 331 million to 692

---

* Some problems of Mexican manufacturers and shippers in making rail shipments are reported in *Technological Audit of Selected Mexican Industries*, Armour Research Foundation (Ann Arbor, 1946), p. 7.

million metric ton-kilometers, and the general director of Pemex
wanted to expand the fleet of tank trucks in order to avoid increasing the load on the railroads.[34] That the railroads had borne a large
share of the burden of carrying petroleum products to market is
shown by the figures for gasoline and fuel oil shipments. Gasoline
and fuel oil constituted an estimated 50 to 60 per cent of all rail
shipments of petroleum products.[35] A very rough comparison indicates that in 1945 domestic rail shipments of petroleum products
amounted to about 12.8 million barrels, compared to 6.3 million
barrels in cabotage traffic, and that in 1946 about 12.6 million barrels moved by rail and 42.9 million barrels by pipeline.[36] These
figures show that, in domestic transport, the physical volume of
petroleum products moved by pipeline was three to four times the
volume moved by rail, and about seven times the volume moved by
sea. Pipe carriage was confined almost exclusively to crude oil,
except for a 37-kilometer line for raw gasoline on the Isthmus. Rail
and sea shipments consisted largely of gasoline and fuel oil, with
very little crude. The predominance of pipeline transport is, of
course, easily explained by its low cost relative to rail transport. It
was estimated in 1944 that the cost of oil transportation by pipeline
was ½ to ¾ centavo per metric ton-kilometer, as against 2 to 3
centavos by rail.[37] Tanker shipments were much less expensive than
rail shipments, but rail predominated over tanker because all the
large consuming centers were high on the central plateau and accessible only by rail or tank truck.

Data concerning tank-truck carriage are not available. Pemex
records show that in 1948 the organization owned 243 tank trucks,
tank trailers, and tractors with semitrailer tanks. The general director in his annual report stated that the tank-truck carrying capacity
was 1.3 million liters (338,000 gallons), which was increased to 1.6
million liters (424,000 gallons) during the year. Transportation
from the Atzcapotzalco refinery, he said, was almost entirely by
truck.

Changes in transportation routes and characteristics and changes
in market conditions called for modifications in storage facilities,
both as to location and size. New transshipment points called for
new construction, and to meet the domestic market requirements
old storage facilities had to be expanded. It appeared, however,
that many old tanks in use at the time of expropriation, or shortly
before, had deteriorated without replacement. In 1936 there were
3,090 steel and concrete tanks with a capacity of 50 million barrels
and, in addition, 19 earthen reservoirs with a capacity of 22 million
barrels, bringing the total storage capacity to 72 million barrels.[38]

In 1946, according to records of Pemex, there were only 1,736 tanks with a capacity of 23 million barrels; since earthen reservoirs remained unchanged, the total dropped to 45 million barrels. It is likely that a large part of the decline was due to nonreplacement of old tanks constructed in the heyday of Mexican production, when crude-oil output was running well over 100 million barrels a year.

It is difficult to trace developments in storage-tank construction. The facts must be gleaned from fragmentary items in the annual reports of the general director of Pemex, from isolated newspaper reports, and from records of construction permits granted by the Secretary of Economy.

There seems to have been no tank construction in the first two years of Mexican operation, judging from the annual reports of the general director. In 1940, to meet Pacific Coast requirements, a loading and storage terminal was built at the port of Salina Cruz on the Pacific side of the Isthmus so that ships could load oil brought by tank car from Minatitlán. The project included storage for 240,-000 barrels of petroleum and facilities for loading and unloading ships and tank cars.[39] This helped relieve the heavily burdened railroads and tankers, since less of the oil going to Pacific ports had to pass through the Canal or over the plateau rail systems. However, it did not completely eliminate such shipments.[40]

Soon after expropriation, Pemex launched a program of building storage plants with sea connections in outlying regions accessible by tanker. By 1948, additional tanks were constructed at Campeche for 77,300 barrels to serve that territory; at Brownsville, Texas, for 60,000 barrels to serve the northern part of the states of Tamaulipas and Nuevo León; at Punta Prieta for 12,700 barrels to serve Lower California in place of shipments by small boat; and at Guaymas, where storage space was increased by 30,000 barrels to give more adequate supplies for the west coast.[41] In 1946, Pemex built 61 tanks at Atzcapotzalco to expand storage capacity at the refinery by about 700,000 barrels.[42]

Developments in transportation and storage must be evaluated together. The transportation system for the petroleum industry was clearly inadequate, and subjected the country to periodic shortages of oil products. But in criticizing its limitations, one must recognize the shortcomings in the complementary function of storage. Storage provides a buffer to absorb slack when refinery output and transportation, or refinery input and crude-oil supplies, cannot be coördinated. The inadequacy of storage space, however, does not explain all the market disequilibrium.

The complementary nature of the various means of transportation, as well as their competitive nature, must also be recognized. Pipelines have the special function of moving very large quantities of fluid products. In Mexico especially, they did not lend themselves well to movements of refined products because of market limitations, and were used primarily to move crude oil. Railroad shipment, on the other hand, was too expensive for moving crude oil, but at the time was the most feasible method of supplying the plateau cities that lacked refineries. Tank ships were particularly useful in moving relatively large quantities, and the shipments could be diversified. Consequently, tankers were the most practicable means of supplying the coastal markets. Even though the markets were small, the low cost of tanker carriage and the possibility of diversifying the shipments made tankers particularly useful to Mexico. However, tanker carriage for domestic distribution seems to have been sufficiently developed, since more than two-thirds of the population lived on the high central plateau,[43] beyond reasonable utilization of tanker service. The urgent need was for more land facilities to meet the industry's transportation requirements. However, even though the railroads were under heavy pressure, expansion of rail facilities did not appear to be the answer. The solution lay primarily in building refineries at large population centers, such as Guadalajara and Monterrey. Then, Pemex would be able to shift the brunt of transportation to pipelines supplying crude oil to the refineries, with tank-truck and rail transportation handling the short hauls to distribution points. However, there was no point in building the pipelines until after the refineries were built. Under the circumstances, the relief of pressure on the railroads did not depend upon further purchases of tank cars, and Pemex recognized this.

The pipeline across the Isthmus of Tehuantepec was a beneficial step. Its value, however, would be severely limited until Pemex built a refinery on the Pacific side because of market conditions on the Pacific littoral and because of the relatively high cost of moving diversified products across the Isthmus.

The final solution to the transportation problem lay in greater use of pipelines. This depended upon the construction of refineries, which could not proceed rapidly until capital could be raised. In his annual report of 1949, the general director spoke confidently of solving the distribution problem within five years. The solution, however, lay within the reach of Pemex only if it found suitable and adequate sources of capital—capital to build both refineries and pipelines.

Chapter VIII

MARKETING
AND CONSUMPTION
PATTERNS

Mexico's desire to retain its natural resources for home consumption was almost rudely fulfilled by expropriation and the subsequent boycott and loss of foreign markets. Marketing was probably the most serious of the immediate problems posed by the far-reaching step of expropriation. The government recognized the seriousness by assigning the job of organizing and directing sales to a separate agency known as *Distribuidora de Petróleos Mexicanos*.

The problem of the domestic market was primarily transportation and coördination of the formerly independent marketing systems of the expropriated companies. The transportation phase was only partially solved by 1950. The organizational phase of coördinating and unifying marketing efforts was solved only after prolonged labor controversy and serious financial difficulties that forced unification as an economy measure. Despite these obstacles, domestic sales increased rapidly and continuously.

However, the most difficult aspect of marketing immediately after expropriation was that of foreign sales, for the effect of the boycott of the oil companies was felt immediately and drastically in the overseas market. Exports of petroleum and petroleum products—which had amounted to 1.6 million barrels in January, 1938, 2.0 million barrels in February, and 0.9 million barrels in the period March 1–18—fell to 95,000 barrels in the period March 18–31, and stood at 311,000 barrels in April. The monthly average for the period from April to December was only 1.1 million barrels (see table 13). The decline in money value was even more precipitous. The value of petroleum exports, which had averaged 12.8 million pesos per month in the year before expropriation, fell to 7.0 million pesos in March and to 1.0 million pesos in April. The monthly average for the remainder of the calendar year was 6.4

97

million pesos (see table 14). Not until 1948 did the annual value of exports exceed the 1937 figure. The virtual collapse of foreign sales was the result of the boycott and of the unavailability of tanker service after the expropriated companies took their ships home.

This chapter will first consider the extent of the monopoly position of Pemex in both the domestic and the export markets; then

TABLE 13

PHYSICAL VOLUME OF EXPORTS OF PETROLEUM PRODUCTS
BY MONTHS, 1938

Month	Thousands of barrels	Per cent of total
January....................	1,650	11.2
February...................	2,011	13.6
March 1–18.................	936	6.4
March 18–31 [a].............	95	.6
April......................	311	2.1
May.......................	1,147	7.8
June......................	865	5.9
July......................	1,039	7.1
August....................	1,373	9.3
September.................	1,171	7.9
October...................	1,460	9.9
November..................	1,319	9.0
December.................	1,360	9.2
Total.................	14,738 [b]	100.0

[a] Figures for March 18–December 31 are for Pemex. Exports of independent origin in this period amounted to about 52,000 barrels, or less than ⅓ of 1 per cent of the year's total.
[b] Column does not add up to total because of rounding.
SOURCE: *Boletín de minas y petróleo*, October, 1939–June, 1941.

it will take up the particular marketing problems that faced Pemex and the policies adopted by Pemex to meet those problems.

During the ten years 1938 to 1947, Pemex distributed about 37.8 million liters of products of a total of 40.2 million liters sold in the home market. Thus, the government agency was responsible for 93.9 per cent of the physical volume of domestic sales, and independent agencies for 6.1 per cent. These percentages were fairly constant throughout the period except for 1938. In that year Pemex operated less than ten months, and the share was only 91.3 per cent (see table 15). Although specific figures of peso income from independent sales are not available, the share of independents in the total value of domestic sales was probably somewhat more than their volume share, because they sold more of the higher-priced

TABLE 14
VALUE OF EXPORTS OF PETROLEUM PRODUCTS, BY MONTHS, 1937–1939
(In millions of pesos)

Month	Exports		
	1937	1938	1939
January	20	10	6
February	11	12	8
March	18	7	7
April	13	1	6
May	18	5	8
June	7	5	7
July	18	7	11
August	10	8	11
September	10	6	4
October	9	7	6
November	14	6	4
December	14	7	5
Total[a]	162	80	83

[a] Some columns may not add up to totals because of rounding.
SOURCE: *Revista de estadística, 1937–1940*.

TABLE 15
PHYSICAL VOLUME OF DOMESTIC SALES[a] BY PEMEX AND BY INDEPENDENTS, BY YEARS, 1938–1947

Year	Millions of liters sold		Percentage of sales	
	By Pemex	By independents	By Pemex	By independents
1938	2,552.9	244.0	91.3	8.7
1939	2,736.1	165.4	94.3	5.7
1940	2,848.3	224.8	92.7	7.3
1941	3,111.0	161.4	95.1	4.9
1942	3,397.2	179.3	95.0	5.0
1943	3,824.4	228.9	94.4	5.6
1944	4,084.3	243.1	94.4	5.6
1945	4,464.8	272.0	94.3	5.7
1946	5,046.3	360.4	93.3	6.7
1947	5,705.2	387.6	93.6	6.4
Total	37,770.5	2,466.9	93.9	6.1

[a] Includes sales of gasoline, fuel oil, gas oil, kerosene, lubricating oil, and greases.
SOURCE: Basic data from Pemex.

products. In the ten-year period 1938–1947, independents sold 7.8 per cent of the gasoline, 46.4 per cent of the greases, 40.3 per cent of the lubricating oil, 8.8 per cent of the gas oil, 8.8 per cent of the kerosene, and only 4.5 per cent of the fuel oil, the relatively cheap item (see appendix table 10). The independents sold more of the higher-priced than of the lower-priced petroleum products because they were more active than Pemex in importing, and imports were for the most part the more valuable items. In the ten-year period, imports of gasoline, fuel oil, gas oil, kerosene, lubricating oil, and

TABLE 16

PHYSICAL VOLUME OF DOMESTIC SALES OF SELECTED PETROLEUM PRODUCTS BY
PEMEX AND BY INDEPENDENTS, DURING THE PERIOD 1938–1947

Product	Millions of liters sold		Percentage of sales	
	By Pemex	By independents	By Pemex	By independents
Gasoline............	8,221.6	686.5	92.2	7.8
Fuel oil.............	26,350.6	1,257.5	95.5	4.5
Gas oil.............	1,506.1	145.9	91.2	8.8
Kerosene..........	1,332.8	129.2	91.2	8.8
Lubricating oil......	333.3	225.2	59.7	40.3
Grease.............	26.1	22.6	53.6	46.4

SOURCE: Basic data from Pemex.

greases amounted to 3,078 million liters, of which independents brought in more than 75 per cent. The domestic market had an especially strong preference for lubricating oils and greases produced in the United States. During this period about 54 per cent of these items were imported (see table 16).

In the period 1938–1947, the share of Pemex in sales of specific products changed significantly (see appendix table 10). The government agency was responsible for 95 per cent of all gasoline sales in the domestic market during 1938–1940, but its share was only 91 per cent in 1946 and 1947. Pemex also lost ground in sales of lubricating oil; its share fell from 74 per cent in 1938 and 1939 to 50 per cent in 1947. In greases, Pemex' sales dropped in about the same degree. However, the government improved its monopoly position in the marketing of kerosene. In 1938 and 1939, Pemex sold about 81 per cent of the total each year. By 1947 it controlled 96 per cent of the domestic market. Its share in sales of fuel oil and gas oil remained fairly constant in the period after 1938.

The effectiveness of Pemex' monopoly was actually greater than percentage figures indicate, because independent sales were largely concentrated in certain specific areas called "free zones" (*perímetros libres*). These zones, which were outlying areas that could not be conveniently supplied from domestic production, included certain towns of the east coast of the Yucatán peninsula, the extreme northwest frontier, and Lower California, where the independents marketed gasoline and other products imported from the United States.

TABLE 17

VOLUME AND VALUE OF DOMESTIC AND EXPORT SALES BY PEMEX, BY YEARS, 1938–1950

Year	Volume (in millions of barrels)			Value (in millions of pesos)		
	Domestic	Export	Total	Domestic	Export	Total
1938	17.1	9.2	26.3	154.7	43.6	198.3
1939	17.9	14.9	32.8	170.0	63.4	233.4
1940	19.3	13.3	32.6	191.4	57.2	248.6
1941	21.0	14.4	35.4	222.1	66.3	288.4
1942	23.2	6.3	29.5	253.3	33.0	286.3
1943	26.0	5.8	31.8	292.2	37.4	329.6
1944	27.6	4.9	32.5	333.0	37.4	370.4
1945	29.4	7.9	37.3	399.8	39.8	439.6
1946	33.5	9.7	43.2	508.0	62.0	570.0
1947	36.8	14.0	50.8	638.1	121.2	759.3
1948	39.8	13.0	52.8	770.9	190.0	960.9
1949	44.6	14.1	58.7	a	a	1,229.4
1950	47.3	23.6	70.9	a	a	1,619.7

ᵃ Figures not available.
SOURCE: *Informe anual*, March 18, 1938; March 18, 1949; March 18, 1951.

The competition facing Pemex in these areas was unique, and had little effect on the government monopoly in other sectors of the domestic market. The only products offering real competition to the government monopoly were greases and lubricating oil imported from the United States, for which there was strong consumer preference. However, the Pemex retail outlets carried imported products as well as domestic brands.

It is likely that Pemex participated less in export trade than in domestic trade, but the data are incomplete. There are also certain irreconcilable differences between the data offered by official government sources and those published by the petroleum agency. During the period 1939–1947, Pemex exported 91.2 million barrels of petroleum. For the same period, official government figures show that total exports of petroleum amounted to 98 million barrels.[1] The difference of 6.8 million barrels is to be attributed to exports by independents. From another approach, production by independents amounted to 12.5 million barrels during the same period; if losses of 6 per cent and domestic sales of 2.2 million barrels are assumed,[2] 9.5 million barrels were exported. Thus, independents exported between 6.8 million and 9.5 million barrels. The share of Pemex, therefore, was roughly between 91 per cent and 93 per cent. It is not possible to make definitive statements as to the participation by Pemex and by the independents in the export of specific products because of discrepancies in the sources; however, it appears that the independents exported mostly crude oil, fuel oil, and gas oil.

In sales trends, Pemex dominated both the domestic and the foreign markets. Between 1938 and 1948, Pemex more than doubled its total volume of sales, increasing it from 26 million to 53 million barrels (see table 17). This rapid expansion was primarily the result of increasing domestic sales, which rose without a break at an average rate of 8 or 9 per cent a year. Export sales fluctuated widely in both value and volume, at first because of the boycott, and later because of the war. The lowest figure after expropriation was that for 1944, when Pemex exported 4.9 million barrels. This was about one-fifth the amount exported in 1936 and again in 1937.[3]

After expropriation, the peso value of sales increased more than eightfold, rising from 198 million pesos in 1938 to 1,620 million in 1950. This extremely rapid rise in value of sales reflected the increasing volume of sales, of course, but even more the depreciation of the peso and the increase in world oil prices.

Gasoline was by far the most important item sold by Pemex. In the nine-year period 1938–1946, gasoline constituted more than 45 per cent of the value of gross sales. Fuel oil was second, accounting for 20 per cent of the total. Gas oil was third with 8 per cent, followed by crude oil and lubricating oil with about 5 per cent each; paraffin, Tractomex (diesel fuel for tractors), and kerosene with about 4 per cent each; asphalt with 2 per cent; liquid gas, greases, solvents, insecticides, and miscellaneous (including vaseline, floor polish, cleaners, stoves, and auto accessories) with less than 1 per cent each.[4]

The most outstanding relative shifts by the constituent products in the value of gross sales included, first, the increase in the importance of gasoline. This product accounted for about 43 per cent of

---

[1] For numbered notes to chap. viii, see p. 248.

gross sales value in 1938, and almost 48 per cent in 1946. This change occurred because of a 184 per cent increase in the peso value of gross sales of gasoline, reflecting a 37 per cent increase in physical volume of sales, from 851 million liters in 1938 to 1,163 million in 1946. Second, fuel oil also increased significantly in relative importance in total gross sales, rising from 19 per cent in 1938 to 22 per cent in 1946. Again, this was due to the increase in volume of sales from 2,458 million liters to 4,055 million liters, a rise of 65 per cent.

Other products that showed significant increases in their relative contributions to gross sales value were kerosene, Tractomex, bottled gas, and certain newly developed products, such as insecticides, cleaning solvents, and polishes. Kerosene, Tractomex, and bottled gas, which had constituted only 5.9 per cent of gross sales in 1938, amounted to 9.6 per cent in 1946.

Items that declined significantly in their relative contributions to gross sales value were gas oil, crude oil, and asphalt. Although sales of these products rose in value from 46 million to 63 million pesos between 1938 and 1946, their relative share of total sales fell from 20.7 per cent to 11.0 per cent. The physical volume of sales of these products actually declined from 1,419 million liters to 1,120 million liters, a drop of more than 20 per cent. Also significant was the sag in sales of these items, both in peso value and in volume, during the war years.

The factors giving rise to these changing relationships, and their significance, may be explained by analyzing first the domestic sales and then the foreign sales.

As mentioned earlier, domestic sales increased at a very impressive rate. The physical volume rose from 2,721 million liters (17.1 million barrels) in 1938 to 6,328 million liters (39.8 million barrels) in 1948, an increase of 133 per cent, or about 9 per cent a year, and the peso value increased from 155 million to 771 million, a rise of almost 400 per cent. By 1950 the volume of domestic sales had reached 7,520 million liters (47.3 million barrels), an increase of 176 per cent over 1938.[5] Most of the increase in physical volume of sales can be attributed to fuel oil, gasoline, and kerosene, which accounted for 2,948 million liters of the total increase of 3,607 million liters of all products between 1938 and 1947. The increase in the three items, therefore, accounted for 82 per cent of the change.

Between 1938 and 1946, about 67 per cent of the physical volume of domestic sales was fuel oil and 20 per cent was gasoline; Tractomex, gas oil, kerosene, and asphalt registered 2 to 4 per cent each. In gross value of sales, gasoline led with 54 per cent; fuel oil was second with 19 per cent; lubricating oil, Tractomex, paraffin, and kerosene followed with about 5 per cent each.

Sixty-three widely scattered agencies handled the distribution of products throughout the republic. Sales, however, were quite heavily concentrated. In 1940, the Mexico City agency, with sales of 48 million pesos, accounted for 25 per cent of the total value of domestic sales, and in 1947, with sales of 177 million pesos, for 28 per cent;

TABLE 18

PERCENTAGE DISTRIBUTION OF SALES OF PETROLEUM PRODUCTS BY PEMEX,
BY SELECTED STATES, 1947

Product	Federal District	Nuevo León	Coahuila	Tamauli- pas	Vera Cruz	Jalisco	Puebla	Total for states selected
Gasoline..	39.5	7.0	4.5	3.1	6.6	4.6	4.1	69.4
Fuel oil...	27.4	a	a	31.5	15.8	a	3.5	78.2
Gas oil....	13.9	a	14.7	14.1	6.3	a	a	49.0
Kerosene.	34.4	4.4	11.3	3.5	7.0	3.9	2.9	67.4
Paraffin...	31.3	a	a	a	a	a	10.7	42.0
Asphalt...	23.0	7.8	5.3	5.3	7.2	a	13.8	62.4
Gas......	80.9	a	2.0	5.0	3.1	2.7	1.1	94.8

a Not specified.
SOURCE: Records of Pemex.

Monterrey was second with 9 million pesos in 1940 and 31 million pesos in 1947, or less than 5 per cent for each year.[6] Agencies in ten cities sold more than 51 per cent of the total in both 1940 and 1947.* The concentration of sales was even greater in 1945, when four agencies sold almost 60 per cent of the total value of sales, and in 1946, when four sold more than 60 per cent. This was apparently due to abnormalities in transportation and to threatened shortages, which caused unusually heavy buying in the vicinity of refineries at Tampico and Mexico City.

A more detailed study of the consumption pattern reveals that, in 1947, the Federal District was by far the most important consumer of petroleum products. This was as might be expected, since the district was the principal center of population and industry. In 1947, Pemex sold 40 per cent of its gasoline, 34 per cent of its kero-

* The ten leading agencies in 1940 were Mexico City, Monterrey, Guadalajara, Torreón, Puebla, Tampico, Chihuahua, San Luis Potosí, Toluca, and Pachuca. In 1947, Toluca and Pachuca lost their places among the first ten to Vera Cruz and Mérida.

sene, 27 per cent of its fuel oil, 23 per cent of its asphalt, 14 per cent of its gas oil, 81 per cent of its bottled gas, and 31 per cent of its paraffin in the Federal District. The exceptionally high percentage of bottled gas sold there was largely the result of a government campaign to substitute petroleum fuels for wood and charcoal, whose use had seriously depleted the forests of the valley of Mexico. Tamaulipas and Vera Cruz, with their large ports, were notable for sales of fuel oil to distributors and shippers. Pemex sold 32 per cent of its fuel oil in Tamaulipas and 16 per cent in Vera Cruz. Coahuila, which included the cities of Torreón and Saltillo, took 15 per cent of the gas oil sold domestically by Pemex and 11 per cent of the kerosene. Puebla, a small state with a moderate amount of industry, took 14 per cent of Pemex' domestic sales of asphalt and 11 per cent of the paraffin. Jalisco, with Guadalajara, the second most populous city of the country, took substantial portions of gasoline, kerosene, and bottled gas. Nuevo León, which included Monterrey, the second most important industrial area and third most populous town, bought significant amounts of asphalt, gasoline, and kerosene.

What were the marketing problems and policies of Pemex?

After March 18, 1938, the government officials in charge of the industry continued the independent distributing systems of the expropriated companies in much the same independent and competitive fashion as before. The companies had operated bulk distributing plants throughout the republic. To retail their products, they had leased service stations and equipment to independent businessmen. To keep oil products moving to markets and to consumers, the government preserved the existing features of the distributing system, in spite of wasteful duplications of effort and lack of coördination.

In July, 1938, to insure a unified over-all organization, the government set up the public marketing corporation, *Distribuidora de Petróleos Mexicanos.* As noted earlier, this organization was able to unify and coördinate the distribution system only after threatened financial collapse forced presidential intervention and broke the resistance of labor leaders to reforms they believed inimical to their interests.

Even after 1940, when the Distribuidora was disbanded and its functions were assigned to Pemex, the essential features of the existing system continued in use. Pemex operated bulk stations and leased out service stations and equipment under one-year contracts, which were automatically renewed unless Pemex gave contrary notification. Under these contracts the lessees could carry only those products specifically authorized by the lessor, and had to meet certain specifications as to maintenance, service, and the wearing of uniforms. The arrangements were not always happy ones for the lessees, who on several occasions threatened to "strike" as an organized group.*

Until 1950, for distribution purposes, the country was roughly divided into three areas, served respectively by the refineries at Tampico, Atzcapotzalco (Federal District), and Minatitlán.⁷ Tampico supplied principally the east coast; Atzcapotzalco served mainly the plateau; and Minatitlán primarily met the needs of the southern areas and the west coast. However, movement between areas appears to have been considerable. When completed in 1950, the Salamanca refinery served northern plateau cities.

It is interesting to observe the general marketing policies of Pemex with respect to price and to variety and quality of products and services.

One of the objectives of expropriation was to advance the nation industrially by keeping fuel costs down. There was a long-standing feeling among labor groups that petroleum products should be made available to the people at low prices, presumably even though the industry was not a financial success.† The presidents of the republic and the general directors of Pemex frequently pointed to the low prices of Mexican petroleum products.

Domestic prices of petroleum products were fixed by the government even before expropriation.⁸ After 1938, the prices were fixed by decrees issuing from the Secretary of Economy. Prices set by the government were based largely on social and political considerations. The government tried to encourage domestic use of petroleum fuels, and the political strength of labor added to the pressure for low prices.

The general financial status of Pemex, of course, influenced the prices of petroleum products; three significant price boosts came at times of financial crisis.‡ However, at least until 1947, specific

---

* The Syndicate of Dealers in Petroleum and Its Derivatives (*Sindicato de Trabajadores del Comercio del Petróleo y sus Derivados*) tried to achieve recognition as a labor organization so as to have the right to strike under the favorable labor laws. Pemex denied having an employer-employee relationship with members of the organization, and was sustained by the Supreme Court (see *Excélsior*, Oct. 25, 1938). Despite this, the Syndicate of Dealers threatened serious "strikes" on at least two occasions (see *Excélsior*, Jan. 12, 19, 1939, and *Novedades*, Oct. 25, 1945).

† In fact, financial success might well have been interpreted by some labor groups as exploitation of the people. See *El popular*, July 24, 1944.

‡ The price increases came in January, 1940, September, 1943, and September, 1946. See *Diario oficial*, Jan. 13, 1940, Sept. 28, 1943, and Sept. 17, 1946.

cost elements appear to have had little effect on prices. The accounting methods of the organization were such as to make rational price-setting on a cost basis an impossibility. After the inauguration of Antonio Bermúdez in December, 1946, cost-accounting techniques were introduced, but it is not known how much progress was made. Cost accounting had been considered unnecessary until that time probably for two reasons: first, it was widely felt, especially by labor, that Pemex was not a business organization required to make ends meet; and second, the management had little incentive to determine specific costs simply because prices were set by the government. Management, squeezed between pressures for low prices and high wages, seems to have developed an attitude of indifference, since both prices and wages were set partly or wholly by government policy, which was subject to political influences.

In pricing petroleum products, the government based its policy principally on the desire to stimulate industrial growth, better transportation, and higher standards of living. In Mexico City, the retail price of kerosene for domestic use was reduced from 17 centavos a liter in 1938 to 14 centavos in 1945.[9] The fall in the price of kerosene was even greater in real terms because of inflation. Consequently, many families converted to kerosene for fuel and lighting, and, between 1940 and 1947, per capita consumption increased more than eightfold, from 2.5 liters to 21.1 liters. The price of fuel oil was kept comparatively low. The average price in 1938 was 1.62 centavos per liter, and 3.82 centavos in 1947.[10] This was an increase of 136 per cent, compared to a rise of 184 per cent in the index of wholesale cost of industrial raw materials in Mexico City.[11] The low average price of fuel oil concealed the fact that even more favorable terms were given the railroads, under the government policy of aiding them.* The price of liquid gas rose from 45 centavos per kilogram in 1938 to only 49 centavos in 1947, or 8.9 per cent, whereas the cost-of-living index for workers in Mexico City rose 205 per cent.[12] Per capita consumption of gas increased almost tenfold as households converted to bottled gas kitchen fuel. Before expropriation, liquid gas sales were confined to Mexico City, but by 1941 most major cities had supplies of the commodity.[13] Consumption was encouraged by the sale of stoves at cost in appliance

---

* A Pemex representative stated that at one time the railroads were charged as little as 1 cent a barrel for fuel oil. This may have been an understatement, but, despite low prices, the railroads became heavily indebted to Pemex. In September, 1947, the debt amounted to 12 million pesos. General Director Bermúdez threatened to stop further deliveries unless a satisfactory arrangement for payment was made. See *El nacional*, Sept. 3, 1947.

stores owned by Pemex. At the same time, the average price of gasoline increased from 16.7 centavos per liter to 25.6 centavos (53.3 per cent), including taxes of 8 centavos per liter in 1938 and 10 centavos in 1946.[14] Thus, the price of gasoline fell appreciably in real terms between 1938 and 1947. Partly in response to this relative decline, consumption increased from 506 million to 1,494 million liters. Per capita consumption of gasoline almost doubled between 1940 and 1947, rising from 32.1 to 64.0 liters. The increasing reliance on motor vehicle travel was reflected in a 40 per cent increase in vehicle registrations from 1940 to 1946.

On September 17, 1946, the government fixed the maximum retail price of gasoline with octane ratings of 57–62 at 26 centavos per liter in Mexico City.[15] The maximum prices ranged from 22 centavos a liter in Ciudad Juárez, where large amounts of gasoline came from the United States, to 34 centavos in Mérida, Yucatán. In setting different maximum prices for different localities, the government made allowances for transportation costs and took cognizance, as noted, of the area's major sources of supply. Mexolina, a superior grade of gasoline running 63- to 72-octane, sold for 4 centavos per liter more.

In the first years of operation, Pemex, absorbed in a struggle for survival and facing problems of organization, administration, labor, and equipment, gave but little attention to variety and quality of output and service. Under the pressure of criticism and of popular protest against shortages and low-quality gasoline, and under the direction of a progressive, businesslike management with more centralized control, the organization began to meet the challenge of changing motor design and of public demand for improved service in the sale of automotive products.

By United States standards, the quality of service in retail stations was poor. This is explained by several factors: first, Pemex had no effective competition; second, management was engrossed in other organizational problems; third, management was weak; and fourth, the public was not educated to demand better service.

Until the end of 1946, general shortages of various products, especially gasoline, struck the country from time to time. Gasoline was scarce along the Laredo–Mexico City highway in 1938 and 1939.[16] In May and September, 1944, there were serious gasoline shortages in Mexico City, requiring informal rationing.[17] During most of January, 1945, there were general shortages of gasoline, and black markets developed.[18] These shortages were due largely to transportation difficulties, but in June and July, 1946, strikes and threats of strike caused panic buying of gasoline and fuel oil in the Federal District.[19] The management, attributing the shortages that developed then to inefficiencies in transportation, announced that supplies were well above the needs of the country.[20] It is likely that sporadic work stoppages at the Atzcapotzalco refinery and the increased needs of the thermoelectric plant at Nonoalco, which supplied Mexico City with power, contributed to the difficulty. The Syndicate of Petroleum Workers, however, assigned the shortage to deficiencies of the railroads and bad management by Pemex.[21]

Until about 1946, there was general indifference to motorists and their needs. After that time, as part of a government campaign to encourage the lucrative tourist trade, Pemex set up model service stations along the Pan-American Highway between Laredo, Texas, and Mexico City. In these, service met high standards, and the tourist received at least as much attention as in the best stations in the United States. In addition to the usual services, courteous Pemex representatives met tourists and gave them pamphlets and verbal information of interest to travelers.

Pemex also paid increasing attention to the quality of products. This was especially true of gasoline. The largest market for gasoline was in the high altitudes of the central plateau, where engine performance was at a disadvantage. At the time of expropriation, gasoline on the market ran 57- to 62-octane. In 1940, a 70-octane gasoline named Mexolina was put on the market.[22] In 1941, Mexolina accounted for 5 per cent of the value of gasoline sales by Pemex. This figure increased gradually, until it stood at more than 37 per cent in 1947.[23] In 1948, Pemex introduced another improved grade of gasoline called Super-Mexolina, which ran between 70- and 80-octane. Small quantities of aviation gasoline also were sold by Pemex, but the quality was relatively low, running between 73- and 100-octane and principally in the lower ranges.[24]

Pemex emphasized the domestic market and exploited the export market only as an outlet for surpluses that were not demanded at home under the government policy of administered prices. The limited refinery capacity curtailed exports of the more highly refined products* as domestic consumption increased;[25] and after World War II, the principal exports were crude oil and fuel oil, which from 1946 to 1948 constituted more than 75 per cent of the total volume, compared to less than 60 per cent in the period 1936–1938.[26] The pressing need for dollar exchange gave Mexico

---

* Exports of gasoline, kerosene, and lubricating oil were less than 10 per cent of the total petroleum exports in 1948, as compared to 20 per cent in 1938.

a greater incentive to increase the margin between petroleum production and domestic consumption so as to participate more extensively in the export market.

Despite Pemex' low-price policies and other measures to encourage consumption of petroleum products, it is doubtful whether Mexico accomplished more in this direction by expropriation and government operation and control than it could have under private ownership and control. Although not conclusive, the evidence suggests that Mexico would have consumed as much had the oil industry remained in private hands.

A comparison of the percentage increase in consumption by ten developing countries in the two periods 1932–1937 and 1937–1950 shows that Mexico lost position in the second period, when the industry was nationalized.[27] Among the ten countries—Argentina, Brazil, Chile, Cuba, Mexico, Peru, Venezuela, Australia, Canada, and New Zealand—in the period 1932–1937, Mexico stood first in the percentage increase in consumption of motor fuel, first in the case of kerosene, and fifth in the case of fuel oil (including gas oil). Mexico also stood fifth in the percentage increase in consumption of all petroleum products; her increase for the period was 48 per cent, compared to a world increase of 44 per cent. In the period 1937–1950, Mexico stood fifth in the percentage increase in consumption of motor fuel, fourth in the case of kerosene, and ninth in the case of fuel oil. Mexico stood seventh in percentage increase in the consumption of all petroleum products with an increase of 136 per cent, compared to a world increase of 62 per cent. Thus, after nationalization Mexico lost position among the ten countries but stood higher above the world average.

In the shifting of position with respect to the percentage increase of all petroleum products in the two periods, Chile dropped behind Mexico. Venezuela, Cuba, and Canada moved ahead of Mexico. It is notable that the last three countries were open to private petroleum development, whereas Chile had taken measures in the late 'thirties to establish a state monopoly.[28] How much significance attaches to these developments is impossible to say without extensive research. The figures given above do not take into account the effects of (1) changes in population, either absolute or relative, or (2) efforts to industrialize in each country. These factors, as well as nationalization, may have been significant in changing the relative positions of the countries.

In conclusion, Pemex had a virtual monopoly in the Mexican market. In the earlier years after expropriation, the problem of coördinating supply with demand was troublesome. The loss of export markets left Pemex with large surpluses to sell at home. In the middle nineteen-forties, the overloaded transportation system created additional difficulties in coördinating supply and demand. The low-price policy of the government, the progressive development of industry, and the rising standard of living no doubt stimulated domestic consumption, but it is a moot question whether consumption increased more than it would have under private ownership. In the late 'forties, it appeared that demand was beginning to press on the supply of refined products.

One may well ask if the price policy established for petroleum products did not in effect subsidize industrial and household users at the expense of development of the oil industry. The answer to this question will become clearer after an examination of the finances of Pemex. If it is true that the price policy did act as a subsidy, one may ask if this was desirable from an economic standpoint or from the viewpoint of broader social policy. (This question will be discussed further in chapter xii.) On the other hand, there is some doubt that, even with Mexico's low-price policy, prices were actually lower than they would have been under private ownership. It is likely that the private companies would have been lower-cost producers than Pemex, as will become more evident in chapters x and xi.

To acquire a complete picture of the market open to Pemex, Mexico's international trade in oil will be considered next.

Chapter IX

INTERNATIONAL
TRANSACTIONS
IN OIL

Historically Mexico's trade in oil was very important. In fact, one of the complaints against the private oil companies was that the industry was geared to export and that, consequently, Mexico retained insufficient oil for her own needs. This complaint ignored the benefits of international trade and the imports that oil exports made possible. The course of events after expropriation profoundly affected Mexico's trade in oil and her net position. In discussing international transactions, we shall consider, first, developments in petroleum export markets and the position of oil among Mexican exports; second, the nature of Mexican import needs; and, third, the net position of Mexico in oil trade and the significance of this position relative to the country's self-sufficiency in oil.

In 1937, exports amounted to more than 25 million barrels.[1] In 1938, the figure was less than 15 million barrels. Even sharper was the fall in money values, from 162 million pesos in 1937 to 80 million pesos in 1938. The story of the struggle of Pemex to rebuild its export markets was a checkered history of a battle against organized foreign companies and against fate. The tough problem of drumming up business in world markets to meet the high production potential was assigned to the special sales agency, *Distribuidora de Petróleos Mexicanos*.

With expropriation, the companies openly announced their intention to boycott Mexican oil exports.[2] They requested that the State Department of the United States take steps to prevent the export and sale of oil produced from the expropriated properties.[3] Although no official response was forthcoming, there is some evidence that the influence of the companies was felt among government agencies: (1) Mexican sellers, even when they were low bid-

---

[1] For numbered notes to chap. ix, see pp. 248–249.

ders, failed to get contracts for oil with United States government agencies, and (2) the "representative year" chosen to set United States import quotas for oil was 1939, when imports from Mexico were at a minimum.[4]

Mexican exports undoubtedly did suffer severely from the boycott.[5] For many months after expropriation, Mexican oil found no favor in the United States market, and even in France shipments were tied up by court action. The first important contracts with United States firms contained clauses certifying that the oil delivered was not from expropriated properties.[6]

Immediately after expropriation, certain American businessmen, trying to take advantage of Mexico's export problems, went to Mexico with the intention of buying up oil at extremely low offerings, but most of them were rebuffed.[7] However, the Distribuidora did finally arrange to handle large amounts of Mexican oil through an American, who negotiated both barter and cash deals abroad.[8] Export markets were so tight that Mexican oil products had to be sold at prices 12 to 15 per cent below posted prices, except asphalt and gas oil, which were in demand at the time.[9]

In the last six months of 1938, exports recovered some of the lost ground, but only under handicap, for shipowners were also threatened with boycott by the companies. No oil products went to the United States until August, when a contract was made with the Eastern States Petroleum Company for the delivery of 360,000 barrels of crude oil a month.[10] Although the price was not advantageous, this contract served as an opening wedge against the boycott. Through the American middleman mentioned above, Mexico made barter arrangements for German machinery and structural steel and for Italian tankers. During the year from August, 1938, through July, 1939, barter was the basis for 52 per cent of oil export sales.[11] The outbreak of the war cut this figure to 15 per cent and prevented fulfillment of part of the existing contracts. The Distribuidora was severely criticized, both at home and abroad, for its marketing policy. At home, the most vociferous condemnation came from the labor syndicate, which felt that more advantageous terms should have been written into the contracts in order that wages might be raised; and condemnation abroad, attributed to the expropriated companies, decried sales of oil to the enemies of democracy.[12] However, the Mexicans had little choice, either in market areas or in price, because of the boycott and the ubiquitous trade barriers of the period. In defense of the export price policy of the Distribuidora, it may be noted that there was no economic

alternative to continuing the production and sale of oil for whatever the limited market would bring. Since labor was strong enough
to prevent the discharge of unnecessary employees if production
were curtailed, wages were largely a fixed cost.[13]

In 1939, world markets for Mexican petroleum began to open.
Large gains were registered in exports to Italy and the United
States, although these were offset in part by declining shipments
to Germany and to English and Dutch interests.[14] The value of
exports accelerated in July and August, but the outbreak of war in
Europe reduced the September figure to the lowest point since
April, 1938 (see table 14). Despite efforts to increase sales to Latin
America, the physical volume sold to that area rose only from
415,000 barrels in 1938 to 478,000 barrels in 1939, as compared to
1,308,000 barrels in 1937.[15]

Late in 1939, the boycott in the United States showed further
signs of weakening, and in 1940 broke down completely. In that
year American buyers took almost 16 million barrels, or more than
three-fourths of the total petroleum exports, as compared to 7.3
million barrels in 1937 and 3.3 million in 1938.[16] The Independent
Petroleum Association protested against the heavy Mexican imports at prices which it said threatened the American industry.[17]
Sales prospects brightened even more when it was rumored that
Japan was seeking to build a pipeline across the Isthmus of Tehuantepec in order to have easier access to Mexican oil,[18] and when it
became known in April that Pemex had signed a contract with a
Japanese-controlled company for the delivery of 2.4 million barrels
of petroleum products within one year at prices averaging 30 cents
per barrel below prevailing market prices.[19] Before the end of the
year, however, after Japan had received about 1 million barrels,
Pemex voluntarily eliminated that market and consigned practically all oil sold abroad to the United States.[20] This step revealed
Mexico's optimism about her position in the United States market.*
The hopeful feeling prevailed despite the decline in exports to
Latin American countries in 1940 which resulted from the shortage
of shipping. The loss of Latin American markets thwarted the plans
of Pemex,[21] which found that exports to the sister republics in each
of the three years 1938 to 1940 were less than half the volume in
1937.[22] In the years after 1940, the United States and Cuba became
by far the two most important markets for Mexican oil exports.

---

* Mexico also acted against Japan by canceling concessions to Japanese companies for exploration for and production of oil on the Gulf Coast, and by for-
bidding exports of petroleum and its products to Japan. See *Excélsior*, Oct. 25, 1940.

TABLE 19

Value of Exports of Petroleum Products from Mexico to the United States, Cuba, and Other Countries, 1941–1947

(In thousands of pesos)

Year	United States	Cuba	Other countries	Total
1941...............	60,323	8,307	1,713	70,343
1942...............	26,870	5,685	1,509	34,064
1943...............	19,462	14,005	3,092 [a]	36,559
1944...............	17,867	6,529	7,431 [b]	31,827
1945...............	23,093	14,137	2,826	40,056
1946...............	37,950	8,795	10,558 [c]	57,303
1947...............	34,564	5,285	5,530	45,379

[a] Exports worth about 2.1 million pesos went to Sweden.
[b] Exports worth about 4.3 million pesos went to Sweden, and worth 1.5 million pesos to Argentina.
[c] Exports worth about 4.6 million pesos went to France.
Sources: 1941–1945, *Compendio estadístico, 1947*, p. 448. 1946–1947, based on *Anuario estadístico del comercio exterior, 1947*.

TABLE 20

Annual Production of Crude Oil and Annual Domestic Consumption of the National Product in Mexico, 1936–1950

(In thousands of cubic meters)

Year	Production	Domestic consumption	Percentage consumed at home
1936............................	6,522	2,696	41
1937............................	7,457	3,150	42
1938............................	6,122	3,137	51
1939............................	6,820	3,420	50
1940............................	7,001	3,800	54
1941............................	6,845	4,519	66
1942............................	5,535	4,530	82
1943............................	5,590	5,256	94
1944............................	6,074	5,610	93
1945............................	6,923	6,035	87
1946............................	7,828	6,466	83
1947............................	7,346	6,687	91
1948............................	9,302	7,241	78
1949............................	9,684	7,865	81
1950............................	11,517	7,914	69

Source: Basic data from Secretaría de Economía Nacional, *Memoria, 1938–1950*.

During the five war years 1941 to 1945, 69 per cent of the value of Mexican petroleum exports went to the United States and 23 per cent went to Cuba. After the war, the United States continued as Mexico's best customer, taking 66 per cent in 1946 and 76 per cent in 1947, but Cuba's share fell to 15 and 12 per cent, respectively, in those years.[23] In 1948 and 1949, when Mexico began to serve a more

TABLE 21

ANNUAL VALUE OF MEXICAN IMPORTS AND EXPORTS OF PETROLEUM PRODUCTS,
1936–1950[a]

(In millions of pesos)

Year	Imports	Exports	Export balance
1936	11.8	152.2	+140.4
1937	16.8	162.4	+145.6
1938	20.0	79.8	+ 59.8
1939	14.0	82.6	+ 68.6
1940	19.4	88.4	+ 69.0
1941	24.8	70.3	+ 45.5
1942	22.6	34.1	+ 11.5
1943	27.2	36.6	+ 9.4
1944	37.6	32.7	− 4.9
1945	48.1	40.6	− 7.5
1946	72.6	57.3	− 15.3
1947	85.5	45.3[b]	− 40.2
1948	108.6	240.4[c]	+131.8
1949	153.0	131.5	− 21.5
1950	171.1	275.7	+104.6

[a] These figures only roughly indicate the true state of exports and imports and the balance. At least rom 1943 on, the data for exports conflict with those given by Pemex.
[b] This figure appears extremely low in view of the 121.2 million pesos given by Pemex.
[c] This figure appears too high (even making allowance for exports of independent producers), when compared to the 190.0 million pesos given by Pemex.
SOURCE: *Anuario estadístico del comercio exterior, 1936–1950.*

diversified market, United States purchases fell off percentagewise.[24]

One factor that helped to get Mexican oil to United States markets during the war years was the agreement that Mexican tankers carrying oil to United States ports be under lease to the War Shipping Administration, which accepted the financial risk by paying insurance costs plus an allowance to Pemex for operating expenses, depreciation, and a reasonable profit.[25] Although of little significance at the time, another opening to United States imports of Mexican oil was the reciprocal trade agreement that became effective on January 30, 1943. This eliminated the oil import quotas and reduced the tariff on kerosene by one-half, in addition to reductions already stipulated by the 1939 trade agreement with

Venezuela.[26] The principal accomplishment, however, was removal of the quotas, although Mexico realized little immediate benefit because of wartime shipping shortages.

The nationalistic and mercantilistic doctrine so emphatically asserted on the façade of the Pemex building, "Consume that which the country produces; produce that which the country consumes,"

TABLE 22

IMPORTS AND EXPORTS OF PETROLEUM PRODUCTS EXPRESSED AS PERCENTAGES OF TOTAL VALUE OF IMPORTS AND TOTAL VALUE OF EXPORTS, RESPECTIVELY, 1934–1949[a]

Year	Imports	Exports
1934	3.1	24.5
1935	2.9	20.5
1936	2.6	19.6
1937	2.8	18.2
1938	2.8	9.5
1939	2.2	9.0
1940	2.9	9.3
1941	2.7	9.6
1942	3.0	3.5
1943	3.0	3.3
1944	2.0	3.1
1945	3.0	3.2
1946	2.8	3.0
1947	2.6	2.1[b]
1948	3.7	9.0[c]
1949	4.0	3.6

[a] See footnotes to table 21 for limitations of the basic data used to derive these figures.
[b] Basic data appear to be in serious error; 6 per cent is probably more nearly correct. See table 17.
[c] Basic data appear to be in error. Probably 7 to 8 per cent is a closer approximation. Pemex reported export sales of 190 million pesos, to which an allowance for exports of independents must be added.
SOURCES: Basic data from *Anuario estadístico del comercio exterior* and, for 1948–1949, from *Compendio estadístico, 1950*, pp. 275, 282.

proved to be a double-edged sword. The motto was a revolutionary doctrine directed especially at the international oil companies, whose particular objective, the Mexicans felt, had been to strip the country of its oil. The crisis in the export market, arising first from the boycott and later from the lack of shipping space, forced the significance of the motto upon the country in a way that had not been anticipated. Pemex found it necessary to develop domestic markets to dispose of its oil. Whereas Mexico had consumed about 40 per cent of its domestic production in 1936 and 1937, it consumed 94 per cent in 1943 (see table 20). Even in 1949, the home

market absorbed more than 81 per cent of the much-increased domestic output, so that petroleum was far from being a commodity
produced principally for export. By that time, however, the increasing difficulties in her balance of payments forced Mexico to
develop export industries. When the Reynosa field was discovered
in 1948, the general director of Pemex expressed the hope that it

TABLE 23

ANNUAL VALUE OF MEXICAN EXPORTS OF CRUDE OIL AND REFINED PRODUCTS
AND THEIR RELATIVE VALUES, 1934–1950[a]

Year	Value (in millions of pesos)			Percentage		
	Crude petroleum	Refined petroleum	Total	Per cent crude	Per cent refined	Total
1934	35.2	122.2	157.4	22	78	100
1935	30.9	122.6	153.5	20	80	100
1936	28.4	123.8	152.2	19	81	100
1937	28.7	133.6	162.3	18	82	100
1938	16.2	63.5	79.7	20	80	100
1939	25.2	57.4	82.6	31	69	100
1940	53.1	35.3	88.4	48	52	100
1941	29.3	41.0	70.3	42	58	100
1942	12.1	22.5	34.6	35	65	100
1943	6.0	31.1	37.1	16	84	100
1944	2.2	30.6	32.8	7	93	100
1945	9.2	31.4	40.6	23	77	100
1946	15.4	41.9	57.3	27	73	100
1947	15.4	30.0	45.4	34	66	100
1948	96.7	153.2	249.9	39	61	100
1949	66.5	65.8	132.3	50	50	100
1950	163.7	114.2	277.9	59	41	100

[a] The figures for total exports for 1943–1948 are incompatible with those given by Pemex, but the relative proportions of crude oil and refined products are probably fairly accurate.
SOURCE: Basic data from *Anuario estadístico del comercio exterior, 1934–1950*.

might prove rich enough to step up exports and improve Mexico's
international position.[27] Although domestic consumption continued to rise in absolute terms, in 1950 it fell to 69 per cent of
total production. The value of Mexico's petroleum exports increased after 1944, but during the three years 1944 to 1946 the
value of imports increased faster and the country became a net
importer in value of petroleum. The net import balance may have
continued into 1947, though it is not possible to say with certainty
because of conflicting data.[28] In 1948 and 1950 Mexico probably
had an export balance, but 1949 showed an import balance of more
than 20 million pesos (see table 21).

Petroleum not only suffered reverses in net trade balance, but also declined relative to total value of exports. In 1934, petroleum had constituted almost 25 per cent of total exports. In succeeding years it declined, amounting to 18 per cent in 1937 (see table 22). Expropriation brought a precipitous decline to less than 10 per cent. In 1942, there was another sharp drop to about 3 per cent, with no evidence of recovery until 1947, when petroleum exports amounted to probably 6 per cent of the total. In 1948 there was a further rise to about 8 per cent, but available data indicate a decline to less than 4 per cent in 1949.

One objective of expropriation was to help the country emerge from its "colonial" economic status. A more detailed study of oil exports will show to what extent the Mexicans achieved their aim of exporting larger amounts of refined products and smaller amounts of crude oil.

Export figures indicate that, both absolutely and relatively, the Mexicans regressed from rather than advanced toward this goal. In the four years before expropriation (1934–1937), the average value of petroleum exports other than crude oil amounted to 126 million pesos per year, compared to 50 million pesos per year in the eleven years 1938–1948. The average value for 1948–1950 was 111 million pesos, but depreciation made the real value small as compared to the preëxpropriation figure. Refined products constituted 80 per cent of the total value of petroleum exports in the four years before expropriation, but only 67 per cent in the eleven years 1938 to 1948. The annual percentage declined radically after 1944, and in 1950 refined products constituted only 41 per cent of total petroleum exports. Exports of the more valuable cuts, including gasoline, lubricants, and kerosene, also declined sharply after March, 1938. Such exports averaged 65 million pesos a year in the four years preceding expropriation, but only 18 million pesos a year in the thirteen years 1938 to 1950.[29] The last three years, 1948–1950, showed some revival, but its significance was offset by the depreciation of the peso in 1948 and 1949. The decline in refined exports was to be expected in view of the great increase in domestic consumption and the inability of the industry to expand its refinery capacity. The increasing dependence upon foreign refined products was also a significant reflection of Mexico's colonial status.

With an insatiable and increasing appetite for petroleum products, the country became more and more dependent upon United States sources. The value of imports increased from less than 17 million pesos in 1937 to more than 108 million pesos in

1948. The average annual value of imports in the four years before expropriation, 1934–1937, was 12.6 million pesos, compared to an average of 43.7 million pesos in the eleven-year period, 1938–1948 (see table 21). Although the available data on the volume of imports are not very accurate, it can be confidently asserted that the average in 1947 and 1948 was about double that in 1936 and 1937.*

A study of specific petroleum imports reveals that the general trend to 1950 was upward.[30] This was especially true of the more highly refined products. After expropriation, gasoline became the principal item purchased abroad. In 1936 and 1937, gasoline imports had amounted to only 125,000 barrels a year and had cost less than 1.5 million pesos. Imports of gasoline mounted rapidly after 1940. By 1948, the 1936–1937 average volume had increased thirteen fold, to 1.6 million barrels, and the value twenty-six fold, to 39 million pesos. These figures declined somewhat in 1949 and 1950.

Up to 1948, developments in lubricants paralleled those in gasoline. From 1936 through 1940, imports of lubricating oils and greases averaged 26 million pounds gross weight a year and cost, on the average, less than 5 million pesos. In the four years 1947–1950, the average annual gross weight was more than 118 million pounds, and the average cost was more than 30 million pesos a year. Fuel oil and paraffin imports also showed significant increases.

Almost all imports came from the United States. From 1938 to 1950, receipts from the United States amounted to between 89 and 99 per cent of the total each year.[31] A large portion of these imports went to areas not easily accessible to national products. Records of Pemex indicate that in 1947 more than 80 per cent of the gasoline and kerosene imports entered the northern border towns and the two west coast ports of Guaymas and Manzanillo, and presumably most of the products were consumed within those general areas. Almost all the asphalt imported in 1947 went through Mexicali and Nogales. Other imported products that were more highly specialized in either production or consumption, such as lubricating oils and greases, paraffin, vaseline, and liquid gas, appear to have gone to the more populous interior of the country, even though most of them also entered border towns.

To what extent did Mexico become self-sufficient in its petroleum requirements in this period? During 1938–1947, the country was supplying smaller and smaller percentages of the domestically consumed gasoline, lubricating oil, and grease. Imports of gasoline

---

* The *Memoria* of the Secretary of National Economy shows 207,700 cubic meters of imports for 1936, 306,000 for 1937, 540,400 for 1947, and 545,500 for 1948. The figure for 1948 is probably incomplete.

rose from 8 per cent of the total consumed in 1938 to 21 per cent
in 1950.[32] Mexican dependence on foreign lubricating oils increased
from 28 per cent in 1938 to 60 per cent in 1947, and on grease from
28 per cent in 1938 to 52 per cent in 1947. In 1947, Mexico imported 82 per cent of its liquid gas, 100 per cent of its vaseline, 49
per cent of its paraffin, 4 per cent of its kerosene, 12 per cent of its
gas oil, and 6 per cent of its fuel oil.[33]

The increasing dependence of Mexico on foreign sources of petroleum products created serious problems and reflected, in part,
upon the government's handling of the industry. The dependence
on imports of expensive refined products in particular put a burden
on the balance of payments. Mexico had the option of expanding its
exploratory program, increasing its refinery capacity, curtailing its
consumption, or reconciling itself to the admission that its petroleum industry could not meet the needs of the country, and that
expropriation was a failure.

Mexico's position as a net importer of oil from 1944 to 1946 was
evidence of the failure of expropriation up to that time. The harsh-
ness of this judgment, however, is mitigated by recognition of events
outside Mexico and beyond its control, such as the war and the
boycotts on Mexican oil and on sales of equipment to Mexico. In
1946, the country had either to put the industry in order or to ad-
mit, perhaps tacitly, that expropriation had been a blunder.
Alemán, choosing the first course, put an experienced businessman
at the head of the industry and cracked a whip over the stubborn
leaders of the petroleum syndicate.

Although Mexico achieved a temporary export balance in value
of petroleum products in 1948, it did not appear likely that this
favorable position could be maintained in the face of increasing
domestic demand and limited refinery capacity, unless these factors
were offset by the discovery of large new pools. Between 1938 and
1947, total domestic sales of gasoline, fuel oil, gas oil, kerosene, and
lubricants (see table 15) increased at the rate of 9 per cent a year.
Between 1938 and 1948, production increased at the rate of only
4.2 per cent. By 1955, at these rates, domestic consumption should
exceed 76 million barrels a year (not counting paraffin, asphalt,
liquid gas, and miscellaneous products or losses in refining and distribution), and production should amount to 78 million barrels.

Such extended prognostications for the petroleum industry are
admittedly flimsy. However, the intangible factors bearing on the
situation were not reassuring. There was little reason to expect any
great slackening of the rate of increase in demand, in view of the

TABLE 24

RELATIVE VOLUMES OF SELECTED IMPORTED AND DOMESTICALLY PRODUCED
PETROLEUM PRODUCTS CONSUMED IN MEXICO, 1938–1947

(Percentages)

Product	1938	1939	1940	1941	1942	1943	1944	1945	1946	1947
Gasoline										
Imported............	8	8	8	16	10	9	10	11	17	20
Domestic............	92	92	92	84	90	91	90	89	83	80
Total..............	100	100	100	100	100	100	100	100	100	100
Fuel oil										
Imported............	7	4	6	3	3	3	3	3	4	6
Domestic............	93	96	94	97	97	97	97	97	96	94
Total..............	100	100	100	100	100	100	100	100	100	100
Gas oil										
Imported............	13	6	5	10	5	5	6	8	7	12
Domestic............	87	94	95	90	95	95	94	92	93	88
Total..............	100	100	100	100	100	100	100	100	100	100
Kerosene										
Imported............	18	18	17	16	13	8	8	8	9	4
Domestic............	82	82	83	84	87	92	92	92	91	96
Total..............	100	100	100	100	100	100	100	100	100	100
Lubricating oil										
Imported............	28	30	39	50	46	52	58	64	60	60
Domestic............	72	70	61	50	54	48	42	36	40	40
Total..............	100	100	100	100	100	100	100	100	100	100
Grease										
Imported............	28	31	37	46	46	43	49	51	58	52
Domestic............	72	69	63	54	54	57	51	49	42	48
Total..............	100	100	100	100	100	100	100	100	100	100

SOURCE: Basic data from Pemex.

Mexican policy of industrializing the country. Petroleum had to be the source of energy for this development because of the scarcity of coal and water power. It was also evident that, unless the country had an unforeseen windfall, there would not be sufficient funds for adequate exploratory and refinery expansion programs. Increased refinery capacity could have temporarily relieved the threatening adverse import balance, but this was not a complete solution because demand was overtaking production.

The only long-run solution to Mexico's problem of maintaining its self-sufficiency in oil appeared to be expansion of the exploratory program. And since capital was not directly accessible from other sources, it seemed that Mexico must offer foreign private companies more liberal terms for carrying on exploration. This solution, however, was highly distasteful to many groups, including the powerful Confederation of Mexican Labor.

General Director Antonio Bermúdez attacked the problem vigorously upon taking office. By 1950 he had made progress, but he was still fighting adverse conditions and the effects of past mistakes. Even with foreign capital, Mexico faced an arduous task of several years if it hoped to restore petroleum to its preëxpropriation position as a lucrative export commodity. The desire to develop oil as a major export was expressed on several occasions by presidents of Mexico and by the general director of Pemex. That this was needed was evident from the fact that in 1948 and 1949 Mexico's international reserves were so depleted that the peso was unpegged and its dollar value fell from 20.6 cents in July, 1948, to 11.6 cents in July, 1949. Without more foreign capital, the industry could make but little contribution to the Mexican balance of payments for many years.

By 1950, Mexico had not achieved its aims of exporting larger amounts of refined products than the private companies had, or of reducing imports of refined petroleum. Mexico had become more dependent on foreign refineries, and it appeared that the country was in serious danger of losing its self-sufficiency in oil.

Chapter X

LABOR RELATIONS

Although the more realistic of the Mexicans hardly expected labor-management relations to become all honey and roses with expropriation, there was a widespread hope that much of the antagonism would subside when the large companies, with their allegedly alien interests, disappeared. Socialists felt that state ownership would harmonize the common interests of workers and public. Syndicalist labor leaders hoped to acquire control of the industry, and thought that this would harmonize management and labor interests. Nationalistic Mexicans, looking little beyond the happy day when the foreigners would depart, did not anticipate serious labor-management controversy. In assessing expropriation, ordinary working-men were generally motivated by two thoughts: higher wages and patriotism. To what extent did various Mexican groups achieve their hopes and aims?

The story of the relations between Pemex and its labor force is rooted (1) in the Mexican Revolution, (2) in Article 123 of the Constitution of 1917, an outgrowth of Carranza's pledge to reform the labor laws in return for labor's support against Villa and Zapata, and (3) in the Labor Law of 1931. The pattern for labor's relations with Pemex was set by the favorable atmosphere that Cárdenas provided for labor; the temper of labor was conditioned by its extreme disappointment in not gaining complete control of the industry. The program upon which Cárdenas rode into presidential power was that of the National Revolutionary party. In its Six-Year Plan, the party set its course toward realization of all provisions of articles 27 and 123 of the constitution. Its attitude toward labor was expressed in sections 74, 75, 77, and 80 of the Six-Year Plan:[1]

Section 74. The National Revolutionary Party recognizes that the masses of city and country workers are the most important factor in the Mexican commonwealth, and that, despite the prostration in which they have lived, they maintain the highest concept of the interests of

[1] For numbered notes to chap. x, see pp. 249–252.

124

the community. The hope of making Mexico a great and prosperous country, by raising the cultural and economic standards of the great masses of the city and country workers, can therefore be rightly based upon the proletariat.

Section 75. The National Revolutionary Party advocates the principles of the right to work and state intervention to enable the individual to exercise this right.

Section 77. Collective bargaining is recognized as the only, or at least most prevalent, form of employer-employee relationship. To that end a clause obligating the employer not to accept non-union workers shall be made compulsory in all collective labor contracts.

Section 80. The government is to accept the same responsibilities as private employers in dealing with labor.

Before expropriation, the petroleum workers were organized along company lines in thirty-two distinct and independent sections. Labor contracts were not at all uniform as to wages and working conditions.[2] In December, 1935, the widespread dissatisfaction of labor and the tutelage of the Cárdenas government brought into being the industry-wide union known as the Syndicate of Petroleum Workers of the Mexican Republic (*Sindicato de Trabajadores Petroleros de la República Mexicana*). As soon as the syndicate had solved its most pressing problems of internal organization, it called a special convention for July, 1936, to draw up demands for a country-wide collective bargaining agreement covering all petroleum workers. The ensuing labor-management controversy ended in the judicial arbitration proceeding known as a "conflict of economic order." The Federal Board of Conciliation and Arbitration made its award in December, 1937. Although toning down the original excessive demands of labor, which would have more than doubled labor costs,[3] the decision provided for very significant improvements in wages and working conditions. This award was to become a focal point of contention in labor-management relations after expropriation. For this reason it is desirable to study briefly the labor conditions prevailing before expropriation, and the nature and extent of the benefits awarded by the Federal Board.

The decision of December, 1937, provided for an increase of almost 9 million pesos in the total basic wage bill of 1936.[4] The average daily wage of 6.97 pesos in 1936 was to be raised an estimated 27 per cent to 8.83 pesos. Total wages and salaries, including allowances for temporary, unhealthful, and overtime work, and for vacation, holidays, and rest days, amounted in 1936 to 45 million pesos[5] and were to be increased under the award to an estimated 61 million pesos,[6] or more than 35 per cent. In addition, various wage allowances under special conditions would push the total wage and salary cost another 6 million pesos above the 1936 figure.

Under the diverse contracts prevailing in 1936, the weekly work period varied from a minimum of 41.5 hours for office employees in certain companies to 48 hours for all employees in other companies.[7] All contracts in the industry called for 6.5 hours' work on Saturday and for payment of ordinary time for overtime not exceeding 1.5 hours. The 1937 award provided for a five-day week of 40 hours. Each worker was to have two rest days each week; if he worked on those days, he was to be compensated at triple time.[8]

Paid vacation periods varied widely in 1936. Some employees of the Huasteca Company received no paid vacation until after four years' service, when they were given 6 days.[9] Thereafter the allowance was increased to a maximum of 18 days after fifteen years' service. The contract with the Dutch-Shell company, "El Aguila," was more liberal to workers. The 1937 decision provided that all companies give 21 days of paid vacation for service periods up to ten years, and 30 days to those employed longer.

In addition, the 1937 award called for increases in pay for hazardous or unhealthful work, and for more liberal indemnification for layoffs and disability.[10] In 1936, indemnification for death due to occupational causes ranged from 730 days' pay to a maximum of 1,095 days' pay, as specified in section 1 of "El Aguila's" contract with labor.[11] The 1937 award called for the equivalent of 1,280 days' wages.[12] The companies were also required to provide each worker with life insurance of 4,000 pesos, to be financed by equal contributions from employer and employee.[13]

Before 1937, a number of wage contracts called for deductions of between 5 and 10 per cent from workers' pay and for equivalent employer contributions to build up individual savings funds for employees, to be delivered if so requested at the end of each year.[14] The 1937 award set the contribution of employee and employer at 10 per cent each,[15] compared to an estimated industry-wide average of 6 per cent contributed by the companies in 1937.[16] This amounted to an estimated increase in company expenditures from 3.2 million pesos in 1937[17] to 4.2 million pesos under the new contract.[18]

There was extreme variation in contractual provisions for housing in 1936.[19] The labor board award provided that companies with more than one hundred workers should provide housing or in lieu thereof 1 peso per day for workers whose daily wages were 10 pesos or less, and 1.50 pesos for workers whose wages exceeded 10 pesos.[20] This represented a great improvement in labor's allowances, for it was estimated that the cost to the companies would be 4.2 million pesos[21] compared to expenditures of 0.6 million pesos in 1936 and of 1.7 million pesos in 1937.[22]

The provisions for medical benefits for workers and their dependents in the new general contract awarded by the labor board marked a significant advance over previous arrangements. Under the awarded contract, the companies were obligated to maintain the following services: medical, surgical, oral and dental, orthopedic and prosthetic, hospital, pharmacy, laboratory, and ambulance.[23] Hospitals were to be established by the companies, and were to meet certain minimum standards. The services specified were to be made available to permanent workers, to temporary workers during periods of employment, and to specified dependents of workers, including wife, progenitors, descendants, brothers, and sisters. Provision was made for continuance of wages during periods of illness.

The award of December, 1937, also provided for a uniform pension system. The maximum allowance for old-age pensions before 1937 appears to have been 75 per cent of wages at age fifty-five and after thirty years' service, or 65 per cent after twenty-five years' service. The contracts also provided that disabled workers aged fifty or more were to be pensioned at 75 per cent of wages after thirty years' service, and at 65 per cent after twenty-five years' service. The new contract provided that retirement pay for workers aged fifty-five should be 70 per cent and 80 per cent after twenty-five and thirty years of service, respectively.[24] For workers with permanent and total disability, the pensions were to be graduated by years of service without regard to age: 65 per cent of wages for fifteen to nineteen years' service, 75 per cent for twenty to twenty-four years' service, and 80 per cent for twenty-five or more years' service.

In addition, the new contract required the companies to provide their workers with training scholarships, libraries, schools, equipment for sports, recreational areas, and other items. The cost was estimated at 1.5 million pesos,[25] compared to annual expenditures of less than 600,000 pesos in 1936 and 1937.[26]

The award of the Federal Board provided that the general executive committee of the syndicate and the local executives of its sections receive free passes on company transportation facilities.

Under the new contract, the cost of benefits other than wages and salaries was estimated at 15 million pesos,[27] compared to 4 million

in 1936 and 6 million in 1937.[28] Total labor costs under the new
contract, estimated at 75 million pesos, were about 26 million pesos
more than 1936 costs, and amounted to 31 per cent of net sales income in 1936.[29] Actual labor costs in 1936 had amounted to 20 per
cent of net sales income. The companies, claiming that the award
would increase labor costs by 41 million pesos, challenged the decision of the Federal Board in the Supreme Court of Mexico. Upon
losing the case, the companies declared themselves unable to pay.
Expropriation followed on March 18, 1938.

Relations between the Pemex management and the labor syndicate were at first cordial and coöperative, but the honeymoon did
not last long. The reason for the initial cordiality was the weakness
and reticence of the first central administration, in contrast to the
aggressiveness of labor leaders, who assumed practically all the
functions of management while the government was organizing
to administer the industry. The position of labor was enhanced by
the appointment of many syndicate officers to high positions in
various branches of the industry.* The history of labor-management relations was to be one of almost continual bickering; of
frequent work stoppages, many of them wildcat and illegal; of
internecine conflict among groups within the syndicate; of bitter
arguments and antagonisms over management's attempt to reorganize the industry on a nationwide basis; and of the seeming
apathy of labor toward the national interests which it had cham-
pioned so vigorously in order to bring about expropriation.

From the beginning, the workers had hoped that the industry
would be turned over to the syndicate to be managed by labor, as
had been done with the railroads. And, in fact, labor enjoyed almost
complete control in the period immediately after March 18, 1938.
The syndicate effected control through the organization of local
administrative councils (consejos de administración) composed of
officers of each section operating in their respective areas.[30] The
General Administrative Council of four government and three
labor representatives functioned principally as an advisory body,
apparently coördinating the industry only in the most superficial
fashion. Its appointed officers found themselves helpless to deal
with syndicate leaders, who rapidly established vested interests in
the local control of operations. The aspirations of the labor syn-

---

* For example, the secretary general of the general executive committee of the
syndicate became personnel manager of Pemex, and the secretary general of section 4
of the syndicate became manager of the Atzcapotzalco refinery. Many of these appointees were incompetent executives. See Jesús Silva Herzog, Petróleo mexicano
(México, D.F., 1941), pp. 237–238.

dicate suffered a severe setback when the law of July 20, 1938, establishing the permanent organization of Pemex, put control into the hands of government appointees on the board of directors and gave labor only a minority voice. However, the syndicate did not lose hope. The first major difficulty between labor and management arose over the degree of control to be retained by labor when the industry was reorganized in 1938–1940.

The first evidence of the breakdown in labor-management goodwill appeared early in August, 1938, when section 1 of the syndicate threatened a 24-hour strike over the central administration's attempt to replace certain local officials in the Ciudad Madero region.[31] Although the strike did not materialize, friendly relations deteriorated rapidly thereafter, as the permanent management pressed for industrial reorganization to bring about coördination and greater economy.

The organization of the industry along the lines of the private companies gave rise to serious duplication and waste in sales, advertising, accounting, engineering, and medical services. In October, 1939, the management announced plans for unifying the various sales agencies under the Distribuidora de Petróleos Mexicanos, so that all wholesaling, retailing, advertising, and certain other functions would be coördinated under one control.[32] The syndicate feared any such streamlining procedure as a threat to the security of workers. A centralization committee with strong labor representation was set up to study plans for unification. By February, 1939, the medical and accounting departments had been centralized, but nearly a year later marketing unification had not yet been completed. This problem merged into the wider problem of general reorganization of the industry and of the formation of a collective labor contract.

The need for general reorganization arose from financial stresses. Shortly after expropriation, the directors of Pemex made the mistake of offering to put into effect gradually the labor board award of December, 1937.[33] This was a rash proposal in view of existing difficulties. In the first place, the suddenness of expropriation left Mexico inadequately prepared to take over the industry without some backward steps, and a transitional period of financial hardship appeared inevitable. Second, the immediate loss of foreign markets entailed a swift decline in revenues, and future prospects were very dim under the cloud of the boycott threatened by the powerful expropriated companies. Third, even with the wages and conditions prevailing before December, 1937, petroleum workers were much better off than other workers. Nevertheless in July, 1938, the pay scales of the 1937 award were put into effect with certain discounts agreed upon by the board of directors.[34]

A very rapid increase in the number of employees accompanied this increase in wage scales. The number of employees, which had been slightly more than 15,000 in 1934 and 1935,[35] increased to 15,895 in April, 1938, to 18,149 in April, 1939, and to 23,073 in October, 1939.[36] In 1938, production of crude oil was 18 per cent less than in 1937, and in 1939 more than 8 per cent less. The result was a rapid increase in labor costs. According to Pemex records, the average daily wage rose from 9.58 pesos in 1937 to 10.69 pesos in July, 1938, and to 12.12 pesos in 1939, and the total labor bill increased from 56 million pesos in 1937 to 69 million pesos in 1938, to 98 million pesos in 1939, and to 100 million pesos in 1940. Even with experienced management and well-established markets, an increase of 42 million pesos in labor costs between 1937 and 1939 would have been serious,* but under the existing conditions a nearly disastrous financial imbalance resulted. In December, 1940, the government was forced to grant Pemex the sum of 60 million pesos, apparently used to cancel tax debts.[37]

Although management committed serious errors, this financial stringency developed largely because of pressures exerted by the syndicate. With expropriation, the central management lost control over hiring, and positions were multiplied to "reward" officers of the syndicate.[38] In January, 1940, a convention of petroleum workers asked that all provisions of the award of December, 1937, be put into effect. Vicente Cortés Herrera, the general manager of Pemex, hotly replied that production had declined despite the increasing number of workers and the rising wage bill.[39] He also accused the workers of failing to maintain discipline, of removing company equipment, and of causing serious waste of oil—wrongs which he said the administration could not correct because local management was too independent. To these charges, the syndicate replied that the disaster facing the industry was due to managerial incompetence.[40] The syndicate leaders, claiming that the Distribuidora had lost 15 million pesos by bungling foreign oil contracts, demanded that Cortés Herrera be dismissed and "brought to justice" for his shortcomings.

---

* Profits, even under the experienced management of the private oil companies, probably would have been wiped out, or nearly so. The average combined profits reported by the expropriated companies (except the Mexican Gulf Petroleum Company) for the three years 1934–1936 were 23 million pesos. The expert commission, in the conflict of economic order of 1937–1938, asserted that the figure was 56.3 million pesos. See *Mexico's Oil* (México, D.F., 1940), pp. 467–468.

With financial problems and labor-management friction threatening calamity, the general managers and the chairmen of the boards of directors of Pemex and the Distribuidora apprised President Cárdenas of their predicament and suggested economy measures. The syndicate also sent a delegation to the President. Late in February, after studying the situation, Cárdenas summoned national and local officers of the syndicate to hear his fourteen-point recommendation for reorganizing the industry and restoring it to a sound financial basis.[41]

The President spoke of his sympathetic bond with workers of cities and farms, and referred vaguely to the coöperative spirit shown by the petroleum workers. However, he charged that the petroleum workers had at times confronted Pemex and the General Administration of National Petroleum with a belligerence reminiscent of their attitude toward the expropriated companies. This, he felt, was a mistake stemming from the failure of certain syndicate leaders to recognize that the profits of the industry now belonged to the nation, that success or failure gravely concerned both the nation and the syndicate, and that injury to the industry would bring injury to the syndicate itself. Appealing to their patriotism, he called upon workers to aid in solving the economic problems of the industry. The President summarized the general needs of the industry as follows:

1. The 1940 budget should be balanced on the basis of an estimated income of 235 million pesos.

2. The development program for the industry should aim at making available for export 200,000 barrels of oil daily, so as to enable the country to pay the expropriation indemnity.

3. The refineries should be expanded and modernized to promote economy and efficiency.

4. Twenty per cent of export sales should be set aside as an indemnification fund for the expropriated properties.

5. The industry should regularly meet its tax obligations and repay advances made by the government for the purchase of new equipment.

6. Steps should be taken to put into effect as soon as possible the labor board award of December, 1937.

The income of 235 million pesos estimated by the President was not unduly optimistic; sales had brought in 233 million pesos in 1939, and 249 million pesos in 1940. However, if the budget was to be balanced at this income level, it must have been evident to all that drastic cuts would have to be made in labor costs. In 1936, labor costs had amounted to about 20 per cent of sales (see appendix table 18). In 1938, they had risen to more than 34 per cent of sales, and in 1939 to 42 per cent. The President's view that labor costs were the chief factor contributing to the financial imbalance of the petroleum industry was revealed by his fourteen specific recommendations. His hopes of saving appreciably on labor costs and of setting aside 20 per cent of income from export sales were supremely optimistic, just as his aim of boosting exports to 200,000 barrels a day was a sanguine expectation in view of the 40,000-barrel daily average in 1939.

President Cárdenas also told the syndicate leaders that it was the government's obligation to outline the measures necessary to reorganize the industry on a sound financial basis. To that end, he specified the following fourteen measures as absolutely essential and undeferrable:

1. To reduce the number of permanent employees to that of March 18, 1938, and to hire temporary employees only for special work and only upon the recommendation of the board of directors.*

2. To eliminate unnecessary positions.

3. To reduce administrative salaries to a more equitable level, since administrators in Pemex enjoyed greater compensation than comparable officials in other industries.

4. To reduce the number of temporary employees to not more than 10 per cent of the permanent employees.

5. To increase the efforts of labor during regular working hours until conditions in the industry improved, so as to avoid unnecessary expenditures for overtime.

6. To suspend for whatever time was necessary the payment of rental allowances to employees receiving more than 10 pesos a day.

7. To suspend the labor award of December, 1937, until such time as the industry could pay off the indemnification and modernize its equipment. Thereafter, that award was to be considered a minimum aspiration.

8. To relax rigid seniority requirements in filling indispensable jobs during temporary absences or vacations.

9. To give the administration discretionary power to designate what positions were indispensable and necessary to fill them when temporarily vacant.†

10. To give the administration freedom to move personnel between zones or to new offices where their services were most needed.

---

* Most of the new employees after expropriation were temporary employees. Between April, 1938, and October, 1939, the number of permanent employees had increased by 1,773, from 14,368 to 16,141, whereas the number of temporary employees had increased by 5,405, from 1,527 to 6,932. See Silva Herzog, *Petróleo mexicano*, p. 242.

† The administration had had little or no discretionary power in this matter, but had had to fill positions from candidates on the seniority lists.

11. To revise administrative assignments in order better to adapt the ability of personnel to the duties of the offices.

12. To weight ability heavily in promotions so as to maintain incentives for advancement.

13. To reorganize the Syndicate of Petroleum Workers to conform to the new nationwide organization of the industry and thus reduce the number of local sections.

14. To include in the collective contract under negotiation a provision giving the administration complete freedom in choosing field superintendents.

The President's measures were a hard blow to the syndicate. They meant a return to preëxpropriation wages and working conditions and, perhaps more significant, a surrender of coveted managerial powers acquired by the aggressive labor leaders who had taken advantage of expropriation difficulties. The leaders felt that Cárdenas, their mentor, had let them down, and they were long in answering him. Time was in their favor, and they fought a delaying action. It was not until April that they sent Cárdenas a reply dealing point by point with his recommendations.[42] With regard to the President's first point, the syndicate claimed that the number of workers employed in 1940 was not so much larger than the number employed in March, 1938, as appeared on the surface. The difference, it was implied, was due largely to differences in methods of classification. (In reality, classification methods had but little effect on the comparative figures.) Furthermore, since the number of employees depended upon developments in the industry, it could not possibly be specified in advance. The syndicate objected to indiscriminate elimination of unnecessary positions as harmful to the legitimately acquired seniority rights of workers. The reduction in administrative salaries was applauded, but with a recommendation that the savings realized should be utilized to implement the labor board award of December, 1937. The syndicate regarded as absurd and impossible the suggested limitation of temporary workers to 10 per cent of the permanent workers. Although agreeing that overtime should be reduced to the indispensable minimum, labor leaders objected to any decrease in housing allowances, for which they had fought long and hard. They could readily accept the President's proposal that the labor board award be the minimum aspiration of labor, but they were reluctant to delay effecting it, especially since many of its provisions had been written into a collective agreement then under discussion with Pemex. The syndicate objected to any evasion or limitation of the vested rights in seniority. The administration's power to fill vacancies and move personnel between zones and offices should be determined by collective agreement. Changes in administrative assignments would be acceptable provided that seniority rights were safeguarded. The syndicate considered that, since ability depends partly upon experience, the incentives for advancement were not normally subverted by seniority rules. But if incapacity was proved, the worker's right to the job should be challenged. The recommendation to simplify the structure of the syndicate was referred back to the component sections. Finally, the syndicate declared that the method of appointing field superintendents had already been determined by a labor-management agreement, issued as a decree of the labor board.

It was evident that the syndicate was committed to rejecting or skirting the essential issues in the President's proposals. Its unwillingness to compromise, despite Cárdenas' manifest favor toward labor and despite conditions in the industry, threatened trouble for the petroleum administration and embarrassment for the government.

The syndicate supplemented its reply to the President with a counterproposal for reorganizing the industry and putting it on a solid basis:[48]

1. To centralize the industry by putting Pemex, the Distribuidora, and the General Administration of National Petroleum under one head.

2. To sever all connections between the administration and ministries of the government.

3. To give the Syndicate of Petroleum Workers majority representation on the board of directors.

4. To repeal provisions of the act creating Pemex which gave the government representation on the board of directors.

5. To prevent anyone outside the industry from participating in management.

6. To permit the Syndicate of Petroleum Workers to participate fully in the reorganization of the industry.

7. To eliminate discounts on effective pay scales.

Early in May, the general executive committee of the syndicate presented an amplified reorganization plan to the President. The new document, incorporating the preceding points and also suggesting that Pemex abolish certain departments handling labor benefits,[44] was essentially syndicalist. In his reply, the President rejected the proposal that the syndicate take over control of the industry. He objected to having a small group handle a natural resource, belonging to the nation, without the controlling voice of the government. The government, he said, would be neglecting its responsibility to the nation. The proposal to remove the discounts on wage scales was rejected as illogical in view of the need to economize. Cárdenas also refused to eliminate those departments providing beneficial services for labor. This, too, was a government obligation that could not be ignored.

The President reiterated four points fundamental to the reorganization of the industry: first, capital was needed to develop the industry; second, funds must be set aside to indemnify the oil companies; third, taxes were due the government; and fourth, the nation as owner of the subsoil should receive profits.[45]

The month of June was replete with meetings, conferences, proposals, and counterproposals by management and by the syndicate, but no agreement was forthcoming. Labor opposition and resentment grew stronger as government insistence on its own reorganization plan increased. The issues were complicated by a threat of schism that developed in the syndicate when employees of the General Administration of National Petroleum, fearful of losing their jobs, objected to the fusion of that organization with Pemex. Meanwhile, the reorganization issue was forced to a head by the report that the combined earnings of Pemex, the Distribuidora, and the General Administration of National Petroleum in the first six months of 1940 amounted to only 143 million pesos, whereas expenditures stood at 211 million pesos.[46]

On July 15, 1940, with financial disaster facing the industry, President Cárdenas ordered government representatives on the boards of directors of the three organizations to take the following steps to restore equilibrium to the industry:[47]

1. To notify the syndicate that, unless conditions in the industry had improved by the end of 1940, bonds would be issued to the workers in lieu of payments from the savings fund.

2. To eliminate rental allowances for those earning more than 30 pesos a day, and to limit them to 30 pesos per month for those earning 20 to 30 pesos a day.

3. To reduce overtime to a minimum.

4. To complete reorganization and consolidation of the industry by July 31.

5. To reclassify administrative personnel in order to reduce wages and salaries.

6. To reduce by 10 per cent earnings in excess of 700 pesos per month.

7. To limit temporarily annual vacations to six days.

8. To fill no temporary or permanent vacancies unless absolutely necessary.

9. To authorize general managers to move administrative personnel anywhere in the country and other employees anywhere in their respective zones.

10. To reduce the number of temporary workers to the absolute minimum.

11. To suspend the policy of paying the wages and expenses of commissions of the syndicate without prior approval by the board of directors, except for the general executive committee, the executive committees of local sections, the collective bargaining commission, and syndicate representatives on the board of directors.

This large bill of particulars struck heavily at the syndicate. The general public support of Cárdenas gave labor a setback, but not for long. When the President's orders were announced to the boards of directors, syndicate representatives walked out, but a quorum remained to comply with the presidential directive.[48] On July 25, the general managers, instructed by their respective boards of directors to carry out reorganization, initiated arbitration proceedings before the Federal Board of Conciliation and Arbitration in a conflict of economic order. Explaining that the loss of export markets resulting from the war necessitated economies, they asked the Federal Board to effectuate the provisions of the presidential reorganization plan.[49] On July 27, 1940, the board complied by suspending all existing work contracts, putting the reorganization plan into effect provisionally, and ordering Pemex to put up a bond[50] to cover wages should the reorganization be subsequently denied.

The request of the syndicate for an injunction against this award was turned down on the ground that the provisional nature of the award in itself supplied a remedy.[51] The syndicate then launched a campaign against the boards of directors of the three government petroleum agencies. It openly accused the general managers of Pemex and the Distribuidora of underhanded tactics in influencing President Cárdenas.[52] The syndicate ordered a 24-hour protest strike, but canceled it when the Confederation of Mexican Labor under the leadership of Vicente Lombardo Toledano intervened in the dispute. Lombardo Toledano, in an executive meeting of the confederation, supported the presidential reorganization plan and accused the expropriated companies of inciting the labor trouble.[53] The general executive committee of the syndicate became more cautious in the face of the unsympathetic attitude of both organized labor and the general public toward the petroleum workers. However, many local sections, antagonized by the official opinion of the Confederation of Labor, regarded as too pliable the attitude of their own general executive committee. Local fulminations of protest broke out in the form of sabotage and of threats against the lives of the general managers.[54] The bitterness of these attacks brought about the resignation of Jesús Silva Herzog, general manager of the Distribuidora. Silva Herzog, a Marxist and an ardent supporter of the proletariat, declared himself unwilling to deal with the "ruffians" in the syndicate and submitted his resignation.

The caution of the syndicate's general executive committee threatened to produce further schism in the ranks of the petroleum workers. A number of the local sections wanted the committee to handle the reorganization problem, whereas other less conciliatory sections preferred to have a special convention deal with it.[55] Among other demands, the recalcitrant sections insisted upon the discharge of all *empleados* (roughly equivalent to white-collar workers) hired since March 18, 1938.[56] They wanted to get rid of all nonunion confidential employees, many of whom had been hired by the administration to replace those installed by the syndicate immediately after expropriation, when employees of the companies had been barred from their offices.

The management groups, conciliated by the favorable attitude of the general executive committee, agreed to modify the Federal Board's temporary award of July 27, 1940. Their agreement with the syndicate, concluded with the aid of the Secretary of Labor, was given official status as an award by the Federal Board on August 7. It gave the general executive committee broader powers in the reorganization proceedings, and provided for the appointment of four commissions to study (1) the temporary reorganization and the application of reorganization procedures, (2) economies proposed by the Syndicate of Petroleum Workers, (3) rules for filling vacancies, and (4) the transfer of workers by the administration.[57] This announcement was followed by a wave of protests from those sections dissatisfied with the general executive committee. Repeated demands for a special convention finally induced President Cárdenas to denounce the proposal as an attempt to obstruct reorganization.[58]

On September 11, 1940, without specifying its reasons, the Federal Board rescinded its award of August 7 and reverted to the presidential reorganization plan of July 27.[59] (The reversal may have been due to government pressure in behalf of its plan of organization, or to the nascent dissatisfaction of the management groups with the powers granted the general executive committee by the later award.) The locals in the Federal District, strongly disapproving the change, met in general assembly within a few days and agreed to strike against Pemex for not observing the agreement of August 7.[60] They asserted that the reorganization plan of July 27 discriminated against workers in the lower categories, and that the industry's problems could be traced to the fact that the general manager of Pemex had a political rather than a business background. The assembly declared in favor of (1) forming a central strike committee, (2) withdrawing from the Confederation of Mexican Labor if its support was not forthcoming, and (3) creating a new petroleum union in the central zone by leaving the Syndicate of Petroleum Workers and electing the officers of the general executive committee to serve the new union. In the meeting, punctuated by cries against Lombardo Toledano and the Confederation of Labor, Rafael Suárez, general secretary of the Syndicate of Petroleum Workers, promised that the executive committee would follow the will of the majority, even though any such strike would undoubtedly be declared illegal.[61]

President Cárdenas condemned the strike movement as unjustified, and was supported by both the Confederation of Labor and the principal industrial unions. These groups, uniting in opposition to the syndicate leaders, specified that the latter must remain in the Confederation of Labor and must submit the dispute to that organization if they desired aid in the reorganization fight.[62] At the same time, the Mexican Revolutionary party (the government party and successor to the National Revolutionary party) condemned the syndicate's opposition to reorganization as damaging and ruinous to the reputation and welfare of the labor movement.[63]

Meanwhile no strike had been called, since the northern and southern zones did not support the central zone. The temporary reorganization got under way in the latter part of September, 1940, and the consequent discharge of workers gave rise to a rash of sporadic strikes in the Federal District.[64] President Cárdenas again intervened, this time giving the syndicate ten days to propose a better plan of reorganization.[65] The syndicate was apparently resorting to delaying tactics, which allegedly[66] would improve its bargaining situation as Cárdenas' term drew to an end and his authority weakened. Meanwhile, the labor board, in accordance with legal procedure in conflicts of economic order, had appointed an expert commission consisting of Enrique Sarro, director of economic studies in the Banco de México, Miguel Manterola, economist and public accountant, and José López Portillo y Weber, petroleum engineer.

On October 31, 1940, the expert commission submitted its report.[67] It pointed to the decline in petroleum production and the deterioration of many of the fields since expropriation. Refining facilities were in bad shape and refining activity was declining. Petroleum exports were down, and their prices had fallen. At the time of the report, the number of Pemex employees had increased by about 25 per cent since April, 1938, and labor costs by 110 per cent. Whereas, in the period 1937 to 1939, the General Administration of National Petroleum had realized increasing profits, amounting to nearly 4 million pesos in 1939, Pemex and the Distribuidora had suffered a decline from profits of 15 million pesos in 1938 to losses of more than 21 million pesos in 1939. This was attributed not to declining income, but to increasing expenditures and, in particular, increasing labor costs. As a consequence, payments of taxes and royalties had ceased.

The award of the labor board was handed down on November 28, 1940. It upheld Pemex on the essentials of reorganization, but approved the syndicate's stand on pay scales and allowances. The board authorized the following temporary measures until financial equilibrium should be restored:[68]

1. Pemex was authorized to discharge permanent employees taken on after April 1, 1938.

2. Pemex was authorized to discharge up to 25 per cent of the doctors, lawyers, pharmacists, and drillers who had joined the company since April 1, 1938.

3. Pemex was authorized to discharge (without consent of the syndicate) temporary workers as soon as their contracts terminated.

4. Pemex was authorized to reduce by 10 per cent the wages of workers receiving more than 700 pesos a month.

5. The company was not to be liable for severance pay or other benefits in any of the preceding changes.

6. Discharges under the temporary award of July 27, 1940, were to be permanent, without further pay or allowances.

7. The petition of Pemex for a collective labor contract was denied.

8. The following additional provisions affected labor directly (only the principal provisions are here included):

a) Confidential employees allowed by the award of December, 1937, were to be listed and forbidden to join the labor syndicate.

b) Rules of seniority were to be established.

c) Pemex was to have complete freedom to fill temporary vacancies when in its judgment replacement was necessary.

d) The workweek was to be 44 hours.

e) Pemex was to have complete freedom to move confidential employees and to shift other wage earners during the reorganization.

f) Vacations, rental allowances, and savings funds were to be continued.

Although the award of the labor tribunal had a semblance of finality, it did not settle the dispute. Dissidence continued, and new obstacles appeared. The award had provided for a mixed commission of labor and management to supervise the details of reorganization. The intervention of President Cárdenas while the case was still pending before the labor board gave the syndicate a lever which it used to maximum advantage. This intervention in legal processes, coupled with the vacillation of the board itself, served not only to vitiate the decision but also to foster aggressiveness in the syndicate and even to lessen the respect of the syndicate and, perhaps, of management for legal procedures.

The dissension remained under cover until after the general manager of Pemex had been relieved by the incoming administration of Avila Camacho. On December 4, 1940, Efraín Buenrostro, the new general manager, announced that reorganization would begin in the north zone with the discharge of 3,500 workers.[69] This was a signal for trouble between the new officials and the syndicate. Late in December, the management petitioned for an injunction against continuing the mixed commission on the ground that it was obstructing the reorganization.[70] The injunction was denied, but the meetings of the mixed commission were suspended in January, 1941.[71] Although Pemex had had to borrow 10 million pesos in December to pay the savings fund allowance, it did not effect all the economy measures authorized by the award of November 28.[72] This was probably due to the strength of labor opposition to the reorganization, for difficulties between labor and management continued. In the latter part of March, 1941, strikes were again threatened, and the President sent federal troops to strategic areas in Poza Rica and Tampico to avert violence.[73] The impending dangers passed, but in May the discharge of seventy workers in the central zone and their replacement by others of greater seniority from the southern zone caused more agitation.[74] As time went on, dissatisfaction spread among the local sections that were particularly affected by the reorganization.[75] In June, a large number of locals voted to strike, and proposed that a general convention of petroleum workers set up a strike committee in the event that the general executive committee of the syndicate opposed the walkout. The general executive committee was inclined to move cautiously because of rumors that Nazi agents were fomenting the strike and that President Avila Camacho was ready to suppress it.[76] Since officials of the Confederation of Mexican Labor also opposed the strike as treason, the danger was again averted. But agitation continued, and reorganization proceeded in desultory fashion as new problems arose to rend labor-management relations.

The next conflict centered about labor's demand for a collective contract. No formal contract had ever governed the relations between Pemex and the syndicate. The haphazard negotiations that had been instituted before the reorganization fight began in 1939 proved sterile, apparently because of syndicate opposition. Pemex' request for a collective contract at the time of the conflict of economic order in July, 1940, had been denied in the November award, since the law requiring employers to engage in collective bargaining at the request of labor did not similarly obligate labor. By 1941, however, the situation had changed, and the syndicate wanted a collective contract. In September, the inertia of the Pemex administration brought protests and renewed threats of strike.[77] The Confederation of Mexican Labor and other independent national unions came to the support of the syndicate and charged the management with obstinately avoiding agreement on a contract.[78] The confederation exacted, as the price of its support, the syndicate's promise not to ask for higher wages.[79]

On October 1, the Secretary of Labor presided over a conference at which the parties discussed the bases for a collective contract.[80] A week later, Efraín Buenrostro announced that agreement had been reached on all points of controversy except (1) the list of confidential employees, (2) the period of medical benefits, and (3) allowances for occupational accidents.[81] These vexatious questions prolonged the negotiations. Although an agreement to resolve the disputed points immediately and to put the collective contract in force within sixty days was signed on October 29, negotiations dragged on for nearly seven months.

The disagreement over confidential employees was particularly significant. A long-standing problem, crucial both in negotiations with the private companies and in reorganization proceedings, it was to cause serious trouble in later years. Confidential employees of the companies had not been required to belong to the syndicate, but their number had been strictly limited. The labor board award of December, 1937, would have allowed the companies an estimated eleven hundred confidential employees.[82] As mentioned previously, all such employees were discharged at the time of expropriation, and their places filled by members of the syndicate. When friction developed between the administration and the syndicate, the former began to replace the syndicate people. This aroused vigorous protests. In the negotiations, the management wanted to establish its right to free choice of confidential employees. The syndicate, hoping to retain its control over the confidential positions, accused the management of appointing excessive numbers in order to dilute syndicate personnel.

With regard to the period of medical benefits and the allowance for occupational accidents, the syndicate demanded that existing discrimination be eliminated by equalizing allowances within each category of worker.[83] The general manager replied that management also desired equalization, but at a level that would not increase total costs. The syndicate wanted all allowances leveled at the maximum in each category.[84]

On May 17, 1942, Pemex and the syndicate signed a collective contract to be effective for two years. It was a compromise document giving the administration firmer control of the organization, and granting the syndicate concessions on various fringe benefits.

The new contract divided confidential positions into three groups.[85] The first group, to be appointed freely by the president of the republic or by the administration, included the principal administrative officers; the leading technicians in accounting, engineering, statistics, law, and medicine; the superintendents of fields and refineries; and the private secretaries of officers. The second group, in which positions might be filled by either members or nonmembers of the syndicate, included geologists, geophysicists, chemists, drillers, and lesser technical employees in accounting, medicine, and engineering. The third group was to be chosen freely by the administration, but from candidates who were syndicate members. It included assistants to superintendents and chiefs in smaller offices and departments in various fields and refineries.

Compared to the award of December, 1937, and to developments before May 17, 1942, the new contract gave management considerable scope. It required the management to fill permanent vacancies in positions normally held by syndicate personnel with syndicate members, but permitted management to use its judgment about filling temporary vacancies, provided that the work of the absentee was not added to the usual load of another employee without extra pay.[86]

Outside the class of confidential employees, seniority was declared to be a vested interest of workers, and strict seniority rules were laid down. The workweek was fixed at 44 hours,* but workers were to receive regular pay for one day of rest each week and also for certain specified holy days and obligatory rest days.[87] If they worked on the weekly day of rest, or on a holy day, or on an obliga-

---

* The award of December, 1937, had set the workweek at only 40 hours.

tory rest day, they were to receive triple pay. When a weekly rest day and an obligatory rest day coincided, they were to receive double pay if they did not work, and quadruple pay if they did work.

The contract gave the management greater freedom in transferring personnel. Wage benefits in cases of illness or accident, both occupational and otherwise, were fixed at a figure below that set by the award of December, 1937. A final major change was the provision that Pemex pay 200,000 pesos per year for wages and allowances for thirty-four officers of local sections of the syndicate, and for transportation expenses of the general executive committee.

Although the collective contract of May, 1942, seemed to have settled relations between the syndicate and the management, new difficulties soon arose. There were complaints against the administration policy of transferring employees from the Isthmus zone to fill vacancies in Poza Rica, instead of using local personnel.[88] In carrying out its newly authorized power to appoint confidential employees, the administration also antagonized labor by replacing certain syndicate members with nonmembers.[89] In November and December, there was another movement within the syndicate to strike over alleged violations of the work contract, and the leaders talked of refusing to arbitrate.[90] The conciliatory intervention of the Secretary of Labor alleviated the danger. In April, 1943, nine sections threatened a work stoppage over the discharge of an officer of local section 3 and over the application of seniority rules.[91] In August, workers in Ciudad Madero walked out on a 24-hour strike in retaliation for three hundred alleged violations of the collective agreement.[92] It was asserted that the instigators of the strike were non-Mexican agitators trying to cause international complications by sabotage.[93] This may have been true, but the workers were especially susceptible to the blandishments of agitators because of the rapidly increasing cost of living.

The cost-of-living index for Mexico City rose from 163 in 1941 to 247 in 1943.[94] This gave rise to considerable unrest among labor groups; and the petroleum workers, still hoping for restoration of the wage scales fixed by the award of December, 1937, began agitating for higher pay. In September, 1943, President Avila Camacho ordered Pemex to put the wage scales of that award into effect; at the same time all wages below 5.52 pesos per day were increased 10 per cent.[95] As a consequence, total wages and salaries rose from 90 million pesos in 1943 to 123 million in 1944, an increase that the industry could ill afford.

The wage increase did not long satisfy syndicate leaders. The general unrest was reflected in recurrent local disturbances and strikes over apparently minor complaints. On February 21, 1944, the general executive committee of the syndicate published in the leading newspapers of Mexico City an open letter accusing the management of seven hundred violations of the collective contract. Among the alleged infractions was the transfer of certain storage plants to private operation on a commission basis, in contravention of the contract's coverage of all stages of production in the petroleum industry.* The syndicate further complained that the labor contract, signed only after five years of strife, denied rights granted to the union by the private oil companies. It also disclaimed responsibility for failure in the industry or for labor unrest produced by management's policies. In the same month, the northern sections carried out a 10-hour sit-down strike for alleged discounts of wages of workers in section 21.[96] Shortly after, there was an 8-hour work stoppage in the Federal District to protest violations of the labor contract.[97]

On March 1, 1944, in another widely published open letter, the syndicate expressed discontent over the relative wage and salary scales after the general increases ordered by President Avila Camacho on October 1, 1943. It asserted that officers had received increases of $33\frac{1}{3}$ per cent, as against increases of only 8 to 15 per cent for various classes of syndicate personnel. The next day the administration published an open letter pointing out that current wages and salaries were in accord with the labor board award of December, 1937, and that officers had received larger raises in October, 1943, to offset their heavier cuts in July, 1938, and August, 1940.

The renegotiation of the two-year labor contract, due to expire May 18, 1944, gave rise to additional friction. Two months before the expiration date the syndicate asked President Avila Camacho to expedite the negotiations.[98] But the parleys lasted until September 8, when the parties signed a new agreement with only minor changes. On July 1, however, during the negotiations, all employees were given a raise of 2.50 pesos per day. The contract increased the rental allowance to 1.50 pesos per day for all employees.[99]

Relations between labor and management remained fairly calm for about a year. Despite rumors of impending strikes,[100] there was no actual work stoppage again until August 20, 1945, when section

---

* The practice of leasing out bulk storage plants seems to have been well established long before this time.

1 in Tampico went out on a 4-hour political strike. On September 12, the same group, joined by two more locals, struck over the same issue, this time for 24 hours.* In October, the locals of the Isthmus zone banded together in a 24-hour protest strike against treatment given workers by a superintendent at Coatzacoalcos.[101] These intermittent work stoppages caused the general director to complain, in his annual report of March 18, 1946, that various locals of the syndicate were engaging in work stoppages "on the most trivial pretexts including intra-Syndicate problems." These strikes, he said, were curtailing production, upsetting distribution processes, and even damaging oil fields. The syndicate delivered countercharges in an open letter published April 17, 1946. It accused the administration of (1) centralizing power in the organization so as to make it a bureaucratic rather than a business institution, (2) failing to coördinate departments despite the excessive centralization, (3) preventing qualified technicians from entering the industry and failing to train personnel adequately, (4) neglecting exploratory work and the tanker fleet, (5) selling oil abroad at disastrously low prices, (6) wasting money in unnecessary lawsuits with labor, (7) hiring foreign drillers who were less efficient than Mexican drillers, and (8) unpatriotically contracting with Standard Oil of New Jersey to sell products in Mexico. The workers showed their growing discontent by asking the President of Mexico to dismiss the general manager.[102]

Although sporadic work stoppages continued, the syndicate had no sharp disagreement with management, probably because it was absorbed in its own reorganization as recommended by President Cárdenas in February, 1940. The shift from company to industry-wide organization, however, was obstructed by the jealousies and vested interests of local section leaders. Intrasyndicate difficulties led to work stoppages in the Federal District in March, 1946.[103] But the reorganization was virtually completed by the middle of 1946, and the original thirty-two locals were reduced to twenty-two.[104]

In the summer and fall of 1946, labor-management relations again reached a crisis. In July, the syndicate requested that the labor contract, due to expire in September, be renewed with certain modifications, including reduction of the workweek from 44 to 40 hours, the right of workers to retire on pensions at the age of forty-five, and the construction of additional medical centers

---

* These strikes were in protest against the Mexican Revolutionary party, which had failed to cancel the election of a senator objectionable to the labor groups. See *Excélsior,* Aug. 24, Sept. 12, 1945.

in the northern and southern zones.[105] The syndicate leaders wanted the new contract to specify higher wages, since the cost-of-living index in Mexico City had risen from 310 in 1944 to 416 in 1946.[106] Intermittent work stoppages at the Atzcapotzalco refinery, coupled with transportation problems, caused petroleum shortages in Mexico City, and more charges and countercharges flew between management and labor.[107]

The administration, still facing serious financial problems, was not able to make any far-reaching concessions, and negotiations broke down. When local strikes occurred in the refineries early in September, the government sent troops to prevent sabotage.[108] The syndicate gave official strike notice to the Federal Board, but the trouble was temporarily avoided by an agreement which included the following principal terms:[109] The existing contract was to be extended until a new one could be negotiated. The deadline for signing a new contract was to be March 8, 1947. Wage scales were to be increased 1 peso per day in the interim. Grievance committees were to be established, and Pemex was to pay their expenses. The syndicate was to rescind its strike notice.

Despite these conciliatory gestures, relations deteriorated; on November 27, so strong a feeling developed at Poza Rica that shots were fired and arrests were made.[110] The principal issue hampering the negotiations was the level at which wages should be equalized. The administration preferred a level that would leave the total wage bill unchanged; labor sought to raise wages in each class closer to the top level of the class, so that no wages would be reduced in the readjustment. The oil workers announced a 24-hour strike for November 28. At the same time, it was disclosed that the general manager, Efraín Buenrostro, had submitted his resignation. This seemed to quiet the workers, who decided to defer their strike until President-elect Alemán took office and appointed a new general manager.

The appointee, who took office December 4, 1946, was Antonio J. Bermúdez, a businessman and former mayor of Ciudad Juárez. One of his qualifications was that he had recently been elected senator from the state of Chihuahua with strong labor support. His reputation for scrupulous honesty and moral fortitude held promise for the future of the industry. His handling of the problems that immediately rose to challenge him vindicated his reputation in the opinion of the general public.

Soon after taking office he was approached by the syndicate with a wage-equalization plan involving an increase of about 14 million pesos in the annual wage bill.[111] Bermúdez countered with an offer reducing the increase to 9 million pesos. This was unsatisfactory to labor, and on December 19 and 20 the syndicate sponsored an illegal 24-hour strike in the Poza Rica and Atzcapotzalco refineries. Bermúdez' response was swift and decisive. He dismissed fifty syndicate leaders responsible for the strike, including all members of the general executive committee. He petitioned the Federal Board of Conciliation and Arbitration to terminate the violated collective labor contracts and instituted proceedings for a conflict of economic order.

In his petition to the board, Bermúdez based existing difficulties in the industry upon the following conditions:[112]

1. The financial crisis faced by Pemex resulted from its heavy responsibilities under the existing labor contract. The work contract caused expenses to exceed revenues.

2. This disequilibrium prevented the organization from meeting its obligations and paying indemnification claims.

3. Financial imbalance prevented the industry from carrying out necessary exploration and refinery expansion.

4. An excess of personnel, due to vested interests in the syndicate, weighed heavily upon the industry and the country.

5. Extreme disorder in the system of job classification was an obstacle to efficient development of the industry.

6. The syndicate had wrested from the administration powers necessary for a program of conservation, maintenance, and development.

7. The effectiveness of management was reduced by the contractual requirement that certain classes of confidential employees needed for administration and supervision be chosen from syndicate personnel.

8. Higher wages were paid in the northern and southern zones because of inclement weather. It was impossible to change the assignments of personnel from either of these zones to the central zone because the contract did not allow any reduction in wages. Therefore, transfers would make wages in the central zone anomalous.

In his report to the labor board, Bermúdez estimated the deficit for operations in December, 1946, at more than 12 million pesos, and the expected deficit for 1947 at 56 million pesos.*

To bring order out of chaos, Bermúdez asked that job classifications be revised, wage scales modified, and excess workers discharged, that management be given a free hand in the exercise of

---

* These figures are unreliable, because they are cash budget deficits and do not take into account depreciation and deferred charges and credits. (See chap. xi.) In addition, the 56 million pesos included 22 million spent on fixed capital, of which an unspecified amount was for depreciation.

administrative duties and in the choice of confidential employees, and that the labor contract be strictly applied to activities directly connected with the petroleum industry, but that the administration be free to carry out other work, such as house construction, with nonsyndicate personnel.

On December 21, President Alemán announced his support of Bermúdez' unprecedented action. This was a hard blow to the syndicate and caused concern to the whole labor movement. The new President, then only three weeks in office, stated that it was his duty to maintain order in accordance with the law, to protect the institutions of the country, and to prevent individuals or groups from undermining the constitutional regime.[113] In justifying the drastic action, the President pointed out that soon after taking office he had ordered the Secretary of Labor to do all he could to settle the long-standing problem between labor and management, but that the syndicate had disregarded this conciliatory effort, had broken off negotiations, and had conducted an illegal strike. The violent measures of the syndicate leaders, he added, had seriously damaged the industry, and he would take the necessary measures to maintain the rights of citizens and ensure the well-being of the country.

The President's course attracted wide support from the public, government circles, and labor. The Regional Confederation of Mexican Labor (CROM), though announcing itself in accord with the government, asked Pemex to make a public statement on the basic issues.[114] The Industrial Syndicate of Mining and Metal Workers (*El Sindicato Industrial de Trabajadores Mineros, Metalúrgicos y Similares de la República Mexicana*) congratulated the President for stopping the illegal strike.[115] After some hesitation, the Confederation of Mexican Labor (CTM) joined in the general disapproval of the petroleum syndicate, although it did not officially support the President's action.[116] The general secretary of the Confederation of Labor, Fidel Velásquez, condemned the attitude of the petroleum workers and expressed grave concern over the mistakes of the leaders, which threatened to harm the whole labor movement; and Lombardo Toledano, though supporting Alemán and appealing for labor unity, condemned the errors of both labor and management in their eight-year-old fight.[117] He denounced the wildcat local strikes, called without approval of the general executive committee, and asserted that bad counselors had pushed Bermúdez into making an issue of this fight.

At a special meeting, the leaders of the Confederation of Mexican

Labor deemed the problem so serious as to require intervention. They accordingly resolved (1) to publish an open letter outlining the issues and the attitude of labor groups, (2) to call a special convention of the petroleum syndicate, (3) to attempt a reconciliation between the administration and the discharged leaders, and (4) to determine the position of the petroleum syndicate in the conflict of economic order.[118]

The surprising and unprecedented action of the management and the widespread hostility to the unruly leaders of the petroleum workers was a serious setback to the syndicate. Within a few days it was reported that the syndicate leaders were attempting a *rapprochement* with the administration of Pemex.[119] Bermúdez replied that he would deal with them but would not put them back on the payroll. A special convention of petroleum workers was called in January, 1947. Alemán, in a conciliatory mood, received a delegation from the convention and agreed to suspend the move for a conflict of economic order for sixty days and to reëmploy those of the fifty discharged leaders who had had no connection with the December strike. However, he reaffirmed his policy of eliminating illegal strikes.[120] On January 11, the convention accepted the resignation of the general executive committee. There followed a series of stormy sessions that brought no satisfactory settlement with the administration, which resumed proceedings in the conflict of economic order.

After the report of the expert commission appointed by the Federal Board, the administration and the syndicate came to an agreement outside the tribunal. The agreement provided for (1) a reduction in the number of confidential and temporary employees, (2) the payment by Pemex of a fixed sum to cover the expenses and allowances of syndicate officers, (3) the appointment of four mixed committees to handle grievances, (4) a 15 per cent increase in the wages of workers in inclement areas, (5) increased freedom for the administration in transferring personnel, (6) the right of the administration to have certain work done on a contractual basis without using syndicate personnel, and (7) mixed commissions to study thirty clauses of the work contract that the administration wanted to modify.[121] This agreement had the force of a new work contract and was to be effective for two years.

The official organ of labor, *El Popular*, approved the agreement and lauded Bermúdez for his sincerity and for his development of the industry without having created a paralyzing bureaucracy.[122] The syndicate claimed that savings up to 80 million pesos a year

should be realized under the agreement,[123] but it is difficult to see
how this could be true. Even if four thousand workers were discharged (as the general secretary of the petroleum workers estimated) and their mean daily wage was as much as 30 pesos, the
annual saving would have amounted to less than 45 million pesos.
Despite the anticipated economies, however, wages, salaries, and
other benefits climbed from 219 million pesos in 1946 to 232 million pesos in 1947, and to 249 million pesos in 1948.[124] The causes
of the increase are not clear, but much of it was apparently spent
for improvements in living quarters and in services to employees.

The events of December, 1946, had left the syndicate shaken but
not broken. Although the leaders became less contentious in their
dealings with the management, their energies did not go unex-
pended. They began to look farther afield. The first step was to
join the Latin American Confederation of Labor (CTAL) in April,
1948.[125] This organization was composed largely of labor groups
led by individuals of strong Marxist, if not Communist, leanings.[126]
Under the joint tutelage of the CTAL and the petroleum syndicate, an International Congress of Petroleum Workers was called
in September, 1948. The keynotes of this congress were (1) opposition to economic imperialism and (2) national sovereignty for
Latin American countries.[127] It was a reflection of the spirit that
had brought on the expropriation and consistently opposed the
return of foreign companies in any phase of the petroleum industry, including the desperately needed exploratory work. The congress extended its hostility to the Inter-American Confederation
of Labor (CIT), a non-Communist labor organization in which
the American Federation of Labor participated.[128] But the syndicate itself was not entirely happy with the Marxist elements. Before the end of the year, the general executive committee proposed
cleaning out the Communists within its own ranks. Local sections
of the syndicate made some effort to rejoin the Confederation of
Mexican Labor,[129] which had recently ousted Lombardo Toledano,
the leader of the CTAL. At the beginning of 1949, this movement
was threatening to rend the syndicate, but it lost importance during the early negotiations to renew the labor contract, due to expire
May 30, 1949.

Although the meetings between labor and management received
little publicity, talks toward a new contract appeared to be breaking down early in May,[130] and there were rumors that the syndicate
would strike if the management did not yield on certain unspecified issues. Finally nine sections agreed to strike, if necessary, to

get their demands.[131] General Director Bermúdez announced on May 29 that Pemex was financially unable to meet labor's wishes, since its budget deficit was 193 million pesos.[132] On May 30, the general executive committee gave strike notice before the Federal Board, presenting minimum demands that would have increased costs by 70 million pesos. Two days later, however, the syndicate reduced its demands so as to cut the costs to about half the earlier figure.[133] With the conciliatory help of the Secretary of Labor, the parties then came to an agreement specifying an increase of about 33 million pesos in wages and allowances. The workweek was reduced from 44 to 40 hours.

The general executive committee had reckoned without the section leaders in making this settlement; sections around Tampico repudiated the agreement as soon as it was publicized.[134] An outbreak of violence brought death to one man, and a member of the general executive committee was attacked. Troops jailed the officers of section 1. Although the leaders of the Confederation of Mexican Labor and of the Alliance of Workers and Peasants expressed satisfaction with the agreement, the syndicate's vigilance committee removed four top members of the general executive committee for being too easy in their dealings with Pemex. The following December the General Convention of Petroleum Workers supported the vigilance committee's ouster of the four leaders.[135] However, the contract of June, 1949, still stood.

The significance of the maneuvering by the four members of the general executive committee is not known. They appear to have been among those of strong Marxist leanings who favored Lombardo Toledano and his CTAL. Why they compromised with the management in the face of active opposition from the sections is uncertain, but they may have remembered the lessons of December, 1946, when the general executive committee was ousted by Bermúdez and Alemán. On the other hand, the syndicate sections may have seized upon the compromise as an excuse to remove leaders whom they distrusted for traveling too close to Lombardo Toledano, the CTAL, and other organizations sympathetic to him.

What benefits did the petroleum workers gain through expropriation? Records of Pemex show that in 1946 the total bill for wages, salaries, and allowances amounted to 219 million pesos. Of this, wages and salaries constituted 180 million pesos (exclusive of certain equalization wages paid retroactively), or about three times the 1938 figure. Of the 180 million pesos, the savings fund received 14.3 million, more than three times the 1938 figure; housing allowances cost 14.2 million, six times the 1938 figure; indemnities took 2.8 million; medical services cost 5.3 million, four times the 1938 figure; syndicate expenses absorbed more than 0.5 million; and miscellaneous expenses cost 1.5 million. In 1947, fifty-nine persons received scholarship payments amounting to 113,000 pesos for study in petroleum and chemical engineering. In 1948, Pemex supported forty-two schools with 17,202 pupils at a cost of 2.8 million pesos. In 1946, the company employed two hundred general practitioners, surgeons, and specialists to provide medical services to employees and their families, and in 1948 it supported eight hospitals. In 1945 Pemex paid wages and salaries for 9.1 million days, of which 6.2 million were days of actual work, and 2.9 million were for vacations, sick leave, accidents, etc.[136]

These were the absolute gains. The relative gains were not so impressive. Although the total cost of wages and employee benefits rose from 56 million pesos in 1937 to 219 million in 1946, the increase did not benefit the individual workman as much as appeared on the surface. The benefits were dissipated among a larger number of workers, and were diminished by the rapidly rising price level. Although the mean value of wages and other benefits per employee of Pemex increased from 3,500 pesos in 1937 to 8,430 pesos in 1946 (an increase of 140 per cent), the index of the cost of living of workers in Mexico City increased from 135 in 1937 to 416 in 1946 (an increase of more than 200 per cent). Furthermore, many of the seeming gains after expropriation were in reality merely the gradual reachievement of wages and benefits won by the syndicate in the labor board award of 1937, which the companies had belatedly accepted on the eve of expropriation.[137] A large part of those wages and benefits had been lost in the difficult period after expropriation, when management was authorized to suspend certain provisions of the award.

Despite these setbacks, petroleum workers held an enviable position among Mexican laborers after expropriation as well as before. In October, 1942, the mean hourly wage of skilled workers in petroleum exploration, production, and refining was 1.23 pesos, compared to 0.77 pesos on the railroads, 0.85 pesos in mining and metallurgy, and 0.70 pesos in textiles.[138] The mean hourly wage of common laborers was 0.82 pesos in petroleum, 0.42 pesos on the railroads, 0.56 pesos in mining and metallurgy, and 0.48 pesos in textiles.[139]

This accounts in large measure for the petroleum syndicate's fight to maintain control of hiring and to preserve the closed shop and closed union. In the early years after expropriation, however, the syndicate was not closed to friends and relatives of influential members.[140] One of the administration's chief headaches was the rapidly increasing payroll. The number of employees jumped from about 16,000 in 1937 to 26,000 in 1946. This rise was excessive even though part of it was attributable to greater production and more exploration.

TABLE 25

WORKER PRODUCTIVITY IN THE PRODUCTION AND
REFINING BRANCHES OF PEMEX, 1938–1946

(In barrels)

Year	Production of crude oil per worker	Refinery output per worker
1938	5,320	4,140
1939	4,730	3,160
1940	4,690	3,200
1941	5,910	3,670
1942	4,680	3,530
1943	4,450	3,670
1944	4,360	3,630
1945	4,640	3,380
1946	4,950	3,920

SOURCE: Basic data from Pemex.

After the relatively harmonious labor-management relations in 1938, worker productivity in the production and refining branches of the industry suffered serious setbacks. Annual crude-oil production per worker declined from 5,320 barrels in 1938 to 4,730 in 1939, or about 11 per cent. The figure rose to 5,910 in 1941, after the reorganization. Thereafter, however, lagging production and the gradually increasing number of employees reduced worker productivity to a low of 4,360 barrels in 1944, from which it rose to 4,950 barrels in 1946. These developments were roughly paralleled in the refining branch (see table 25).

Another personnel problem that confronted Pemex, though it was not directly related to labor relations, concerned retailing. Pemex leased retail stations to individual enterprisers. During the era of the private companies, the retailers had organized as a labor syndicate (*Sindicato de Trabajadores del Comercio del Petróleo y sus Derivados de la República Mexicana*) and had been legally recognized as such, with all the accompanying rights and privileges.

This organization remained outside the Syndicate of Petroleum Workers, though the hired labor of the retailers was organized as a part of the syndicate.

After expropriation Pemex consistently refused to recognize the retailers' syndicate as a labor organization or to deal with it collectively. In January, 1939, the issue was brought to a head by Pemex' announcement that rental rates on the retail stations and equipment would be raised.[141] The Syndicate of Retailers gave notice of intention to strike on February 4 in order to obtain the following demands:[142] (1) a collective work contract, (2) lower rental rates, (3) a paid day of rest each week, (4) provision of housing allowances, medical services, and work uniforms, (5) shorter hours, and (6) restriction of gasoline sales to members of the retailers' organization.

At this juncture, the organized employees of the retailers threatened to strike against Pemex if the latter recognized the Syndicate of Retailers, and the Syndicate of Petroleum Workers announced its intention of blocking recognition by placing the issue before the Federal Board of Conciliation and Arbitration.[143] However, Pemex refused to recognize the organized retailers as a labor group, and declared that any strike would result in cancelation of contracts.[144] The matter was finally settled without a strike, after Pemex had made certain voluntary concessions to placate the retailers. In the fall of 1945, again, there were unsuccessful efforts to force Pemex to recognize the retailers as a labor group.[145]

In conclusion, it may be said that labor-management relations in the petroleum industry were difficult both before and after expropriation, but that in the later period they more clearly exposed the true nature of labor's objectives. Before 1938, the common antagonism to large, foreign economic interests concealed the real motives of syndicate leaders. The postexpropriation controversies, however, revealed the traditional syndicalist doctrine that motivated many of the leaders. Their conflicts with management in the period up to December, 1946, were more deeply rooted than the issues of private versus public ownership or of foreign versus Mexican ownership. The syndicate leaders wanted complete control of the petroleum industry. Other advocates of expropriation, such as Jesús Silva Herzog, had hoped that the nation would reap the full benefit of (1) ousting the foreign interests, which they felt took exorbitant profits from the country, and (2) establishing government ownership so that the profits could be used to advance the welfare of the whole Mexican people. Silva Herzog, as manager of the Distribuidora, ran headlong into the conflicting doctrine of the syndicate leaders. When it became evident that the government was determined to control the industry, the syndicate-management struggle broke out afresh, in a pattern very like that of the preëxpropriation period. It was an understatement when President Cárdenas, mildly rebuking the syndicate, said that the petroleum workers had sometimes confronted their own government with the same attitude they had shown toward the foreign companies. Cárdenas, who had socialist but not syndicalist leanings, blocked the syndicate's aim to gain complete control of the industry.

To a large extent, the industry's dire financial straits after expropriation were attributable to the policies of the syndicate. Early encroachments of the leaders impaired the managerial function; vested interests blocked reorganization; and excessive labor costs necessitated government subsidies and prevented the accumulation of reserves for exploration. The methods of syndicate leaders were so ill-considered that on at least two occasions they elicited the disapproval of leading labor groups, who complained that the repercussions were harmful to all organized labor. In the years after expropriation, the syndicate's campaign was evidently intended to wreck the industry financially. However, until December, 1946, the management and the presidents of the republic could not be drawn into an all-out fight to keep wages down to a level consistent with the marginal productivity of labor. They acted to save the industry only under great duress. Finally President Alemán, recognizing the general hostility of organized labor to syndicalist doctrine, decisively ended the threat of syndicalism within the industry.

Obviously, expropriation did not solve the labor problem. In fact, from the standpoint of the government, labor difficulties multiplied and political stresses intensified in the absence of a strong foreign element in the industry against which all parties could spontaneously unite. The government was torn between its sympathy toward labor and its obligation to operate the industry successfully. After expropriation it had to assume new functions, such as handling finances and achieving a nice balance between contending interests in the industry. Before 1938, the government could limit its concern mainly to the well-being of the petroleum worker, for the companies had to shoulder the problem of making ends meet.

One of the problems of labor-management relations was the intrusion of politics into the machinery for handling disputes. Cárdenas, and to a lesser extent Avila Camacho, meddled in the legal processes of arbitration. This intervention diminished the respect of both parties for the Federal Board of Conciliation and Arbitration, and encouraged the belief that any adverse decision of the board could be hurdled by direct appeal to the executive power. The fact that the Federal Board was itself a cog in the legal machinery was seemingly ignored by labor, management, and even the presidents of Mexico. President Alemán's handling of the illegal strike of December, 1946, was a step toward rectifying prevailing attitudes.

After the war the Mexican labor movement lost strength,[146] and there can be little doubt that the activities of obstreperous leaders, including those of the petroleum syndicate, contributed to the decline in prestige. However, the syndicate seemed to learn from experience. After 1946, although complete harmony did not reign on the labor-management front, relations were more peaceful. There were few illegal strikes, and in 1948 the syndicate went so far as to sign a pact of solidarity with the railroad and mine workers.[147] The full significance of this alliance was not clear, but the objectives appeared to be further nationalization of Mexican industries, opposition to the reëstablishment of foreign economic interests, and, perhaps, the regaining of the syndicate's lost prestige through more conservative policies.

Even though all elements in the syndicate did not become reconciled to the existing organization of the industry, there were few voices heard after 1946 in favor of complete labor control. The industry continued under the direction of a more powerful management, subject to government supervision, and the prospects of successful development therefore appeared brighter.

Chapter XI

FINANCIAL ASPECTS

In 1938, most Mexicans who thought about the finances of the expropriated industry expected it not only to provide good wages and other benefits to labor, but also to be self-supporting and contribute high tax yields to the government. These people generally felt that Mexico had great wealth in oil and that the main reason why the country did not derive more benefit from it was because the private oil companies carried tremendous profits out of the country. It is the purpose of this chapter to investigate the extent to which Pemex achieved self-support and contributed to the government in taxes and other payments.

For the outsider, an accurate assessment of the finances of Pemex is difficult. Until 1950 the organization never published a systematic statement in which the public could have confidence. To evaluate the financial status of Pemex, one must rely on sporadic data given in the general director's annual reports, a few published balance sheets and statements of earnings and expenditures, and the very general reports of the expert commissions appointed to study the industry in the two postexpropriation conflicts of economic order.

With these documentary aids, it is possible to analyze certain aspects of the industry's finances and to draw some inferences concerning the status of Pemex. Yet the problem remains complicated. First, accounting techniques were rather primitive, and cost accounting was not used at least until 1947. Finances were managed on a hand-to-mouth basis. The principal concern was to obtain enough cash income to meet necessary cash outlays, and there was apparently little regard to apportioning deferred charges to the appropriate accounting periods, or to making allowances for depreciation of equipment or depletion of reserves. Second, public statements on investment did not clearly distinguish between gross and net investment or among expenditures for repairs, replacement, or expansion of fixed capital. Third, in its accounting the management ignored the significance of the initial investment

157

represented by the costs of indemnification for expropriation. Fourth, Pemex did not pay its taxes regularly, and was at times far in arrears. Even the gasoline consumption tax, for which Pemex was merely the collection agency, was in default. In the early years, the finances of Pemex were hopelessly entangled with those of the government.

Before analyzing Pemex' finances, it will be helpful to review briefly the highlights of its financial history. The story properly begins with the value of the investments expropriated by the Mexican government, but this is not known with any degree of precision. The value of the expropriated properties was the focal point of such heated controversy that it is not possible to say what figure was correct.* However, the significant item for this investigation is the amount of the indemnity payment finally agreed upon.

The first step in settling the oil companies' claims was completed in May, 1940, when the Sinclair group agreed to accept payments totaling $8.5 million over a period of about three and one-half years.[1] The second step came in April, 1942, with the agreement between the United States State Department and the Mexican government covering the claims of the remaining expropriated American companies. The amount agreed upon was $23,995,991,† to be paid over a period of five years, plus interest amounting to over $5 million.[2] The final step, agreement with the Dutch-Shell interests, did not come until August, 1947, when the Mexican government agreed to pay $81,250,000 over a period of fifteen years, plus interest at 3 per cent retroactive to March 18, 1938.[3]

* The total amount of capital invested in the petroleum industry to December 31, 1936, was estimated by the petroleum division of the Department of National Economy (*La industria petrolera mexicana*, p. 39) at 983 million pesos, distributed as follows:

American companies	511 million pesos	52.0%
English-Dutch companies	408 million pesos	41.5%
Mexican companies	49 million pesos	5.0%
Others	15 million pesos	1.5%
	983 million pesos	100.0%

At the time of expropriation, Mexican estimates placed the value of the expropriated properties, after allowance for depreciation, between 222 million pesos (Miguel Manterola, *La industria del petróleo en México* [México, D.F., 1938], pp. 45–46) and 234 million pesos (Jesús Silva Herzog, *Petróleo mexicano* [México, D.F., 1947], pp. 152–156). The values claimed by the companies were much higher. The American companies alone claimed $120 million, or 432 million pesos at 27.75 cents per peso. (See Secretaría de Economía Nacional, *Memoria, 1941–1942*, p. 147.) The Mexicans asserted that $86 million of this was for oil in the subsoil and was, therefore, constitutionally invalid.

[1] For numbered notes to chap. xi, see p. 252.

† See the asterisk (*) footnote on next page.

The annual installments were to be $8,689,258 each. The sum of expropriation payments on principal thus amounted to approximately $113 million.†

This $113 million represented the value placed upon the nation's stake in the oil industry at the time of expropriation. The figure does not necessarily represent the historical, reproduction, or prudent investment value of the assets acquired by the Mexican government, because the final agreement appears to have been subject to political influences. No balance sheets for the first seven years after expropriation are available, but later statements valued the expropriated assets at considerably less than the expropriation payments.‡ Some deviation, of course, was to be expected, since there was no way of anticipating the amounts that would be agreed upon.

However, the expropriation payments did enter the balance sheet in another form. On December 31, 1947, after agreement with the Dutch-Shell interests, a credit to income of 796.5 million pesos was shown payable to the government for reimbursement for the expropriated properties. This figure was very close to the peso outlay that would have been necessary at 1950 exchange rates to make the expropriation payments, which were payable in dol-

---

* The amounts allowed for the American companies and their subsidiaries were as follows:

Standard Oil (New Jersey) group	$18,391,641
Standard Oil of California group	3,589,158
Consolidated Oil Company group	630,151
Sabalo group	897,671
Seaboard group	487,370
	$23,995,991

Although payments to the United States government on this amount began in July, 1942 (*El nacional*, July 2, 1942), at least one company did not announce its acceptance of the agreement until October, 1943 (*Excélsior*, Oct. 3, 1943).

† This estimate is reached by adding the principals of the sums agreed upon:

Sinclair group	$ 7,500,000
Other American companies	23,995,991
Dutch-Shell group	81,250,000
	$112,745,991

Although the terms of the Sinclair agreement are not known, it seems reasonable to assume that about $1 million of the $8.5 million was interest over the five-year period, and that $7.5 million was principal.

‡ There is no direct method of determining the value at which the expropriated properties were initially carried, but that the value was well below the amount of payments agreed upon is quite certain. The value of the expropriation payments amounted to more than 400 million pesos, even at the preëxpropriation value of the peso (27.75 cents); and in 1949, with the majority of the expropriation payments still to be made, the peso stood at less than 14 cents. Over against this 400 million pesos, the value of fixed assets and inventories as of March, 1938, is estimated to have been

lars. Of the 796.5 million pesos, 157.7 million were charged off as already paid, and 638.8 million were to be charged to future operations.

In addition to the payments for the initially expropriated properties, 20 to 30 million pesos were invested in the General Administration of National Petroleum* and an unknown amount was paid for small companies bought or expropriated after 1938.

During its first two years of operation, Pemex published very little detailed information concerning its financial operations. The general statements of the managers indicated extreme difficulty, and this led to thorough administrative reorganization. The first specific official statements came from the expert commission on October 31, 1940. Its report showed profits of 15 million pesos in 1938, and losses of 22 million pesos in 1939.[4] These figures, however, are only a general indication of the financial condition. It is likely that profits were less and losses greater than indicated, since Pemex operated pretty much on a cash income and outgo basis, and construction was at a low level at the time. The figures create the same general impression as the general manager's annual report of March, 1941, which revealed an unsatisfactory financial status in 1938, attributable to poor equipment, the boycott, and the administrative problems of the transition period. The situation, the general manager continued, had been improving in 1939, until the war and the consequent loss of European markets unbalanced income and expenses. Then Pemex fell behind on its general taxes and even faced the prospect of being unable to liquidate the gasoline consumption taxes it had collected. Pemex

---

less than 350 million pesos. This estimate is based upon the following considerations. The balance sheet of December 31, 1947, shows that the fixed assets delivered to Pemex by the Mexican government after expropriation were valued at 152 million pesos in March, 1938. (See App. C-3.) It is estimated that inventories at the time of expropriation did not exceed and were probably less than those carried at the end of 1947, which stood at 201 million pesos. This estimate is based upon the assumption that inventories of oil and other products in March, 1938, were not more than double their value at the end of 1934, 1935, and 1936, when they were consistently valued at less than 40 million pesos. (See *Mexico's Oil* [México, D.F., 1940], pp. 470–472.) At the end of 1947 they stood at 96 million pesos. The value of inventories of materials at the end of 1934, 1935, and 1936 did not exceed 33 million pesos (which incidentally seems very high for an organization allegedly suffering from a materials shortage). The total value of inventories on December 31, 1947, was 201 million pesos which, added to the value of fixed assets as of March, 1938, amounts to 353 million pesos.

* This estimate is based on data in Silva Herzog, *Petróleo mexicano*, p. 289. He indicates that the profits of 3.8 million pesos, made by the General Administration of National Petroleum in 1938, were 18.44 per cent of its capital investment, which would thus amount to 20.6 million pesos. The balance sheet of December 31, 1947, shows that the value of this organization's assets was 29 million pesos.

was also in debt for freight, raw materials, and equipment. Early in 1940, it became obvious that reorganization of the industry was necessary to prevent a complete breakdown. In addition to such outside factors as the boycott and loss of markets, labor costs had soared from 56 million pesos in 1937 to 98 million in 1939.[5] In July, 1940, the management was forced to institute proceedings for a conflict of economic order before the Federal Board of Conciliation and Arbitration. The board's temporary award gave considerable relief, for it reduced by 10 per cent all wages and salaries over 700 pesos per month, suspended payments into the savings fund, restricted rental allowances, suspended vacations, and reduced overtime pay. Consequently, Pemex was able to meet some of its more pressing obligations. In September, the 12 per cent tax on the value of petroleum exports was eliminated, and President Cárdenas asked Congress for a reduction in other petroleum taxes.[6]

The retroactive restoration of wages and allowances to labor in the Federal Board's award of November 28, 1940, put Pemex back into the financial disequilibrium of six months earlier. The federal government was forced to intervene to save the corporation. The Secretary of the Treasury suspended the payment of taxes, which were charged to the Pemex account, and gave "special economic aid" to the organization to help it meet pressing demands for cash outlays. The government granted Pemex 60 million pesos, allegedly to repay it for certain additions to fixed capital, and these funds were used to liquidate tax debts.

A law passed on December 31, 1940, provided that some of the Pemex profits go to the national treasury.[7] Apparently to offset in part labor's demands for higher wages, the law attempted to guarantee the government a minimum return of 3 per cent on the capital invested by the nation (to be charged as an expense of operation), and a royalty to be fixed by the Secretary of National Economy at between 10 and 35 per cent of the value of the oil produced. Profits beyond these returns to the government were to be distributed as follows: 20 per cent to Pemex reserves, 60 per cent to the federal government, and 20 per cent to labor. At the end of 1944, a new law ordered Pemex to reimburse the government for indemnification payments on account of expropriation, which the government had carried up to that time.[8] These payments were to be given precedence over interest and royalties. To meet them, 10 per cent of the gross revenues less taxes was to be set aside.

During the first years of Pemex, there was a crying need for capital to rebuild and modify refineries, pipelines, and storage facilities to meet the new market conditions. The report of the general manager in March, 1943, claimed that Pemex' investments up to that time (exclusive of indemnities) amounted to 145 million pesos, of which the federal government had provided 60 million and the industry 85 million from earnings. These figures apparently covered gross investment in fixed assets, including expenditures for repairs and replacements, since there appear to have

TABLE 26

ANNUAL INVESTMENT[a] OF PEMEX, 1938–1946

(In millions of pesos)

Year	Investment
1938	7.5
1939	18.1
1940	48.2
1941	20.0
1942	23.3
1943	16.8
1944	38.3
1945	55.9
1946	95.9

[a] Whether investment is net or gross is not specified, but the figures probably include replacement of some items of depreciated equipment.
SOURCE: *Revista de economía continental*, November 20, 1947, p. 603.

been no corresponding additions of new equipment in this period. It is impossible, from available data, to determine precisely the net addition to capital. In 1947 a statement by the general director (formerly called the general manager) indicated that between March, 1938, and the end of 1942 Pemex invested about 117 million pesos in the industry (see table 26),[9] but it is likely that much of this was spent to replace depreciated equipment. Another aspect of the capital accumulation of Pemex will be analyzed when the balance sheet is considered.

In the years 1942 to 1945, little was heard about the finances of Pemex. Cash balances were probably good, because income was rising rapidly and there was little drilling or construction during the war when materials and equipment were hard to get. During the three years 1942 to 1944, investment expenditures amounted to 78 million pesos.[10] When funds were needed to purchase equipment, which again became available in 1945 and 1946, financial hardship once more began to pinch the industry. Meanwhile, labor costs had again rapidly increased, rising from 109 million pesos in 1943 to 219 million pesos in 1946, and syndicate leaders were pressing for higher wages at a time when the industry needed cash for its expansion program.

During 1945 and 1946, Pemex invested 152 million pesos in the industry; late in 1946 plans for extensive exploration and refinery construction made the financial problem acute and culminated in a conflict of economic order in December. The general director, in his report to the Federal Board of Conciliation and Arbitration, outlined a plan for pipeline and refinery expansion costing in the neighborhood of 190 million pesos. This program, he said, could not be carried out because of financial difficulties; and, he added, it had been necessary to get a bank loan to meet tax obligations, to distribute savings funds to workers, and to pay for necessary raw materials and equipment.[11] He announced a deficit of over 12 million pesos from operations in December, 1946, and a prospective deficit of 56 million pesos in 1947, even without any expansion.

The settlement of the conflict of economic order on June 1, 1947, gave Pemex a little relief in wage payments and greater freedom in signing contracts for exploratory drilling. The reduction in labor costs was probably not large, but the amount is uncertain because the mixed commissions responsible for the application of wage agreements have notably failed to harmonize labor-management conflicts. However, the greater freedom in signing contracts for exploratory drilling, necessitating smaller cash outlays, relieved some of the financial pressure.

This general view of the finances of Pemex will be illumined by a more detailed analysis of specific aspects. Let us first consider income. Gross revenues after expropriation increased from 242 million pesos in 1939, the first full year of operation, to 568 million pesos in 1946, or by 135 per cent (see table 27). The increase was not spectacular, because 1939 had been an unusually bad year for Pemex, and because costs were rising rapidly and the value of the peso was falling. Between 1939 and 1946, Pemex' labor costs increased 124 per cent, whereas the price indexes for industrial raw materials and for construction supplies increased 135 per cent and 218 per cent, respectively.[12] However, the total income of Pemex had probably been limited by the government policy of keeping fuel prices low.

Analysis of available data on the expenses of the organization reveals that the two principal items were labor costs and payments to the government. In the nine years 1938–1946, both together took 65 per cent of gross revenues, labor costs accounting for 37 per cent and payments to the government for 28 per cent. In this period labor costs amounted to 1,128 million pesos, of which 83.0 per cent was for wages and salaries, 6.8 per cent was paid into savings funds, 5.8 per cent was for housing allowances, 2.8 per cent for medical services, and 1.6 per cent for other benefits.[13] A breakdown of labor costs by branches of the industry shows that 36.7 per cent was paid out in production, 41.4 per cent in refining, 7.3 per cent

TABLE 27

INCOME OF PEMEX, 1938–1948

(In millions of pesos)

Year	Income
1938	154.9
1939	242.3
1940	278.7
1941	311.5
1942	307.3
1943	344.5
1944	392.9
1945	460.5
1946	568.0
1947	759.3[a]
1948	960.9[a]

[a] Includes only income from sales.

SOURCES: Pemex, *Informe anual*, March 18, 1948; March 18, 1949; Antonio J. Bermúdez, "Mexico's Program of Oil Expansion," *World Petroleum*, January, 1948, pp. 48–49.

in sales, 10.1 per cent in administration, and 3.6 per cent in shipping (0.9 per cent was paid to employees of the General Administration of National Petroleum before 1940).

Payments to the government, amounting to 863 million pesos in the period 1938 to 1946, included general taxes, the gasoline consumption tax, interest, and royalties; and it is impossible to disentangle these completely for the entire history of Pemex. However, the breakdown can be at least partly reconstructed. The most complete information comes from the few available office records of Pemex, covering the seven years 1941 to 1947 (see table 28). In this period, total payments to the government amounted to 875 million pesos, of which 594 million, or 68 per cent, came from the gasoline consumption tax (for which Pemex was only the collection agency), 171 million, or 19.5 per cent, from other taxes (including taxes on production, exports, and imports, and certain minor taxes), and 110 million, or 12.5 per cent, from royalties, interest on the government investment, and possibly, for 1945 to 1947, from the indemnification payment of 10 per cent of gross income less taxes. The available data do not show whether or not these figures included the assessment for indemnification, though it is hardly

TABLE 28

COMPOSITION OF PAYMENTS BY PEMEX TO THE FEDERAL GOVERNMENT, 1938–1948
(In millions of pesos)

Year	Gasoline consumption tax[a]	General taxes[b]	Royalties and 3% return on government investment[c]	Total payment to government[d]
1938........................	38.2	e	e	41.1
1939........................	42.8	e	e	64.3
1940........................	53.8	e	e	96.6
1941........................	62.8	13.4	24.2	100.4
1942........................	69.0	7.5	9.6	86.1
1943........................	82.9	10.0	29.8	122.7
1944........................	81.1	11.2	1.3	93.6
1945........................	90.6	18.6	15.0	124.2
1946........................	98.5	38.2	−2.5 [f]	134.2
1947........................	108.7	72.5	32.2	213.4
1948........................	e	e	e	311.7

SOURCES AND NOTES:
[a] Gasoline consumption tax for 1941 to 1947 from Pemex records, and for 1938 to 1940 computed by multiplying gasoline sales of Pemex (see appendix table 10) by tax of 8 centavos in 1938 and 1939 and 9 centavos in 1940. (See *Compendio estadístico, 1948*, p. 128.)
[b] General tax payments for 1941 to 1947 from Pemex records.
[c] Amounts toward royalties and 3 per cent return on government investment computed by subtracting the gasoline consumption tax plus general taxes from total payments to the government. It is likely that from 1945 on part of this figure should be imputed to reimbursement to the federal government on account of the expropriation payments.
[d] Total payments to government according to annual reports of the general director and to the statement by Antonio J. Bermúdez, "Mexico's Program of Oil Expansion," *World Petroleum*, January, 1948, pp. 48–49.
[e] Not available.
[f] Claimed payments on account of gasoline consumption tax and general taxes total more than total payment to government. See note c.

likely that the general manager would have failed to list all payments to the federal government in his claims. However, there is an inexplicable discrepancy if this is true, for the balance sheet of December 31, 1947, shows payments of 158 million pesos to the government on the expropriation account.

More detailed examination of these payments shows that the gasoline consumption tax, which stood at 8 centavos per liter in 1938, was increased to 9 centavos in 1940 and to 10 centavos in 1946. This, coupled with the rising volume of gasoline sales, increased the tax yield very rapidly after expropriation. The general manager boasted that the government collected more from the petroleum industry in 1941 than ever before.[14] His assertion, however, ignored the fact that in 1941 more than 82 per cent of the government collections came from the gasoline consumption tax, and that the direct contribution of Pemex to government support was less than 14 million pesos (see appendix table 23), compared to an annual average of almost 23 million pesos paid by the private companies in the three years 1934 to 1936.[15] With the possible (but not likely) exception of 1940, there was no year from expropriation to 1946 when the general tax payments of Pemex exceeded those of the companies (see table 28). From 1941 to 1947, import duties accounted for 41 per cent of the general tax payments, export duties for 26 per cent, production taxes for 32 per cent, and miscellaneous taxes for 1 per cent.

As noted above, the law of December 31, 1940, provided that Pemex pay the government 3 per cent interest on its investment, plus a royalty on production to be fixed by the Secretary of National Economy between 10 and 35 per cent. A rough but conservative calculation shows that, before 1948 at least, Pemex did not fulfill its obligations under this law. Based on the published figure of approximately 325 million pesos for the capital and surplus of Pemex in 1946 and 1947, the imputed interest of 3 per cent on the government investment for the seven years from 1941 to 1947 would have amounted to at least 68 million pesos. (This computation ignores the government investment of 425 million pesos in indemnification payments and its additional investment of 324 million pesos in the industry during 1938–1946.) Royalties during the same period, at the minimum rate of 10 per cent on the production of 300 million barrels of crude oil valued at 3.50 pesos per barrel,* would have amounted to 105 million pesos. Total interest plus royalties for the period 1941 to 1947, under the law of December 31, 1940, would thus have amounted to at least 173 million pesos, whereas actual payments were less than 110 million pesos. Moreover, payments toward indemnification for the three years 1945–1947 would have amounted to 136 million pesos (see table 29). Reimbursements to the federal government for expropriation indemnities were probably included in the total payments to the government as shown in table 28. If this is true, the amount in default for the period 1941 to 1947 was at least 199

---

* A value of 3.50 pesos per barrel is considered a minimum figure and a very conservative estimate. The Secretary of the Treasury, for tax purposes, valued crude oil at 25.02 to 38.85 pesos per cubic meter, depending upon its specific gravity. This is equivalent to between 3.98 and 6.18 pesos per barrel. See *Boletín de minas y petróleo*, Sept., 1942, pp. 98–99.

million pesos. But if total payments to the government did not include indemnification reimbursements, and if 157.7 million pesos were paid as indicated on the balance sheet of December 31, 1947, Pemex was still in arrears by more than 40 million pesos.

The financial shortcomings of Pemex were also apparent from its failure to maintain an adequate exploratory program or to build up financial reserves for that purpose. During the eight years 1939 to 1946, Pemex produced about 320 million barrels of crude

TABLE 29

ESTIMATED REIMBURSEMENT PAYMENTS DUE THE FEDERAL GOVERNMENT FROM PEMEX ON ACCOUNT OF INDEMNIFICATION, 1945–1947

(In millions of pesos)

Year	Gross income[a]	Taxes[b]	Income after taxes	Due government[d]
1945	460.5	109.2	351.3	35.1
1946	568.0	136.7	431.3	43.1
1947	759.3 [c]	181.2	578.1	57.8

SOURCES AND NOTES:
[a] See table 27.
[b] See table 28.
[c] Includes only income from sales.
[d] Ten per cent of income after taxes.

oil. At the minimum estimate of 30 centavos per barrel for the rate of field depletion,* at least 96 million pesos should have been allowed for exploration merely to maintain crude-oil production without increasing the rate; the actual expenditure was less than 68 million pesos.[16] Furthermore, reserve funds apparently had not been built up because one of the reasons for the conflict of economic order beginning in December, 1946, was that the industry had insufficient funds for expansion. In 1947, Pemex spent 36 million pesos on exploration, more than the estimated minimum annual requirement for maintaining production. However, this figure was well below the 60 million pesos needed to drill the seventy-five exploratory wells that were deemed necessary each year to keep production ahead of demand.[17]

Pemex published balance sheets for December 31, 1945; August 31, 1946; and December 31, 1947 (see App. C).[18] These state-

* The oil companies were said to have allowed 30 to 40 centavos per barrel for field depletion (see Manuel A. Hernández, "El fracaso en México de la expropiación petrolera es una valiosa enseñanza," El economista, Mar.–Apr., 1946, pp. 123–126), and the subdirector of the department of exploration of Pemex estimated costs of exploration at 36 centavos per barrel in 1947 (see Jorge D. Cumming, "El problema de las reservas petroleras de México," Servicio de información, Jan., 1948, p. 84). Thus a depletion allowance of 30 centavos is very low.

ments, though not completely reliable, will, if analyzed and compared, yield reasonable inferences about the financial condition
of Pemex.

Over the two-year period there was a considerable rise in both
current assets and current liabilities, but liabilities increased more
than assets. The ratio of current assets to current liabilities fell
from 4.4 on December 31, 1945, to 2.2 on December 31, 1947. The
latter figure, however, marked an advance over the unfavorable
ratio of 1.7 as of August 31, 1946. Working capital amounted to
about 160 million pesos at the end of both 1945 and 1947, although
dropping to less than 90 million pesos in the interim report. In-
specting the details more closely, one is struck by the relatively
low cash balances held. Also impressive is the relatively large stock
of stored materials and accessories (*materiales y accesorios alma-
cenados*), ranging in value from 88 million to 105 million pesos, or
between 35 and 42 per cent of the current assets. For an organization suffering from chronic shortages of materials and equipment,
the figures seem very high. It is likely that the values were inflated.

The ratio of fixed assets to fixed liabilities was favorable, amounting to 4.1 on December 31, 1945. Although it declined slightly to
3.7 on the 1947 report, fixed assets increased by nearly 115 million
pesos, whereas long-term debt increased by only 38 million pesos.
This favorable development had a counterpart; the ratio of owned
capital to borrowed capital fell from 1.59 to 0.85, since there was
no appreciable change in the capital and surplus of the organization.

The balance sheet shows that between March, 1938, and December 31, 1947, 524 million pesos were invested in fixed assets, and
probably between 40 and 90 million pesos in working capital.*
The net investment of new capital in the industry, from expropriation to the end of 1947, amounted to between 560 million and 610
million pesos. It is not possible to specify exactly the sources of this
capital, though it is known that funds came from the Export-
Import Bank of Washington, the *Nacional Financiera* (a long-
term credit agency of the Mexican government), the Mexican government, and the earnings of the industry. The balance sheet of
December 31, 1947, shows capital and surplus of Pemex amounting

---

* The estimated investment of working capital is determined as follows: Working
capital as of December 31, 1947, was approximately 160 million pesos. The expropriated companies left practically no cash or claims to cash in Mexico, but they
left inventories of petroleum products estimated at 40 to 80 million pesos, and inventories of materials estimated at 30 to 40 million pesos. This indicates that Pemex
added 40 to 90 million pesos to working capital.

to 326 million pesos. This figure includes the earnings of the organization returned to the business and the direct and indirect contributions of the federal government. At that time the long-term debt (*Deuda a Largo Plazo*) amounted to 107.9 million pesos. Of this, 72.4 million pesos were in bonded indebtedness, 25.4 million in other promissory notes, 6.5 million in claims for interned ships acquired by Pemex, and 3.5 million in foreign obligations frozen by the war. In addition to the long-term debt, there is an unexplained item under the contingent liabilities called "Provision for Miscellaneous Obligations" (*Provisión para créditos diversos*), amounting to 64.6 million pesos.

The annual reports of the *Nacional Financiera* indicate that, at least after 1942, this institution contributed heavily to the petroleum industry. In the five years 1943 to 1947 it made loans amounting to 163 million pesos. This figure includes 48.5 million pesos ($10 million) lent by the Export-Import Bank through the *Nacional Financiera*. It is likely that appreciable amounts were supplied by the *Nacional Financiera* in earlier years, but data are not available. The balance sheet of December 31, 1945, indicates that Pemex' long-term debts, all owed to *Nacional Financiera*, amounted to slightly less than 59.9 million pesos. Two years later the bonded indebtedness, in two series, totaled 72.4 million pesos. Series "B," amounting to 20.6 million pesos, payable in six years at 5.14 per cent interest, was due the *Nacional Financiera*.[19]

It is impossible to distinguish between the capital originating in the federal government and that arising from earnings. It is known that at the end of 1940 the federal government granted Pemex 60 million pesos. In addition, there probably were hidden contributions in the form of tax adjustments. At the end of 1947, the federal government held the Series "A" bonds, amounting to 51.8 million pesos payable in six years at 3 per cent interest.[20] There is also an unexplained balance due the federal government (*Gobierno Federal, saldo acreedor*), amounting to 26.6 million pesos.

In his report to the Federal Board of Conciliation and Arbitration in the conflict of economic order of December, 1946, the general director of Pemex did not include the account due the Export-Import Bank in the bonded indebtedness. According to the schedule of repayments, on December 31, 1947, Pemex would have owed 29.1 million pesos on the principal of the loan. It is impossible to determine from the balance sheet how this account was carried—it may have been included in the item "Provision for Miscellaneous Obligations."

Mexican nationals, as individual investors, were conspicuously reluctant to commit their capital directly to the petroleum industry. Some private capital undoubtedly went into the oil industry through the channels of the *Nacional Financiera*. However, apparently only once after expropriation did a Mexican national show an inclination to participate directly on a significant scale. This was in 1946, when a Mexican was awarded a contract for exploring and developing a tract in Sinaloa, but the contract lapsed.

The scarcity of capital funds forced Pemex to turn to the United States for aid. To meet its exploratory needs, Pemex first attempted to contract with small American companies for work to be performed in Mexico, rather than for cash loans.[21] Failing in this, Pemex tried to make contracts with larger American companies that were still acceptable to labor for exploratory drilling and cash loans. In April, 1948, a 10-million-dollar loan and a coördinated exploratory program were agreed upon with the Cities Service Company, and in March, 1949, a second contract was made with the Mexican American Independent Company.[22]

These contracts helped to meet the pressing needs of Pemex in the exploratory field, but there were still serious capital shortages for the refinery and pipeline programs. Since other large American companies were unacceptable in Mexico, Pemex turned to the United States government with a request for $200 million to rehabilitate the industry. However, lengthy negotiations in the spring and summer of 1949 finally fell through. (See page 49 above.) This rebuff turned Mexico to its own financial resources, and the general director confidently asserted that the Mexicans would provide their own capital needs.

In accepting this attitude, Pemex set itself a difficult task. If the demands of labor were kept within reasonable bounds, it appeared in 1950 that the industry would expand and prosper under the capable guidance of General Director Antonio Bermúdez. Up to 1947, financial affairs of the organization had been subject to recurrent crises. Contributing factors included (1) the perversion of the functions of Pemex to the limited interests of the Syndicate of Petroleum Workers or of its leaders, (2) the appointment to many high administrative offices of persons with political rather than technical or managerial qualifications, and (3) a pervasive feeling that Pemex was a service organization for the Mexican community rather than a business enterprise that had to show profits. Bermúdez, however, felt that the organization's two responsibilities—to serve the public and to become a financially in-

dependent, self-sustaining business—were not incompatible. In ap-
plying for a loan in Washington, Bermúdez was not asking succor
for a dying industry, but rather looking for capital to speed the development of a natural resource that could make a valuable economic contribution to the country. Without the loan, the industry could still develop under capable direction, but the pace
would obviously be much slower.

In conclusion, until 1948 Mexico did not realize the popular
expectation (1) that expropriation would keep the large earnings of
the oil industry at home, and (2) that the industry would pay substantially larger taxes to the government. Not only did Pemex fail
in these respects, but it was apparently subsidized by the government. For a number of years Pemex was in arrears on taxes, including the gasoline consumption tax for which it was merely the collection agency. It received one outright grant in 1940 and probably
received indirect subsidies through tax remission. To 1946, Pemex
paid less annual taxes (not including the gasoline sales tax) than
the companies paid in any one of the three years 1934 to 1936. The
organization was in default on its reimbursement payments to the
government for expropriation indemnification, and it had failed
to build financial reserves for exploration sufficient to keep production ahead of rising demand. Pemex found it necessary to cut wages
and other benefits temporarily below those awarded by the Federal
Board in 1937 against the private companies. Even after the returns to employees had recovered in peso terms, real wages were
lower than before expropriation.

Since financial data for 1948 to 1950 are lacking, it is not possible
to draw any exact conclusions about this period. Apparently, however, the business acumen of General Director Bermúdez stood the
industry in good stead. Finances improved as a result of better
labor discipline, superior accounting techniques, and more aggressive business methods.

Chapter XII

SOME BROADER EFFECTS
OF EXPROPRIATION

Mexicans expected profound social changes to result from expropriation. Among their avowed aims had been the achievement of economic independence or freedom from "economic imperialism." They were suspicious of the large foreign companies and wanted a new entrepreneurial agent without ulterior motives, an agent whom they could trust not to restrict production or upset the economic and social life of the nation. Many Mexicans with strong humanitarian feelings hoped that expropriation would improve the well-being of the lower classes by ensuring a fairer distribution of wealth and income and by offering more equitable economic and social opportunities. Nationalists saw expropriation as a method of reëstablishing the Mexican nationality as the dominant element in economic life. To what extent were these objectives achieved? To what extent did expropriation result in other broad social and economic effects that were not anticipated or were only tacitly recognized?

It was inevitable that the expropriation of an industry of such absolute and strategic importance in the Mexican economy as petroleum would have extensive repercussions in other areas of economic, political, and social life. Petroleum, as a chief source of energy in Mexico, was a key to the industrial development of the country. Realization of the strategic significance of the industry was a factor prompting the expropriation. The industry was also of great absolute importance. In 1936 and 1937, almost 60 per cent of the Mexican production of crude oil was exported. Its value was more than 150 million pesos each year, and constituted nearly one-fifth of the total value of exports. In 1937, petroleum and its derivatives contributed more than 3 per cent to the net national income.[1]

On the economic side, expropriation seriously influenced invest-

[1] For numbered notes to chap. xii, see pp. 252–253.

ment decisions of owners of capital, both at home and abroad and within and outside the petroleum industry; and, as noted earlier, patterns of consumption and the balance of payments were also affected. On the political side, the results of expropriation and of subsequent developments in the industry can be seen in both the domestic and international spheres, and there were additional diffused social effects on real income and the standard of living.

In its economic aspects, the act of expropriation had a twofold repercussion on investment. First, it resulted in the repatriation of large amounts of foreign capital in Mexico; and, second, it was a serious deterrent to additional new investment, both domestic and foreign.

The expropriation, involving property settlements of about $113 million, called for the repatriation of about 440 million pesos (at the March, 1938, rate of exchange of 25.597 cents per peso), or more than 8 per cent of the estimated national income for 1938. Since repayment extended over twenty-four years, the average rate of repatriation of funds was approximately 18 million 1938 pesos a year. However, the delay in paying Dutch-Shell claims and the depreciation of the peso had raised the annual installment to approximately 75 million pesos by 1949.

Although this sizable movement of capital out of the country would normally have been detrimental to the Mexican balance of payments, two factors tended to nullify the net effect of the voluntary repatriation of capital. First, the oil companies were taking funds out of the country even before expropriation. For the three years 1934–1936, they reported average annual profits of 22 million pesos.[2] Since these profits* were in all likelihood removed from the country, expropriation caused less outflow of capital than would have occurred had the oil companies been allowed to remain and take their profits home.

The second nullifying factor was the declining interest of some large companies, especially American ones, in Mexican oil. This indifference had been developing ever since the middle 'twenties. Growing pressures from the Mexican government made the companies fear that expropriation would follow, and the more cordial atmosphere and the lucrative deposits found in Venezuela, Colombia, and the Near East, for example, convinced them that superior earning opportunities existed elsewhere. The result was liquida-

---

* The expert commission in the conflict of economic order of 1937 estimated average annual profits for 1934–1936 at 56 million pesos. It also asserted that "El Aguila" and Huasteca together exported capital amounting to 45 million pesos in 1936. (*Mexico's Oil* [México, D.F., 1940], pp. 260, 468, 476.)

tion of assets, or disinvestment, through the process of limiting replacements of depreciated capital to bare necessities. This disinvestment was similar, in its net effect on the balance of payments, to the capital repatriation undertaken voluntarily by the Mexicans. Although the extent of liquidation of investments through depreciation cannot be precisely determined, the sad state of the refineries in 1938 and the decline in exploration after 1934 suggest that it was substantial. Such a policy of disinvestment was probably less true of "El Aguila," which wanted to protect its rich stake in the Poza Rica field, than it was of the other large companies.

It might be contended that, had expropriation not taken place, the oil companies would have stepped up their investment under the stimulus of war demands. The validity of this argument is doubtful. The rigors of the German submarine campaign forced the United States to rely heavily on its own petroleum resources in 1942 and 1943, and not until 1944 did its imports from Venezuela, the Netherlands West Indies, and Colombia reach the prewar level.[3] Since these areas were just as accessible as Mexico to east coast ports of the United States, the war would probably have occasioned little new investment in Mexico.

A less direct effect of expropriation was its deterrence of new investment in other lines of industry. The expropriation climaxed a series of acts and policies of the Cárdenas administration that had made both foreign and domestic capital wary of the country.[*] Foreign capital tended to disinvestment rather than expansion, and domestic investors were inclined to hoarding. A flight of capital from Mexico followed expropriation. Cárdenas, whose principal interest was in land reform, perhaps did not regard this as serious; but Avila Camacho and Alemán found that the chary attitude instilled in potential investors by the Cárdenas regime was a hurdle obstructing the road to industrialization.

It cannot be said that, if Cárdenas and his advisors had not expropriated the oil companies, foreign capital would have found Mexico completely hospitable. As has been noted, there had been a traditional antipathy toward foreign capital. This feeling had found expression in the revolutionary objective of Mexicanizing industry. In the late 'thirties, a new group of rising industrialists, who were anxious to industrialize Mexico in order to raise its plane of living and to establish its economic independence, again gave voice to this revolutionary aim.[4] The group sided with labor in its

---

* For some of the wider effects of the policies of the Cárdenas administration see Sanford A. Mosk, *Industrial Revolution in Mexico* (Berkeley and Los Angeles, 1950), pp. 53–60, 83–84.

general hostility to foreign capital. Presidents Avila Camacho and Alemán tried to offset this growing sentiment by official statements of cordiality toward foreign investors. However, even though the expropriated companies undoubtedly would have returned, given the opportunity and certain guarantees by the Mexican government, the tide of resentment was too strong against them. A similar but much more moderate feeling against all foreign private capital was prevalent.

TABLE 30

INDEX OF WHOLESALE PRICES IN MEXICO CITY, 1932–1942
(1929 = 100)

Year	Index	Per cent increase over previous year
1932	82.6	− 8.2
1933	88.3	+ 6.9
1934	91.2	+ 3.2
1935	90.6	− 0.7
1936	95.5	+ 5.5
1937	112.3	+17.6
1938	115.8	+ 3.1
1939	118.5	+ 2.3
1940	120.2	+ 1.4
1941	127.2	+ 5.8
1942	140.1	+10.1

SOURCE: *Anuario estadístico, 1942*, pp. 1206–1208.

The deflationary effects that might have been expected to follow expropriation were shown at most only by a slight decline in the rate of increase in the rapidly mounting wholesale price index (see table 30). That the effects were not more in evidence was due to three principal factors. First, expropriation payments were not begun immediately. Payments to the Sinclair interests did not begin until 1940, and settlements with the American and Dutch-Shell interests were not arranged until 1942 and 1947, respectively. Second, the heavy buying of Europe and the United States in the rearmament race helped to keep Mexican industry active. In 1938, the surplus of exports over imports stood at 344 million pesos.[5] Third, the domestic economy was in a strongly expansionist stage as a consequence of heavy government investment beginning in 1937,[6] and this offset the otherwise possibly depressive effects of expropriation. Planned expenditures in the federal budget rose steadily from 406 million pesos in 1936 to 837 million pesos in 1942, whereas the domestic debt of the federal government increased from 579 million pesos in 1938 to 1,029 million pesos in 1942, and its foreign debt increased from 1,186 million pesos to 1,340 million pesos during the same period.[7] Between June, 1936, and June, 1937, demand deposits and money held by the public increased from 589 million pesos to 735 million pesos.[8] In April, 1938, the figure dropped to 660 million pesos, but by December, 1939, it had reached 920 million pesos. The index of physical volume of industrial production increased from 112 in 1936 to 122 in 1937, faltered slightly in 1938, and then increased to 132 in 1942.[9]

Insofar as the expropriation contributed to disorganization in the oil industry and thus to recurring shortages of fuel supplies, it hampered manufacturing and discouraged investment. Much of the industrial activity in the vicinity of Mexico City relies on petroleum fuel. During the war period, the lack of fuel frequently forced factories to suspend operations.[10] However, an offsetting factor was the government policy of keeping fuel prices low in order to encourage industry. From 1938 to 1947, the average domestic price of fuel oil increased only 135 per cent, whereas the wholesale price index for raw materials increased more than 184 per cent.[11] Official public policy tended more and more toward reliance upon petroleum fuels for industrial development,[12] a trend evidenced by construction of the Poza Rica–Mexico City gas pipeline to serve industry in the Federal District. The low-price policy is seen in the very moderate price increases on other petroleum products. In the period 1938 to 1947, the average price of asphalt increased only 51 per cent; of gasoline, 54 per cent; of tractor fuel, 38 per cent (for the period 1938 to 1946); of lubricating oil, 64 per cent; and the price of kerosene actually declined 13 per cent.

The declining relative cost of fuels probably contributed significantly to the development of electrical energy, production of which increased from 2,064 million kilowatt-hours in 1935 to 3,970 million in 1948. (See table 31.) After expropriation, there was a notable increase in the relative amount of electricity generated in thermoelectric as compared to hydroelectric plants. Between 1935 and 1938 thermoelectric plants produced slightly more than one-fourth of Mexico's electrical energy, but well over one-third in 1946.

Some effects of expropriation on the transportation network have been indicated in chapter vii. A less direct result was the interrelated growth of highways and increase in consumption of petroleum products. In 1935, the federal government embarked on an extensive highway development program, and expenditures for repairs and new construction increased rapidly. In 1934 new highway construction cost 13 million pesos, a record amount up to that time; by 1943 this expenditure had increased to 138 million pesos.[13] Total expenditures on roads, including maintenance, increased from 20 million to 174 million pesos during the same period. In the years 1941 to 1945, 400 miles of highway, on the

TABLE 31

Generation of Electric Energy by Type of Plant, 1933–1948
(In millions of kilowatt-hours)

Year	Total	Hydroelectric	Thermoelectric
1933.	1,528	1,269	259
1934.	1,834	1,479	355
1935.	2,064	1,512	552
1936.	2,245	1,674	571
1937.	2,480	1,822	658
1938.	2,512	1,871	641
1939.	2,462	1,618	844
1940.	2,529	1,698	831
1941.	2,524	1,652	872
1942.	2,625	1,938	687
1943.	2,739	1,892	847
1944.	2,750	1,721	1,029
1945.	3,068	2,092	976
1946.	3,317	2,121	1,196
1947.	3,598	a	a
1948.	3,970	a	a

a Data not available.
Sources: 1933–1946, *Compendio estadístico, 1948*, p. 130. 1947–1948, *Revista de estadística*, April, 1949.

average, were paved each year.[14] The extension of good roads was reflected in the rising domestic sales of asphalt and gasoline and in the increasing numbers of motor vehicle registrations. From 1934 to 1936, the average annual sale of asphalt by the expropriated companies was about 15 million kilograms;[15] from 1938 to 1945, the average annual sale by Pemex was 73 million kilograms.[16] Gasoline consumption in Mexico increased from 505,000 cubic meters in 1937 to 1,286,000 cubic meters in 1946.[17] The number of registered vehicles increased from 123,000 in 1937 to 209,000 in 1946, a rise of 70 per cent.[18] It cannot be assumed, of course, that these advances would not have been made without expropriation. Highway development and increased petroleum consumption were interrelated objectives of the revolution, and it is not possible to draw any causal sequence between them and the nationalization of the oil industry. In fact, the rapid increase in gasoline consumption began long before expropriation took place. The cheapness of gasoline undoubtedly contributed to maintaining the rate of increase after 1938. However, it is likely that the result would have been much the same under some alternative to expropriation, such as rigorous application of existing price controls to the private companies. This conclusion is supported by Mexico's loss of position, among ten developing countries, in percentage increase in consumption of petroleum products after expropriation. (See above, page 110.)

In the political field, the expropriation caused repercussions both at home and abroad. The expropriation was the first critical test of the friendly Latin American relations initiated by Hoover and popularized by Roosevelt as the "Good Neighbor" policy. The United States had sought to establish friendship by withdrawing occupation troops from various Latin American countries and by revoking treaty rights of intervention. In the Inter-American Conference of Foreign Ministers, the Latin Americans had finally induced the United States to accept the principle of nonintervention in Latin American republics. To further their aim of sovereignty, certain Latin American nations had introduced a statement known as the Calvo Clause into their concessions to foreigners. Under this clause a foreigner agreed with the government, in return for a contract or a concession, not to request his home government to intervene in any disputes over property rights in connection with the contract or concession.[19] Despite the fact that this clause was specifically written on their stock certificates, the owners of "El Aguila" did appeal to the British government and received support. After an exchange of sharp notes between Great Britain and Mexico, diplomatic relations were broken.[20] The American interests also sought the intervention of their government. The ensuing diplomatic correspondence between the United States and Mexico was pointed, but more moderate than that between Britain and Mexico. After some hesitation and uncertainty, the policy of nonintervention won out, despite vigorous protests from the expropriated companies that the Mexican government had infringed upon the bounds of good neighborliness. Effecting expropriation without armed intervention was evidence of vast progress in hemispheric relations during the preceding ten years. It could not be said that Mexico had established its political sovereignty, but the political pressures on Mexico emanating from the "Colossus of the North" were thenceforth more likely to be incentive inducements rather than the pointed coercions of earlier times. Expropriation and the subsequent developments evidenced full acceptance by the United States of the nonintervention policy.

One of the aims of expropriation had been to bolster the political freedom and sovereignty of Mexico through economic independence. It was felt that a country too closely tied to another in economic affairs had a weak foundation for political independence, and that the solution lay in industrialization. Large supplies of fuel at low prices would aid industrial development, and, according to the Mexican argument, would be assured by government ownership. It is obvious that expropriation of the oil industry did not halt industrialization, but there is a real question whether nationalization was an aid or an obstacle. Pemex' costs rose very rapidly after expropriation, and, despite the low-price policy, it is doubtful that prices were lower than they would have been under private operation. Comparisons of Mexico with other developing countries suggest that expropriation slowed down the rate of increase in consumption of petroleum products.

In addition, Mexico's international trade showed that the country had not yet become independent of other countries in supplying the domestic demand for petroleum products. Although the oil industry expanded notably after 1938, demand increased much faster than refining capacity. Consequently, Mexico still relied heavily upon foreign productive capacity, and in the period 1944 to 1947 was a net importer by value.

One benefit of expropriation was that the large oil companies had much less incentive to create domestic political pressure than before, when they had vested interests to serve. On the other hand, similar pressure was exerted after expropriation by the Syndicate of Petroleum Workers. Its energy, formerly directed against private managers, came to be set against government managers; and, as pointed out earlier, the feelings and activities of labor generated strong political pressures which each new government had to take into account. But the Mexicans did not have to put up with the foreign intervention that was so repugnant to them. The progress toward economic independence will be considered further in connection with economic imperialism.

The government's inability to realize immediate and unqualified success in managing the petroleum industry and the railroads undoubtedly deterred further adventures in nationalization. It also tempered the attitude toward other industries, especially those with large foreign investments. In mining and smelting, for example, less than 5 per cent of the invested capital was Mexican before the war, and in public utilities and merchandising less than 50 per cent was Mexican.[21] Succeeding presidents progressively retreated from Cárdenas' position that industrialists who were "tired of the class struggle" might turn their businesses over to the government or to labor. Under Avila Camacho and Alemán, private capital was strongly encouraged to undertake the industrialization of the country, and threats of expropriation no longer issued from official sources. At the same time, foreign capital, having seen the temper of an aroused populace, realized the value of treading the straight and narrow way. The animus against foreign capital still smoldered in organized labor and in the rising group of new industrialists. Foreign investors knew that adverse publicity might give these pressure groups the strength necessary to force the government into action against them, despite the need for capital. The foreigners also knew that their home governments would no longer back them to the hilt. Consequently, both sides moved circumspectly.

After expropriation, the foreign companies feared that the Mexican example would be copied by other Latin American countries, especially since Mexico was a sort of laboratory for social experimentation. The possibility did not materialize. Aside from Mexico, only Venezuela, Colombia, Argentina, Peru, and Ecuador produced appreciable amounts of oil. None of these countries took significant measures toward expropriation as a consequence of Mexico's action. The laboratory experiment was not successful enough to convince others beyond a reasonable doubt. Most of the steps toward nationalization in other countries were taken before March, 1938. A year earlier Bolivia had resorted to expropriation by seizing the Standard Oil interests.[22] In Argentina, it was a government agency, *Yacimientos Petrolíferos Fiscales,* that had made the first oil discovery in 1904, and private companies did not participate in oil production until 1916.[23] In 1949, the government agency produced more than 70 per cent of the crude oil.[24] Although government regulation of private companies was gradually tightened in Argentina, the Mexican experience appeared to have had little influence on this development. In Chile, a law of 1934 had authorized nationalization of the petroleum industry, but there was no commercial production before 1949, when a government agency made the oil strike. In 1950 this agency was the sole producer.[25] The first oil discoveries in Brazil were made in 1939 by a government agency established the preceding year, and in 1946 the entire petroleum industry was under government operation. The government of Peru participated in oil production in a small way, but most of the activity was undertaken by private capital operating under relatively favorable laws. It did not appear likely that private exploitation of oil resources would be terminated. The same was true of Ecuador, where development was carried on by private companies operating under laws more favorable to private exploitation than those of any other important producing country of Latin American, except Venezuela.

In the years just before 1950, the most serious threat of government action against private petroleum companies appeared in Colombia. Instead of expropriation, however, the government announced that concessions of the Tropical Oil Company (a subsidiary of Standard Oil, New Jersey) expiring in 1951 would not be renewed. Then, allegedly admitting its inability to operate the concession, the government asked Tropical to remain and to train Colombian personnel to take over three to five years after the expiration date. By that time the Colombian government would have established a new company with itself as major stockholder.[26] Meanwhile Tropical received new concessions to exploit, and the Minister of Mines and Petroleum announced a series of amendments liberalizing the oil laws.[27] Any Mexican influence on Colombia was apparently in the direction of a slower and less painful ingression into the industry than expropriation.

In Venezuela, foreign oil companies had had more freedom of operation than in any other Latin American country, and there seemed little likelihood of extensive government intervention so long as the industry remained prosperous. Prosperity obscured potential differences between the companies and the government. The stability of the government and of the economy was dependent on the oil industry. The backwardness of agriculture constituted a serious imbalance in the economy; this inherently unstable equilibrium was thinly disguised by the tenuous supporting threads of postwar prosperity. If prosperity faltered, increasing government intervention was probable; but such intention was not likely to extend to expropriation without more intensive training of Venezuelans for the task of management.

It appears that, for Venezuela and Colombia, the Mexican experience was more of a warning than an invitation to expropriate. Despite the popular feeling, especially in Colombia, against absentee capital that took little interest in domestic investment and development, both countries seemed to realize their limitations in managing industry, and to recognize the benefits of measures short of expropriation, such as heavier taxes, greater sharing in royalties, and the formation of companies of mixed foreign and domestic capital.

Oil expropriation in Mexico was not an isolated incident, but rather one aspect of a general reform movement that affected wide areas of economic and social life. The roots of this reform sprang from an impoverished and suppressed lower class. It would not be proper to leave the study of the petroleum industry without considering briefly some of the social implications of nationalization.

Certain fringe benefits for employees of Pemex and their dependents, such as medical, educational, and recreational facilities, have already been pointed out. The Syndicate of Petroleum Workers, as one of the three most powerful independent unions, set a precedent for others in its wage and welfare demands, especially since the Cárdenas administration accepted the responsibility of enforcing labor tribunal awards, even if this course led to expropriation. However, the radicalism of the syndicate helped to create the popular resentment and internal disunity that greatly reduced the strength of the labor movement after the war. Not only did labor organization suffer a setback, but the prospects for further progress in labor legislation deteriorated. The weakening of the labor front, coupled with rapid industrialization and wartime shortages, contributed to the 15 per cent decline in real wages in manufacturing between 1939 and 1949.[28]

One of the objectives of expropriation was to resist economic imperialism and foreign exploitation. Mexicans used these terms loosely to refer to all foreign investments, especially large ones; but there was little effort to specify clearly what "economic imperialism" and "exploitation" meant. The terms were highly charged with emotional connotations. Some Mexicans took advantage of such emotionalism by using the terms to vilify all foreign investors. Apparently few Mexicans analyzed the concepts objectively or saw the fundamental causes of conflict. Basically this problem is closely related on an international scale to the general problem of functional distribution of income. Wendell C. Gordon has rightly pointed out that it is a mistake to consider the conflict of *economic* interests involved in economic imperialism as a clash between political units;[29] rather, it is a struggle between interest groups over functional shares of income.* The identical problem that Mexico

---

* However, it must be recognized that the opponents may range themselves along international lines if the principals in the contest appeal to political values or to spurious economic objectives.

faced and complained of (to the point of making it a motive for expropriation) is present whenever outside capital enters an under-developed area, even when the people in that area live under the same flag and enjoy the same political rights as the capitalists.

It will clarify this issue to present some differing concepts of economic imperialism and to evaluate expropriation as a means of combating it.

Ultranationalistic groups are inclined to use the term "economic imperialism" to denote the mere presence of foreign capital in a country. With this interpretation, the conflict of interests may have national or geographic lines of demarcation, but, as will be pointed out, the conflict of *economic* interests does not follow national or geographic lines. Traditionally, many influential labor groups have adopted this concept of economic imperialism. It is perhaps the simplest and most understandable definition. Its simplicity has popular appeal for the uneducated, and its clear-cut distinction and emotional connotations attract highly nationalistic groups.

Lombordo Toledano, the Mexican labor leader, said:

Only . . . when the Mexican people are masters of what their land contains, of what their land produces, when all belongs to the Mexicans, will we be able to look forward to a day in which it will be possible that our public services shall be at the service of the Mexican people.[30]

A group of rising Mexican capitalists during and after World War II became conscious of a certain homogeneity of interest with labor groups in their hostility to foreign capital. They accepted this concept of economic imperialism and supported the labor groups.[31]

The conflict of economic interests in the case of Mexico was not between national entities. It is at least questionable, if not deniable, that the equity returns to foreign corporations were higher than those to domestic Latin American firms.[32] By and large, the level of prospective returns considered necessary to induce entry of domestic enterprisers into industry was very high by the standards of industrially advanced countries. If foreign capital were cheaper than domestic capital, there would be no conflict of interests along national lines, but only between foreign capital and domestic capital. Domestic capital apparently wanted a monopoly in domestic investment in order to increase its functional share. This was contrary to the nation's economic interest.

Those who opposed the oil companies simply because they represented foreign capital and who also favored larger functional shares for labor were holding to inconsistent objectives. The Cárdenas regime, labor groups, and the expert commission of 1937 regarded maldistribution of income as one of Mexico's principal social problems. And, in truth, the pitiful share and small absolute amount of national income received by the low-income groups present a serious socioeconomic problem. As a general policy, the ousting of foreign capital is not conducive to more equitable sharing in the national income, nor does it tend to increase the absolute amount received by labor. To the extent that the profit and interest returns to domestic capital are higher in the absence of foreign capital, distribution has been adversely affected by expropriation. In this respect, expropriation was inconsistent with the social objective of more equitable distribution of income. To the extent that expropriation reduced foreign investment, it adversely affected the marginal productivity of labor and the total income as well. The effect on distribution was not plainly visible, because the government financed the petroleum industry at low rates of return and virtually suspended royalties. However, the opportunity cost was a significant factor because, had the government not invested in the petroleum industry, the capital could have gone into industries which had been financed by other high-cost domestic capital.

If economic imperialism meant to the Mexicans the mere presence of foreign capital, then economic imperialism was present, of course, and expropriation helped Mexico divest itself of this undesired element. However, the policy had two adverse features. First, the exclusion of foreign capital was a political aim attainable only by incurring economic and social losses; as a consequence of expropriation, capital costs tended to increase, total income to fall, and the distribution of income to be more inequitable. Second, as it turned out, the rebuff to foreign capital was only temporary and was largely reversed by succeeding political administrations, which again encouraged foreign investment.

A second concept defines economic imperialism as investment by foreign companies, particulary large corporations, in underdeveloped areas so that functional shares in the form of profit, interest, and rent must be paid to foreigners. This definition is especially applicable when such returns are considered exorbitant. Here the conflict is economic, but it does not neatly array the contending interests on opposite sides of national borders. It is not a clash of geographic interests; it is again a clash over shares of income. This time, the principals in the struggle are not competing capitalists, but competing nonhomogeneous agents of production. This kind of economic imperialism can take place even within national borders. Almost every region of the United States has complained, at one time or another, of the New York capitalists who invested in that region and then drew out profits and interest. The region was not worse off for having had the investment. On the contrary, the normal result was that wealth increased and living standards improved. If the return to the investors was "excessive," the wealth of the region might have increased faster if the functional share of the capitalists had been less and that of local agents more. The solution to the problem of increasing regional wealth is not to bar foreign capital. Rather it is to retain in the region the portion of the capitalists' return that is in excess of the amount necessary to attract outside capital at a rate consistent with the desired rate of economic development in the region. The necessary return to outside capital would be that demanded, under competition, by capitalists who brought their investment funds to the region. Any payment above this competitive standard would presumably be "excessive."

A serious difficulty complicates the empirical application of this principle in the attempt to determine whether a given return is excessive. Capital markets may not be competitive.* Suppliers of capital may be extremely large or collusive, or for other reasons may be able to influence their rate of return. However, the mere fact that one country gives a higher return to capital than do other countries is not necessarily proof that the return is excessive. The anticipated return necessary to attract capital will have a direct relationship to political and economic uncertainties. For this reason (among others), underdeveloped areas would do well to minimize these uncertainties, insofar as possible. Such a policy would pay, for these areas could gradually place restrictions upon the present flow of returns to suppliers of capital without impairing the immigration of new capital needed in development.

The areas of interest are not defined by national boundaries because, if domestic capital were available for development at

---

* It may be possible to determine, within limits, at what point interest returns are excessive, but at what point profits and rents are excessive is probably indeterminate. Past experience may possibly lead to the conclusion that economic profits have been excessive if they continue over long periods of time during which the entry of new firms has been restricted. But, whatever the definition of profits, empirical difficulties arise in determining whether profits exist in a given situation; it is not easy to measure adequate money compensation for risk, uncertainty, or innovation, or for whatever basis has been chosen for the definition. It is also difficult to segregate profits from other implicit returns, especially economic rent to owners of natural resources.

lower rates of return than those received by outside capital, the foreign capital could not enter. When foreign capital does enter an underdeveloped area, there is the presumption that domestic capital is scarce and at least as costly as foreign capital. Income per worker is therefore increased by the entry of foreign capital which competes with domestic capital. As pointed out above, the inducements necessary to attract domestic capital in Mexico were relatively high.

If economic imperialism meant to the Mexicans that the large corporations were drawing out of the country exorbitant functional shares in the form of profits, rent, and interest, then the problem of determining whether the oil companies represented economic imperialism is more serious. The report of the expert commission studying the labor-management conflict of 1937 reveals that the percentage ratio of profits of the oil companies to capital, reserves, and surplus was 22.7 per cent in 1934, 24.9 per cent in 1935, and 21.8 per cent in 1936.[33] It is impossible to say for certain that this level of returns was excessive. There was some evidence that oil companies with investments in the more rewarding area of Venezuela were losing interest in Mexico. On the other hand, "El Aguila" was still expanding in the 'thirties. Presumably the returns obtained by "El Aguila" were sufficient, and perhaps large enough to justify an attempt to increase the Mexican share of the revenues.

The Syndicate of Petroleum Workers sought a more equitable distribution of earnings, and the Federal Board of Conciliation and Arbitration gave legal authority to the workers' claim to a larger share in the income of the companies. Enforcement of this decision would have modified the undesirable aspects of economic imperialism. Perhaps the Mexicans were too quick to expropriate, since that act did not solve the question of inequitable distribution, which is basic to this type of economic imperialism. On the contrary, expropriation was retrogressive; it intensified maldistribution through repatriation of foreign capital, as pointed out above. It seems that government regulation, to increase labor's share of revenues or to prevent or tax away excess profits, interest, and rents, would have yielded superior economic benefits to the country.

A third concept of economic imperialism refers to economic penetration for the purpose of extracting natural resources for export with little or no processing. This tends to perpetuate the "colonial" status of the country containing the natural resources.

The underdeveloped country wants more investment in the processing industries, an idea frequently found in Mexican writing and speeches. Complaints against such economic imperialism are apt to be particularly vehement if the raw materials are processed abroad and resold to the country of origin. Normally, foreign capital engaged in such exploitation would process the natural resources in the country of origin if it were economic to do so. (However, in an imperfectly competitive situation a producer might not do this, because of nonprofit motives or because he was not alive to actual profit opportunities.)

In attacking this sort of imperialism, the underdeveloped country might require that raw materials be processed before export. If this policy were applied to foreign capital not receiving "excess" returns (as defined above), capital would emigrate. However, if this policy were applied to capital receiving excessive returns, the country could build its processing industries without adversely affecting its capital requirements. There might, of course, be political repercussions if the affected capitalists, by cries of confiscation, induced their home governments to intervene and bring pressure to bear on the underdeveloped country. In past times, this was more than a remote possibility.

If the Mexicans interpreted economic imperialism as the companies' refusal to develop processing industries, they could have accomplished more to their economic advantage by regulation than by expropriation. In fact, the Mexican government did make progress in this direction when it induced "El Aguila" to build the Atzcapotzalco refinery. Expropriation did not substantially benefit the country with respect to increased refinery facilities; Mexico fell behind in meeting its own demand for refined products, and refined products came to constitute a smaller proportion of total petroleum exports than before expropriation.

A fourth concept of economic imperialism refers to the development of export industries in a backward country where the good exported is also consumed at home and where real want exists for the good.[34] It is perhaps profitable for investors to export the goods, despite the real need in the backward country, because the purchasing power in the domestic market is low relative to the purchasing power in foreign markets. Whether the underdeveloped country can modify or prevent this practice by embargoes or quotas on export, without repelling needed capital, again depends on whether the returns to capital are excessive. In any event, restrictions on exports would force economic losses on the country by eliminating the advantages of international specialization and trade, provided that returns to foreign capital were not excessive.

If the economic imperialism the Mexicans were attacking was the exporting of goods needed in the domestic market, then expropriation at least gave them direct control over their exports. Although home consumption increased very rapidly after expropriation, there is some question as to how much of this was due to (1) expropriation, (2) normal increase as purchasing power and living standards rose, or (3) the relative decline in prices of petroleum products. The experience of other developing countries suggests that the increase in consumption was despite expropriation rather than because of it.

It is conceivable that the Mexicans could have achieved long-run economic gains by selling fuel at home at prices below world market prices. If the low fuel prices acted as a subsidy to an industry that, once established, could and would maintain itself, then the temporary uneconomic restriction on export may have been justified on long-run grounds similar to the infant industries argument. The Mexicans did try to accomplish this. However, to be economically justified, the subsidized industries must in the long run be able to pay fuel prices consonant with world market prices. If Mexico wanted to retain exports at home and to subsidize industry, it could have achieved these ends by regulatory measures short of expropriation, such as export quotas and domestic price regulation.

A fifth concept of economic imperialism is associated with investing companies that have tremendous financial resources. Their power may be such that their operations have widespread repercussions on the economic and political life of the underdeveloped country. From a democratic viewpoint, this is at best an undesirable situation. At worst, a foreign company can create both economic and political crises. If, in attacking economic imperialism, the Mexicans were opposing the concentrations of foreign economic power that caused disturbances in their economic and political life, expropriation did yield benefits to them, as has already been pointed out.

Probably most Mexicans who objected to economic imperialism were under the impression that expropriation would tend to make the distribution of income more equitable. As previously indicated, this was a hope based on unsound economic policy. In addition, the concern for more equitable distribution ignored the importance of augmenting total national income.

To the extent that capital had to leave the country to pay for indemnification and that foreign capital was frightened away, investment was reduced and productivity and real income failed to make the advances that would otherwise have been realized. Insofar as the Mexicans tried to carry out industrialization with less foreign capital, current consumption and the plane of living were depressed. The fact that the expropriation payments tended to increase exports, by increasing foreign holdings of Mexican pesos and by depressing Mexican exchange, was of little advantage to Mexico. Full or near-full employment was quite consistently maintained after expropriation as a consequence of monetary expansion and the pressure of consumption spending, and the net result was an adverse effect on real income. One important beneficial effect of expropriation on the level of real income partly offset these adverse factors. Whereas a large part of the foreign exchange acquired by the companies through exporting oil had never served Mexico directly because the companies owned, held, and spent it abroad, the foreign exchange acquired by export after expropriation (over and above the amount needed for indemnification payments) was the property of the Mexicans and thus became available for foreign purchases that would benefit the country.* However, the same result could have been achieved by taxation or other devices short of expropriation.

Another social effect was the influence of nationalization upon the use of petroleum products and consequently upon the plane of living. The government carried on a campaign to substitute kerosene and liquid gas for wood and charcoal as household fuels by offering petroleum products at exceptionally low prices and by selling cooking stoves through Pemex agencies at moderate prices. The relative simplicity and cleanliness of petroleum fuels, compared to wood and charcoal, can be fully appreciated only by those who have used both. Between 1938 and 1946, while the general price level soared, the average price of kerosene fell 13 per cent and that of liquid gas 5 per cent. That the populace responded to the low prices and other encouragements is shown by the increase in domestic consumption of liquid fuels, nearly ninefold for kerosene and twelvefold for liquid gas.

Again, it cannot be said unequivocally that this would not have

---

* In theoretical terms, the additional foreign exchange obtained by Mexico from the expropriated properties should not have exceeded the excess returns received by the companies. Otherwise, there would have been exploitation of the exploiters. That is, the indemnification payments would have been inadequate reimbursement, and expropriation would have been confiscation.

happened under private operation of the petroleum industry. It can be argued that government regulation would have produced similar results. However, it is not likely that the government would have been so keenly interested in making petroleum products generally available to the public if Pemex had not taken over, and if the boycott and the war had not prevented the disposal of surpluses in foreign markets.

In conclusion, the social changes expected from expropriation were not entirely realized. Some of the changes were contrary to the expressed aims of the Mexicans. Whether the aim of ending economic imperialism was achieved depends upon what is meant by the term. Of course, the presence of the large oil companies, with their potential economic and political influence, was terminated. The export of significant amounts of capital in the form of profit, interest, and rent from oil was largely ended. The country gained complete control of oil resources, which it could devote directly to its own uses provided it was ready to incur the necessary costs and sacrifices.

However, Mexico was not able to engage in the spectacular program of building processing plants that many Mexicans had hoped for. In fact, the country became increasingly dependent upon foreign processing plants because refinery construction did not keep pace with demand. Although the companies no longer carried large profits, interest, and rent from the country, Mexico had to make sizable indemnification payments, which had adverse effects on the country's economic development. This was accentuated by the fears that nationalization instilled into foreign and domestic capital. Although Mexico hoped to improve the position of low-income groups, economic analysis shows that expropriation did not further this objective because increasing scarcity of capital raised the relative shares received by domestic owners of capital and, at the same time, the decline in available capital reduced the total income.

The standard of living in Mexico tended to rise with the increasing use of petroleum for producing electricity, paving roads, providing fuel for automobiles, replacing wood and charcoal as household fuels, and mechanizing agriculture. However, it is not possible to attribute these advances (except, possibly, in the case of household fuels) to expropriation, because many other developing countries whose oil industries remained in private hands had even more spectacular increases in consumption than Mexico.

Perhaps the most significant noneconomic benefit derived by the country was progress in the Mexicanization of industry. Mexicans learned that their economic life and destiny were dependent upon their own initiative and effort. However, this benefit involved a significant economic sacrifice.

Chapter XIII

SUMMARY AND CONCLUSIONS

The purpose of this investigation was to discover the objectives of Mexico in expropriating its petroleum industry and to determine the extent to which the country achieved those objectives.

The aims of expropriation were complex and deeply rooted in the history of the Mexican nation. Nationalization was the fruit of a long-delayed reform movement with economic, political, and social aspects. Mexicans felt that they were economically too dependent upon the industrialized countries of the world, and that they were consequently subject to the pressures of foreign moopolies and "economic imperialism." Many Mexicans regarded the large oil companies as irresponsible and unmindful of the basic economic, political, and social interests of the country, and as contributory to unrest and instability by periodically creating uncertainty and alarm. The companies carried from the country oil and profits that many Mexicans thought should be devoted directly to national development. The companies' loss of interest in the Mexican fields had brought on a serious decline in production. The foreigners had operated under special privileges, granted many years before, that barred Mexicans from effective participation in this basic industry. Influential Mexicans thought these conditions caused undesirable distortions in the distribution of income. A few Mexicans feared a collapse of production as a result of the antagonisms and open conflicts in labor-management relations. Legal action before the Federal Board, and the response of management to the decisions handed down by the board, led a large segment of the population to feel that the larger oil companies had challenged the processes of Mexican law and threatened to precipitate a disastrous strike that would paralyze the economy. The efforts of the oil companies to maintain their property rights in the subsoil appeared to many Mexicans to contest the sovereignty of the nation and its rights to its natural resources. Whether these fears and animosities were justified is beyond the scope and purpose of the present study. It is significant that Mexicans believed these things to be true, and that in 1938 they felt that nothing short of expropriation could rectify matters.

The drastic step of expropriation threw the problem of organizing and administering more than 90 per cent of the petroleum industry into the hands of the Mexican government. The heavy reliance upon labor in the initial period of government operation was a blessing at the time, for it kept the industry going, but it raised serious problems later when the government attempted to consolidate its administration. The permanent organization, the government corporation *Petróleos Mexicanos* (known as Pemex), gave labor four of the nine appointees on the board of directors, but the government retained voting control. The officers of Pemex and the government generally regarded the corporation as a self-supporting business enterprise. Its virtual monopoly in the oil industry was protected by highly restrictive legislation, enacted to meet the demands of powerful nationalistic groups, especially organized labor.

Physical conditions in the industry presented extremely difficult problems in view of the state of international markets. Production and refinery output suffered from expropriation. Although the production potential was high, production had to be drastically curtailed because foreign markets were seriously reduced, first by the boycott of the expropriated companies, and later by wartime shipping shortages. Possession of a tanker fleet would have alleviated these problems; but Mexico acquired a fleet only with difficulty, and the ships obtained were needed to supplement the domestic transportation system. Refineries were in such a deplorable state that they were able to meet the demands upon them only with the utmost exertion. As Pemex improved the refineries and gradually expanded the domestic market to absorb larger quantities of the production potential, the limitations of the transportation network hampered the industry. The foreign oil companies had built the major pipeline systems for export purposes, except the one between Poza Rica and Atzcapotzalco (Mexico City). The railways, burdened by age and mismanagement, failed to meet the needs of the country as consumption increased. The rising domestic demand revealed basic weaknesses of Pemex in meeting exploration and refining requirements. In 1944, Mexico began to import more petroleum than it exported, measured by value.

The situation was enormously complicated by the radical character of the Syndicate of Petroleum Workers, which, disappointed in its effort to get full control of the industry, made inordinate demands out of all consonance with the conditions and problems faced by management. Since management was undoubtedly inefficient and ill-prepared for the magnitude of the task thrust upon it, Pemex reached the verge of financial prostration. It appealed to the government and to the Federal Board of Conciliation and Arbitration for a reduction in labor benefits and for an extension of managerial powers. The board gave Pemex a financial respite and also somewhat extended its authority.

Until 1945, Pemex would have been judged a failure by almost any test, but the end of the war and its associated shortages eased the situation. At the end of 1946, the appointment of a successful businessman and highly capable executive, Antonio Bermúdez, as general director marked a significant advance. President Alemán's support of the management during an illegal strike shortly after Bermúdez' appointment brought a rigorous disciplining of labor through the discharge of unruly syndicate leaders. In 1947, exploration and production rapidly expanded. To step up exploration, Pemex engaged American companies through loan-drilling contracts that were payable in oil but that gave the driller no rights to subsoil deposits. In 1950, production exceeded 72 million barrels, the highest figure in twenty-four years, but it was still doubtful that the 217 wells drilled in that year, the largest number in twenty-one years, could maintain the production potential ahead of the rising demand. Although refinery capacity in 1948 was 37 per cent more than in 1937, it was lagging seriously behind the needs of the country; and Mexico imported nearly 100 million pesos' worth of expensive refined products in 1948. Pipeline systems were being slowly extended and modified to meet the special needs of the domestic market, but lack of capital obstructed efforts to improve service to the north central and west coast areas, which the overloaded railways could not adequately handle. With increasing production, petroleum exports regained some of the lost ground. Increasing imports partly nullified this gain. Labor discipline reached at least the minimum standards consistent with effective operation of the industry. Pemex appeared to be in financial equilibrium and was contributing increasing financial support to the government, although it was in arrears on past payments due the government. Not until 1946 did Pemex' general taxes (excluding the gasoline consumption tax) exceed those paid by the private companies in 1936, and until 1948, at least, the company did not meet the legally required royalty payments to the government or the 3 per cent interest on government investments. In 1950, the industry was suffering from capital starvation. Domestic investment funds available to Pemex were inadequate, and direct foreign investment in petroleum was effectively barred. There was little prospect either that direct foreign investment in the industry would be permitted or that private Mexican capital would volunteer. On the basis of its petroleum experience, the government was not likely to resort to expropriation of other foreign-owned properties. Other Latin American governments did not follow the lead of Mexico in expropriation, and there was little prospect that they would. In short, to speak metaphorically, Pemex had survived the traumatic shock of birth, and after twelve years was giving some assurance that it could grow.

To what extent were the objectives of expropriation accomplished?

There is little doubt as to the almost complete realization of the short-run objectives. The general economic paralysis threatened by the final labor dispute of the ejected companies was avoided; Mexican law and legal procedures prevailed against the large foreign economic units; and the nation's ownership of subsoil deposits of oil was established. Against these accomplishments must be weighed the facts that, at least until the end of 1946, the chronic labor-management disputes contributed to the repeated shortages or threats of shortage that at times caused local paralysis, and that in the early years labor, and sometimes management, showed considerable indifference toward Mexican law and legal procedures.

As to the long-run objectives, expropriation, by repulsing "economic imperialism," gave Mexico more independence in the sense of greater national control over her own economic destiny. The Mexicans gained a sense of being active rather than passive participants in the petroleum phase of the world economy. The alleged monopolistic position of the private oil companies was destroyed. Although a greater monopoly replaced them, it was fortunate that those in charge of Pemex were dedicated to the policies of reducing prices and of expanding output. After 1946, definite progress in rebuilding the industry became evident, and standards of living rose as consumption of petroleum products increased. However, these gains could not be attributed to expropriation. Other developing countries showed similar progress, and the evidence suggests that those countries which left the petroleum industry in private hands enjoyed greater relative increases in consumption than Mexico did. Real costs of production appear to have increased after expropriation.

The repatriation of oil capital and the alienation of other

capital, through fears engendered by expropriation, undoubtedly hurt total production in Mexico and accentuated the maldistribution of income. The harmonious labor-management relations expected from expropriation did not develop, for the antagonisms lay deeper than the question of organized labor versus private management. The retention of the formerly exported private profits was largely, if not completely, offset by indemnification payments and a decline in labor productivity.

The alternative to expropriation was closer regulation. To the extent that the oil companies' profits, interest, and rent were "excessive," Mexico could have imposed regulation without adverse effects on investment. Although it can be argued that regulation tends to discourage investment, well-considered regulatory steps might have been used to attack specific problems without serious damage to investment incentives. However, three factors stood in the way of this approach to Mexico's oil problems. First, there was not sufficient agreement among Mexicans as to what the specific economic problems were, nor was there sufficient understanding of the economic principles involved. Second, some of the companies were already losing interest in Mexico for investment purposes, which suggests that these companies were not receiving "excessive" returns. Third, the oil problem was not simply economic. There were political and social aims as well. Mexicans were willing to make economic sacrifices, if necessary, to achieve these other ends.

Expropriation almost completely accomplished the Mexicanization of the oil industry, although those who had hoped to see the industry controlled by private Mexican enterprisers were disappointed. The nation established its ownership of the subsoil deposits. The government ended what many considered a flaunting of Mexican law and legal procedures by foreigners. Ousting the large oil companies removed a significant disturbing, or potentially disturbing, foreign influence from Mexican political and social life. Although it could be argued that Pemex and the Syndicate of Petroleum Workers possessed an even greater disturbance potential, the Mexicans felt less frustration and international tension when only their own people were involved and when the application of controls did not cause complications with more powerful nations.

Mexicans wanted liberation from the large companies. This assertion of economic independence suggests the modern man who wants individual freedom so strongly that he turns to a self-sufficient, subsistence type of economic activity. Shunning specialization and economic interdependence, he foregoes a higher standard of living and economic satisfactions but gains other values associated with freedom and individualism. Henry David Thoreau weighed a higher standard of living with less individualism against fewer economic satisfactions and greater individualism, and found his balance favoring the latter. The balance of values of other persons of his day swung the opposite way.

Undoubtedly, from a purely economic standpoint, Mexico could have better solved its petroleum problem by more extensive regulation and other steps short of expropriation, but it is unlikely that such measures would have satisfied the basic political and social aspirations of the people. Revolutionary principles and hostility to the large foreign companies were too deeply imbedded in Mexican consciousness to stop short of expropriation. Like Thoreau, the policy-makers of a society, rather than the social scientists, must weigh and choose among political, social, and economic values to the extent that they are mutually exclusive. Mexican policy-makers made such a choice. They apparently erred in their assessment of the economic values to be attained by expropriation. However, at the end of twelve years of experience, extremely few voices expressed regret for the act of expropriation, and the fundamental will to consummate the objectives of expropriation seemed as strong as in 1938.

APPENDIXES

Appendix A

FINDINGS OF THE EXPERT
COMMISSION AND REPLY

1. FINDINGS OF THE EXPERT COMMISSION IN THE
CONFLICT OF ECONOMIC ORDER SUBMITTED
TO THE BOARD OF CONCILIATION AND ARBITRATION,
1937

1. The principal oil companies operating in Mexico form part of large North American or English economic units.

2. The principal oil companies operating in Mexico have never been fully integrated to the country and their interests have always been alien, and at times even opposed, to the national interests.

3. The principal oil companies operating in Mexico have left in the Republic only wages and taxes, without in reality having cooperated in the social progress of Mexico.

4. The principal oil companies operating in Mexico have earned enormous profits in the exploitation of the subsoil. It is impossible to calculate the total amount; but it may be affirmed, at a conservative estimate, that the majority of the companies recovered their invested capital more than a decade ago.

5. The oil industry, considered on a world basis, is financially more important than any other great industry.

6. The great petroleum interests have, on more than one occasion, influenced national as well as international political events.

7. Oil production began in Mexico in 1901 on an insignificant scale, reached its highest point in 1921, and then declined constantly to 1932. Since that time a slight improvement is noted due to the exploitation of the fields of Poza Rica and El Plan.

8. The decrease in oil production in Mexico is due to the depletion of oil deposits, especially those of the Golden Lane and Cacalilao; to the lack of new and intensive exploration to discover other fields; and possibly also to the policy of the oil companies.

9. Drilling activities have decreased alarmingly in recent years. Drilling operations in 1936 are considerably less than in 1926, although the

percentage of productive wells drilled is greater at present than ten years ago.

10. All the oil fields in Mexico are about to be exhausted, with the exception of those of Poza Rica and El Plan, the production of which is estimated at a probable fifty million barrels a year during a period of from ten to twelve years.

11. The exploration of new fields and the drilling of new wells are a great national problem which must be solved. Otherwise, there is danger that Mexico will face a petroleum shortage in a relatively short period, and will be obliged to import oil.

12. There are large zones of possibly oil-bearing lands along the coastal plain of the Gulf of Mexico, in the northern part of the states of Coahuila, Nuevo León, and Tamaulipas, and in certain other parts of the country.

13. Production in 1936 increased 7.48 per cent as compared with that of 1934, due to a very important increase, 26.17 per cent, in the production of light crude, while heavy crude production decreased 33.14 per cent.

14. The characteristics of the petroleum industry in Mexico have been modified in recent years. From 1920 to 1924, and even in subsequent years, the major portion of production was exported, while in 1936 national consumption represented 15.86 per cent of heavy crude oil, 99.9 per cent of light crude, and 43.50 per cent of refined products.

15. Nearly 60 per cent of Mexican crude oil production and derivatives is exported to the United States and England.

16. The Compañía Mexicana de Petróleo "El Aguila," together with its affiliated companies, represented, during the year 1936, 59.33 per cent of total production. This fact reveals a tendency toward monopoly.

17. In recent months the price curve for petroleum and derivatives has been rising, which indicates excellent prospects for the industry, at least during the next few years.

18. The prices of articles of prime necessity which make up the "basket of provisions" of a worker's family composed of five members, in the oil zones, had increased 88.96 per cent in June, 1937, in comparison with the 1934 averages.

19. The real wages of the great majority of oil workers at the present time are lower than those earned by workers in the mining industry.

20. The real wages of the great majority of oil workers at the present time are lower than those earned by workers of the National Railways of Mexico.

21. The real wages of the great majority of oil workers at the present time are lower than those which they earned in 1934 by at least 16 to 22 per cent, the decrease varying in inverse ratio to the amount of the nominal wage.

22. The real wages of the American oil workers during the second

quarter of 1937 were 7.84 per cent greater than those which they earned in 1934.

23. According to the books of the oil companies, the prices at which they sell their products are invariably lower than the price quotations in trade publications which accurately reflect the conditions of the market.

24. The prices at which the companies sell petroleum derivatives in Mexico are considerably higher than the prices at which these same products are sold in foreign markets.

25. The price at which the Compañía "El Aguila" (and the same may be said of other companies) sold gas oil in Mexico (average of 1934–1936), was 171.75 per cent higher than the price at which it sold the same product abroad.

26. The price at which the Compañía "El Aguila" (and the same may be said of other companies) sold gasoline in Mexico (average of 1934–1936), less the gasoline consumption tax, was 134.40 per cent higher than the price at which it sold the same product abroad.

27. The price at which the Compañía "El Aguila" (and the same may be said of other companies) sold kerosene in Mexico (average of 1934–1936) was 341.18 per cent higher than the price at which it sold the same product abroad.

28. The price at which the Compañía "El Aguila" (and the same may be said of other companies) sold lubricants in Mexico (average of 1934–1936) was 350.76 per cent higher than the price at which it sold the same products abroad.

29. The prices at which the oil companies sell their products in Mexico are so high that it is evident that they constitute an obstacle to the economic development of the nation.

30. The yearly average of the capital stock of the defendant oil companies, with the exception of the Mexican Gulf, which did not permit a revision of its books, was 164,000,000 pesos during the three year period 1934–1936.

31. The yearly average of unamortized invested capital of the defendant oil companies, with the exception of the Mexican Gulf, was 335,000,000 pesos during the three year period 1934–1936.

32. The reserves and surplus of the defendant oil companies (average of 1934–1936), with the exception of the Mexican Gulf, was 79,000,000 pesos.

33. The annual rate of profit on the capital stock of the defendant oil companies, with the exception of the Mexican Gulf, averaged 34.28 per cent during 1934–1936.

34. The annual rate of profit on the unamortized invested capital of the defendant oil companies, with the exception of the Mexican Gulf, averaged 16.81 per cent during 1934–1936.

35. In 1935, the principal oil companies in the United States earned a profit of 6.13 per cent on their invested capital.

36. The profits of all the oil companies in the United States on their invested capital were: in 1931, 2.76 per cent; in 1932, losses instead of profits; in 1933, 1.70 per cent; in 1934, 2.20 per cent; and in 1935, 1.44 per cent.

37. The profits of the oil companies operating in Mexico are considerably higher than the profits of those operating in the United States.

38. The capital invested in the petroleum industry in Mexico in 1935 represented only 0.73 per cent of the capital invested in the petroleum industry in the United States, whereas oil production in Mexico represented 4.05 per cent of production in the latter country.

39. In 1935, an investment of 8.64 pesos was necessary to produce a barrel of crude oil in Mexico, as against 48.12 pesos in the United States. The investment required in Mexico amounts to 17.96 per cent of that required in the United States.

40. During the last three years (1934–1936), the defendant oil companies have earned very large profits; their financial condition must be considered as being extraordinarily sound and, in consequence, it may be asserted that, without prejudice to their present or future condition, at least during the next few years, they are perfectly able to accede to the demands of the Union of Oil Workers of the Mexican Republic up to an amount of approximately 26,000,000 pesos a year.

SOURCE: *Mexico's Oil* (México, D.F.: Mexican Government, 1940), pp. 591–592.

2. "EL AGUILA'S" REPLY TO THE FINDINGS OF THE EXPERT COMMISSION

It is not directly a concern of this study to evaluate the arguments used by Mexicans in the controversy with the oil companies. However, it is significant to the history of Mexican petroleum to note that the oil companies also had a case. The Compañía Mexicana de Petróleo "El Aguila" formally answered the charges of the expert commission, which reported to the Federal Board of Arbitration and Conciliation on August 3, 1937 (see pages 20–21). "El Aguila" responded at the hearings before the Federal Board August 27 to September 20, 1937 (see *Mexico's Oil,* pp. 608–615).

1. To the charge of the expert commission that the oil companies were parts of large British and American enterprises, "El Aguila" answered that it was a Mexican commercial corporation organized in accordance with laws of the country and was not part of any foreign economic unit.

2. To the charge that the large British and American companies had never become integrated with the country, that they left only wages and taxes in the country and did not coöperate in social progress, and that their interests were alien or even hostile to those of the country, "El Aguila" replied by pointing to the large tax payments to the

country, to loans made to state governments and advances to the federal government on taxes, to royalties to individuals, and to the freight payments to Mexican railways. "El Aguila" referred to the roads and airfields opened by the companies in their operating districts and to the economic and social opportunities offered to workers as evidenced by labor contracts.

3. To the charge that the oil companies had made enormous profits, "El Aguila" objected that the expert commission had picked a most favorable group of years, 1934–1936, and requested that profits be studied for the more representative period 1927–1936.

4. To the charge that the companies had influenced national and international political events, "El Aguila" replied that it had remained aloof from politics and that its activities were strictly industrial, as its continued expansion even during the revolutionary period testified. The company said that it had differed with the Mexican government over the question of whether or not the constitutional provision asserting the nation's ownership of subsoil deposits could legally be retroactive.

5. To the charge that the companies had possibly restricted production and exploration and allowed the oil industry to decline, "El Aguila" claimed that the companies had wanted to intensify exploration but that the Secretary of National Economy had obstructed this by not granting the necessary permission. "El Aguila" referred to the huge expenditures made by various companies in exploratory work.

6. To the charge that "El Aguila" showed monopolistic tendencies, the company objected that the expert commission was inconsistent. The experts had complained that the industry was declining because the company failed to intensify its activity, and at the same time that the industry was being monopolized because of the company's excessive activity.

7. To the charge that real wages were declining as indicated by the increasing cost of the workers' "basket of provisions," "El Aguila" objected to the statistical technique used. The company asserted that the syndicate itself made the computations and that the increase in cost was due not so much to increase in the cost of the articles as to the addition of new items to the basket and to the substitution of higher quality items. "El Aguila" declared that in reality no appreciable change in the cost of living had taken place.

8. To the charge that real wages of the majority of petroleum workers were lower than those of miners and of national railway workers, "El Aguila" stated that the expert commission had used for comparison the mining wage scales of only three areas and not the average for the whole industry. The company took the commission to task for failing to take into account the shorter workweek and the greater social ("fringe") benefits enjoyed by petroleum workers as compared to miners.

As for the higher wages of the railway workers, "El Aguila" pointed out that the commission itself had admitted that semiskilled and unskilled oil workers received higher pay than railway workers of comparable skill (see *Mexico's Oil*, p. 233). Therefore the company contended that, since the majority of workers were semiskilled or unskilled, elementary logic disposed of the charge of the experts. With regard to the decline in real wages, "El Aguila" pointed out that in 1934 the oil companies paid wages of 27 million pesos to 23,034 workers, whereas in 1936 the companies paid wages of 43 million pesos to only 18,006 workers. In addition, social benefits had increased in this period.

9. "El Aguila" denied the charge that the oil companies sold products at higher prices in Mexico than abroad, and offered its books and literature on world prices to prove that its prices were not out of line with world prices. "El Aguila" pointed to the very favorable prices at which it sold fuel to the National Railroads. Far from being an obstacle to development, "El Aguila" asserted, the oil companies had contributed to economic progress, as indicated by the increasing domestic consumption of oil.

10. "El Aguila" also denied the assertion of the expert commission that the companies' financial condition enabled them to meet the demands of labor, and offered its books as evidence. The company also attacked the legal competence of the Federal Board to decide the case.

The Standard Oil Company (N.J.) and other interests that lost in the expropriation attacked the Mexican position in a series of pamphlets published in 1939 and 1940. However, these works did not deal with the Mexican charges in the specific detail found in "El Aguila's" arguments.

Appendix B

207

TABLE 1

PETROLEUM PRODUCTION IN MEXICO, BY YEARS AND CUMULATIVE TOTAL,
1901–1950
(In thousands of barrels)

Year	Annual production	Cumulative total[a]
1901	10	10
1902	40	51
1903	75	126
1904	126	251
1905	251	503
1906	502	1,005
1907	1,004	2,009
1908	3,931	5,940
1909	2,712	8,652
1910	3,632	12,285
1911	12,546	24,831
1912	16,550	41,380
1913	25,682	67,063
1914	26,222	93,285
1915	32,893	126,179
1916	40,545	166,724
1917	55,293	222,016
1918	63,828	285,845
1919	87,073	372,918
1920	157,069	529,986
1921	193,398	723,384
1922	182,278	905,662
1923	149,585	1,055,247
1924	139,678	1,194,926
1925	115,515	1,310,440
1926	90,421	1,400,861
1927	64,121	1,464,982
1928	50,150	1,515,132
1929	44,688	1,559,820
1930	39,530	1,599,350
1931	33,039	1,632,389
1932	32,805	1,665,195
1933	34,001	1,699,195
1934	38,172	1,737,367
1935	40,241	1,777,608
1936	41,028	1,818,636
1937	46,907	1,865,543
1938	38,506	1,904,048
1939	42,898	1,946,946
1940	44,036	1,990,982
1941	43,054	2,034,036
1942	34,815	2,068,851
1943	35,163	2,104,015
1944	38,204	2,142,218
1945	43,547	2,185,766
1946	49,235	2,235,001
1947	56,284	2,291,285
1948	58,370	2,349,655
1949	60,736	2,410,391
1950	72,118	2,482,509

[a] There may be slight discrepancies due to rounding.

SOURCES: 1901–1947, Secretaría de Economía, *Compendio estadístico.* 1948–1950, *World Oil*, July 15, 1950, July 15, 1951.

TABLE 2

OIL WELLS DRILLED IN MEXICO, TOTAL, SUCCESSFUL, AND ABANDONED,
BEFORE 1917 AND BY YEARS, 1917–1950

Year	Total	Successful	Abandoned
1901–1917.............	279	174	105
1917..................	79	43	36
1918..................	43	28	15
1919..................	41	31	10
1920..................	112	69	43
1921..................	321	206	115
1922..................	265	158	107
1923..................	467	259	208
1924..................	699	296	403
1925..................	801	298	503
1926..................	808	318	490
1927..................	570	204	366
1928..................	340	148	192
1929..................	218	114	104
1930..................	133	71	62
1931..................	87	57	30
1932..................	50	31	19
1933..................	93	53	40
1934..................	145	57	88
1935..................	80	35	45
1936..................	67	37	30
1937..................	45	29	16
1938..................	31	15	16
1939..................	24	15	9
1940..................	33	23	10
1941..................	25	14	11
1942..................	14	6	8
1943..................	16	9	7
1944..................	31	20	11
1945..................	49	31	18
1946..................	52	31	21
1947..................	50	28	22
1948..................	80	43	37
1949..................	158	96	62
1950..................	217	127	90

SOURCES: 1901–1947, Secretaría de Economía, *Compendio estadístico*. 1948–1950, *World Oil*, July 15, 1950; July 15, 1951.

TABLE 3

Annual Production of Crude Oil by Fields in Mexico, 1941–1949

(In thousands of cubic meters)

Field	1941	1942	1943	1944	1945	1946	1947	1948	1949
North Tampico region (Pánuco-Ebano)									
Altamira	11	7	4	6	10	8	4	27	22
Ebano, SLP	55	26	20	13	30	49	53	56	60
Ebano, Ver	279	102	88	85	148	280	324	290	248
El Limón, SLP	5	5	1	.....	.....	13	22	16	16
El Limón, Ver	10	10	3	.....	.....	24	38	39	39
Cacalilao	293	196	175	233	322	523	641	614	564
Pánuco, Ver	250	196	187	202	281	433	471	538	514
Topila, Ver	57	45	26	39	51	44	47	48	43
S. Sebastián, Ver	.....	2	3	4	3	4	3	3	3
South Tampico region (Golden Lane)									
Tantoyuca, Ver	.....	.....	.....	.....	.....	.....	.....	.....	.....
Dos Bocas	6	6	5	5	.....	6	1	.....	.....
Chiconcello and S. Miguel, Ver	4	1	3	3	.....	3	4	19	17
Tepetate, Chinampa, Amatlán, Zaca-mixtle, Ver	351	243	380	455	537	377	335	308	281
Juan Felipe, Ver	49	23	40	48	56	30	25	20	17
Toteco and Cerro Azul, Ver	300	229	398	546	613	510	494	543	498
Moralillo, Ver	5	4	4	4	4	1	.....	46	84
	4	5	5	5	5	5	5	6	5
								16	13

.....					248	208	160	140
.....	6	3	3	3	4	5	3	2	2
Paso Real	13	5	36	27	24	22	21	19	18
Poza Rica region									
Macatepec, Ver.	62	24	333	541	604	896	1,075	1,116	909
Poza Rica, Ver.	3,984	3,496	2,960	2,801	3,044	3,271	4,005	4,354	4,378
Escolín, Ver.	....	1	....	....	....	1	....	....	....
Isthmus region									
Tonalá, Ver.	302	271	246	233	239	214	217	209	201
El Plan, Ver.	580	422	411	502	490	602	706	633	601
Filisola, Ver.	52	56	58	54	49	39	40	44	45
Teapa, Ver.	....	10	8	4	....	....	2	2	1
Acalapa, Ver.	9	57	35	36	56	73	57	77	96
Ixhuatlán, Ver.	....	....	1	1	....	....	....	....	8
Northeast region									
Reynosa, Camargo	....	....	....	....	....	....	....	11	41
Total[a]	6,845	5,535	5,590	6,074	6,923	7,828	8,948	9,302	8,923

[a] There may be slight discrepancies in totals due to rounding.
SOURCE: Secretaría de Economía Nacional, *Memoria*.

TABLE 4

DEVELOPMENTAL AND EXPLORATORY WELLS DRILLED UNDER AUSPICES OF PEMEX,
BY REGIONS, 1938–1950

	Region				Total
	North of Tampico	South of Tampico	Isthmus	Poza Rica	
1938					
Developmental..............	9	0	7	2	18
Exploratory.................	0	0	0	0	0
1939					
Developmental..............	7	1	10	8	26
Exploratory.................	0	0	0	0	0
1940					
Developmental..............	8	1	8	8	25
Exploratory.................	0	0	0	0	0
1941					
Developmental..............	6	0	11	4	21
Exploratory.................	0	0	0	0	0
1942					
Developmental..............	9	2	0	4	15
Exploratory.................	0	0	0	0	0
1943					
Developmental..............	8	0	5	5	18
Exploratory.................	1	1	1	0	3
1944					
Developmental..............	11	0	16	5	32
Exploratory.................	1	1	0	0	2
1945					
Developmental..............	16	3	14	6	39
Exploratory.................	2	5	3	0	10
1946					
Developmental..............	8	4	18	8	38
Exploratory.................	7	0	4	0	11
1947					
Developmental..............	8	1	14	9	32
Exploratory.................	7	5	6	0	18
1948					
Developmental..............	20	12	16	15	63
Exploratory.................	3	8	6	0	17
1949					
Developmental..............	54	46	38	7	145
Exploratory.................	6	1	6	0	13
1950					
Developmental..............	58	89	37	26	210
Exploratory.................	3	2	2	0	7
Total					
Developmental..............	222	159	194	107	682
Exploratory.................	30	23	28	0	81
Grand Total.................	252	182	222	107	763

SOURCES: 1938–1946, Pemex. 1947–1948, *World Oil*, International Section. 1949–1950, *World Oil*, July 15, 1951.

TABLE 5

REFINERY CAPACITY IN MEXICO, BY REFINERIES, 1937

Refinery	Owner	Daily input capacity in barrels	Type of plant
Arbol Grande...................	Sinclair Pierce Oil Company	10,330	Complete
Mata Redonda..................	Huasteca	24,000	Complete
Ciudad Madero.................	"El Aguila"	50,000	Complete
Minatitlán....................	"El Aguila"	30,000	Complete
Atzcapotzalco.................	"El Aguila"	7,500	Topping
Bella Vista...................	Mexican Govt.	2,000	Topping
Laredo Refinery...............	Independent	160	Topping
Mexico Refinery...............	Independent	60	Topping
Union Refinery................	Independent	160	Topping
Santa Catarina Refinery.......	Independent	190	Topping
Total....................		124,400	

SOURCE: *Mexico's Oil*, pp. 113–117.

TABLE 6

Products Obtained from Refinement of Petroleum in Mexico, 1936–1950
(In thousands of cubic meters)

Product	1936	1937	1938	1939	1940	1941	1942	1943
Petroleum and derivatives submitted to distillation[a]	6,430	7,091	6,866	6,770	6,367	7,006	6,634	7,193
Derived products	6,173	6,838	6,672	6,557	6,154	6,773	6,441	7,052
Losses	257	253	195	213	214	233	193	141
Derivative products:								
Fuel oil	3,106	3,271	2,944	2,906	2,928	3,192	2,889	3,156
Gas oil	606	620	512	660	644	681	707	794
Crude gasoline	421	765	1,709	1,623	1,313	1,570	1,498	1,435
Refined gasoline	1,106	1,154	837	794	662	706	733	874
Crude kerosene	115	138	270	287	281	313	350	423
Refined kerosene	113	133	53	58	78	84	80	88
Oil and grease	91	83	58	40	56	29	39	49
Crude paraffin	6	1	1	1	1	2	2	4
Refined paraffin	19	18	18	17	16	15	14	14
Asphalt	360	551	209	127	129	106	92	160
Gas	.....	.....	.....	.....	.....	.....	.....	.....
Miscellaneous	230	106	60	43	45	75	39	55
Total products of refinement[a]	6,173	6,840	6,672	6,557	6,154	6,773	6,441	7,052

[a] There may be slight discrepancies due to rounding.
SOURCES: 1936–1945, Compendio estadístico. 1946–1950, Secretaría de Economía Nacional, Memoria.

TABLE 6—*Continued*

Product	1944	1945	1946	1947	1948	1949	1950
Petroleum and derivatives submitted to distillation[a]	7,715	8,344	9,206	10,655	10,359	11,218	11,671
Derived products	7,556	8,161	9,023	10,485	10,206	11,037	11,472
Losses	159	183	183	170	153	181	199
Derivative products:							
Fuel oil	3,500	3,749	4,096	4,910	4,848	5,156	5,360
Gas oil	792	809	800	876	778	922	926
Crude gasoline	1,545	1,650	1,834	1,999	1,801	1,858	1,828
Refined gasoline	873	950	1,032	1,346	1,456	1,662	1,823
Crude kerosene	444	461	497	582	600	678	728
Refined kerosene	135	226	261	332	373	397	423
Oil and grease	58	56	53	57	65	65	59
Crude paraffin	11	18	16	16	19	19	22
Refined paraffin	15	17	17	17	15	14	14
Asphalt	132	170	352	258	60	69	66
Gas	……	1	1	31	120	138	172
Miscellaneous	51	55	63	62	70	60	52
Total products of refinement[a]	7,556	8,161	9,023	10,485	10,206	11,037	11,472

[a] There may be slight discrepancies due to rounding.
SOURCES: 1936–1945, *Compendio estadístico*. 1946–1950, Secretaría de Economía Nacional, *Memoria*.

TABLE 7

REFINERY CAPACITY IN MEXICO, BY REFINERIES, 1948

(In barrels)

Refinery	Daily input capacity	Cracking capacity
Ciudad Madero......................	55,000	8,500
Atzcapotzalco......................	50,000	11,070
Minatitlán..........................	27,500	2,500
Arbol Grande.......................	20,500	......
Mata Redonda......................	11,500	5,500
Poza Rica..........................	6,400	......
Total...........................	170,900	27,570
Salamanca (under construction).......	30,000	......

SOURCES: Adapted from *World Oil*, July 15, 1949, p. 93, and from records of Pemex.

TABLE 8

ANNUAL REFINERY OUTPUT OF MEXICAN REFINERIES AS GIVEN BY OFFICIAL GOVERNMENT SOURCES, COMPARED TO ANNUAL OUTPUT OF PEMEX AS PUBLISHED BY THE LATTER, 1938–1948

(In millions of barrels)

Year	Government figure[a]	Figure of Pemex[b]	Approximate discrepancy[c]
1938........................	42.0	33.7	8.3
1939........................	41.3	31.8	9.5
1940........................	38.7	29.9	8.8
1941........................	42.6	34.9	7.7
1942........................	40.5	33.0	7.5
1943........................	44.4	34.4	10.0
1944........................	47.5	35.9	11.6
1945........................	51.3	39.2	12.1
1946........................	56.7	44.0	12.7
1947........................	65.9	46.4	19.5
1948........................	64.2	47.6	16.6

SOURCES:
[a] Total production of Mexican refineries as given in *Memoria* of Secretaría de Economía.
[b] Production of Pemex as shown in records of Pemex and annual reports of the general director.
[c] Discrepancy is only approximate because of rounding and because of small amounts of production by independent refineries for which data are not available.

TABLE 9

MOVEMENTS OF GASOLINE AND FUEL OIL BY RAIL IN CARLOAD LOTS, 1937–1947

Year	Gasoline		Fuel oil	
	Thousands of metric tons	Millions of metric ton-kilometers	Thousands of metric tons	Millions of metric ton-kilometers
1937........................	266	155.1	450	135.3
1938........................	235	140.6	582	190.7
1939........................	242	149.4	654	229.7
1940........................	250	164.4	767	350.0
1941........................	272	172.9	849	369.0
1942........................	330	194.6	635	250.2
1943........................	324	211.7	825	308.7
1944........................	299	168.7	705	291.8
1945........................	338	186.5	901	408.3
1946........................	339	193.3	887	443.1
1947........................	401	202.4	1,071	489.2

SOURCE: *Revista de estadística.*

TABLE 10

Annual Physical Volume of Sales of Selected Petroleum Products by Pemex and by Independents, 1938–1947

(In millions of specified units)

Product	1938	1939	1940	1941	1942	1943	1944	1945	1946	1947	Total	Per cent
Gasoline (liters):												
Pemex	477.5	535.1	597.4	700.6	773.7	830.6	836.1	949.3	1,163.1	1,358.2	8,221.6	92.2
Independents	28.0	33.3	34.2	43.3	56.8	75.8	72.2	88.1	119.4	135.4	686.5	7.8
Total	505.5	568.4	631.6	743.9	830.5	906.4	908.3	1,037.4	1,282.5	1,493.6	8,908.1	100.0
Fuel oil (liters):												
Pemex	1,929.9	2,033.8	2,077.5	2,216.3	2,404.1	2,737.6	2,936.7	3,089.3	3,369.3	3,556.1	26,350.6	95.5
Independents	180.9	104.3	157.7	69.8	87.6	112.0	122.6	114.7	157.6	150.3	1,257.5	4.5
Total	2,110.8	2,138.1	2,235.2	2,286.1	2,491.7	2,849.6	3,059.3	3,204.0	3,526.9	3,706.4	27,608.1	100.0
Gas oil (liters):												
Pemex	88.8	105.0	104.0	119.2	129.2	144.5	153.6	169.8	218.3	273.7	1,506.1	91.2
Independents	17.1	8.7	7.4	18.4	8.4	9.5	12.3	15.5	17.5	31.1	145.9	8.8
Total	105.9	113.7	111.4	137.6	137.6	154.0	165.9	185.3	235.8	304.8	1,652.0	100.0
Kerosene (liters):												
Pemex	29.0	33.0	40.7	46.2	57.1	73.7	119.3	212.7	251.3	469.8	1,332.8	91.2
Independents	7.7	8.2	9.3	9.7	9.5	7.8	10.7	18.8	26.4	21.1	129.2	8.8
Total	36.7	41.2	50.0	55.9	66.6	81.5	130.0	231.5	877.7	490.9	1,462.0	100.0
Lubricating oil (liters):												
Pemex	25.6	27.0	26.6	26.5	30.5	35.1	35.9	40.7	41.2	44.2	333.3	59.7
Independents	9.5	9.9	14.9	18.3	14.8	21.6	22.7	31.8	35.3	46.4	225.2	40.3
Total	35.1	36.9	41.5	44.8	45.3	56.7	58.6	72.5	76.5	90.6	558.5	100.0
Grease (kilograms):												
Pemex	2.1	2.2	2.1	2.2	2.6	2.9	2.7	3.0	3.1	3.1	26.1	53.6
Independents	.8	1.0	1.3	1.9	2.2	2.2	2.6	3.1	4.2	3.3	22.6	46.4
Total	2.9	3.2	3.4	4.1	4.8	5.1	5.3	6.1	7.3	6.4	48.7	100.0

TABLE 11
ANNUAL PHYSICAL VOLUME OF SALES BY PEMEX, BY PRODUCTS, 1938–1946
(In millions of units)

Product	1938	1939	1940	1941	1942	1943	1944	1945	1946	Total	Per cent[a]
Asphalt (kilograms)	180.4	149.2	163.6	127.8	123.7	98.4	80.6	76.6	124.9	1,125.2	2.49
Fuel oil (liters)	2,458.4	2,596.1	2,878.5	2,915.1	2,686.3	3,214.8	3,290.2	3,706.5	4,055.3	27,801.2	55.38
Crude oil (liters)	724.3	1,363.4	1,361.1	1,202.3	490.9	218.2	104.2	386.6	524.9	6,375.9	12.70
Gasoline (liters)	850.6	790.9	732.1	877.9	836.2	832.0	836.4	949.6	1,163.2	7,868.9	15.67
Gas oil (liters)	514.0	439.4	664.1	451.4	254.8	356.0	470.5	456.7	470.7	4,077.6	8.12
Gas (kilograms)	.8	1.4	2.3	4.0	5.2	6.2	6.9	7.9	9.6	44.3	0.10
Greases (kilograms)	2.1	2.2	2.1	2.2	2.6	2.9	2.7	3.0	3.1	22.9	0.05
Insecticides (liters)	b	b	b	.2	.2	.3	.3	.5	.3	1.8	b
Kerosene (liters)	52.6	40.7	73.5	76.3	57.3	74.1	119.1	212.9	251.4	957.9	1.91
Lubricating oil (liters)	39.6	27.3	26.8	26.6	30.5	35.0	35.9	40.7	41.1	303.5	0.60
Paraffin (kilograms)	21.7	16.4	11.8	14.4	17.4	12.3	12.9	11.6	14.1	132.6	0.29
Solvents (liters)	b	b	2.4	3.5	3.4	3.4	4.8	6.3	7.8	31.6	0.06
Tractomex (liters)	92.1	100.0	113.7	135.9	166.3	189.7	196.8	156.1	169.5	1,320.1	2.63
Miscellaneous (various)	b	.2	.2	.1	b	b	b	.1	b	.6	b
											100.0

a Percentages figured on basis of 1 kilogram equal to 1.1 liters.
b Less than one-half the unit specified.
SOURCE: Basic data from Pemex.

TABLE 12

ANNUAL GROSS VALUE OF SALES BY PEMEX, BY PRODUCTS, 1938–1946

(In millions of pesos)

Product	1938	1939	1940	1941	1942	1943	1944	1945	1946	Total	Per cent
Asphalt	8.5	7.0	7.5	6.0	6.8	5.7	6.0	5.9	10.9	64.3	2.10
Fuel oil	43.2	47.5	55.2	56.5	51.6	66.7	73.3	93.6	126.8	614.4	20.07
Crude oil	14.5	35.0	31.8	26.6	11.0	7.7	3.4	10.9	17.4	158.3	5.17
Gasoline	96.3	99.4	111.6	131.3	140.6	157.7	174.4	212.4	273.7	1,397.4	45.64
Gas oil	23.2	23.0	36.7	25.2	17.2	25.1	33.0	31.9	34.8	250.1	8.19
Gas	0.4	0.6	0.9	1.6	2.0	2.4	2.8	3.4	4.1	18.2	0.59
Greases	0.9	1.2	1.3	1.3	1.5	1.9	1.8	2.0	2.7	14.6	0.48
Insecticides	......	......	0.4	0.3	0.3	0.5	0.5	0.7	0.5	3.2	0.10
Kerosene	5.5	5.4	7.7	8.2	7.5	9.6	14.6	25.5	32.5	116.5	3.80
Lubricating oil	11.8	11.1	11.9	12.1	14.6	18.3	18.5	21.1	23.0	142.4	4.65
Paraffin	9.7	8.1	8.3	9.7	15.3	12.0	18.7	19.2	23.1	124.1	4.05
Solvents	......	......	0.7	1.0	0.9	0.9	1.4	1.9	2.3	9.1	0.30
Tractomex	7.3	9.0	10.3	12.2	14.8	17.2	18.3	16.4	18.6	124.1	4.05
Miscellaneous	2.3	2.0	1.3	2.0	2.2	3.9	3.7	3.9	4.3	25.6	0.84
Total	223.6	249.3	285.6	294.0	286.3	329.6	370.4	448.8	574.7	3,062.3	100.03

SOURCE: Basic data from Pemex.

TABLE 13

ANNUAL PHYSICAL VOLUME OF DOMESTIC SALES BY PEMEX, BY PRODUCTS, 1938–1946

(In millions of units)

Product	1938	1939	1940	1941	1942	1943	1944	1945	1946	Total[a]	Per cent[b]
Asphalt (kilograms)	53.3	72.1	82.2	63.3	81.6	90.6	71.4	73.2	72.6	660.3	1.93
Fuel oil (liters)	1,929.9	2,033.8	2,077.5	2,216.3	2,404.1	2,737.6	2,936.7	3,089.4	3,369.3	22,794.6	66.54
Crude oil (liters)	....	....	....	....	....	....	....	....	....	....	....
Gasoline (liters)	477.4	535.1	597.5	700.6	773.7	830.6	836.1	949.3	1,163.1	6,866.3	20.04
Gas oil (liters)	88.8	105.0	104.0	119.2	129.2	144.5	153.6	169.8	218.2	1,232.3	3.60
Gas (kilograms)	0.8	1.4	2.3	4.0	5.2	6.2	6.9	7.9	9.6	44.3	0.13
Greases (kilograms)	2.1	2.2	2.1	2.2	2.6	2.9	2.7	3.0	3.1	22.9	0.07
Insecticides (liters)	....	....	0.3	0.2	0.2	0.3	0.3	0.5	0.3	2.1	0.01
Kerosene (liters)	29.0	33.0	40.7	46.2	57.1	73.7	118.9	212.7	251.3	862.6	2.52
Lubricating oil (liters)	25.6	27.0	26.7	26.5	30.5	35.0	35.9	40.7	41.1	289.0	0.84
Paraffin (kilograms)	21.7	16.4	11.8	14.4	17.4	12.3	12.9	11.6	14.1	132.6	0.39
Solvents (liters)	....	....	2.4	3.5	3.4	3.4	4.8	6.3	7.8	31.6	0.09
Tractomex (liters)	92.1	100.0	113.7	135.9	166.3	189.7	196.8	156.1	169.5	1,320.1	3.85
Miscellaneous (kilograms)	....	....	0.1	....	....	....	....	....	....	0.1	....

[a] Small discrepancies in totals are due to rounding.
[b] Percentages computed on the basis of 1 kilogram equal to 1.1 liters.
SOURCE: Basic data from Pemex.

TABLE 14

GROSS VALUE OF DOMESTIC SALES BY PEMEX, BY PRODUCTS, 1938–1946

(In millions of pesos)

Product	1938	1939	1940	1941	1942	1943	1944	1945	1946	Total[a]	Per cent
Asphalt	2.44	3.17	3.69	3.31	4.18	5.18	4.59	5.33	5.34	37.23	1.47
Fuel oil	31.37	34.04	34.23	38.97	42.46	51.86	61.76	75.24	99.49	469.42	18.58
Crude oil	...	...	...	...	...	...	...	...	...	...	...
Gasoline	79.53	88.89	105.13	124.30	137.93	157.44	174.34	212.37	273.67	1,353.60	53.59
Gas oil	7.08	7.40	7.60	8.93	9.74	11.09	12.12	14.18	18.37	96.51	3.82
Gas	0.36	0.57	0.94	1.61	2.02	2.37	2.76	3.41	4.07	18.11	0.72
Greases	0.94	1.20	1.29	1.32	1.53	1.89	1.75	1.96	2.72	14.60	0.58
Insecticides	...	...	0.40	0.28	0.32	0.51	0.54	0.74	0.45	3.24	0.13
Kerosene	4.33	4.77	5.76	6.48	7.46	9.53	14.62	25.48	32.47	110.90	4.39
Lubricating oil	9.28	11.02	11.87	12.04	14.60	18.28	18.45	21.12	23.04	139.70	5.53
Paraffin	9.71	8.06	8.32	9.70	15.34	11.96	18.72	19.19	23.12	124.12	4.91
Solvents	...	...	0.67	0.98	0.93	0.92	1.41	1.89	2.35	9.15	0.36
Tractomex	7.34	9.03	10.25	12.24	14.85	17.21	18.28	16.41	18.60	124.21	4.92
Miscellaneous	2.28	1.81	1.22	1.95	2.02	3.92	3.66	3.86	4.29	25.01	0.99
Total	154.66	169.95	191.37	222.11	253.39	292.18	333.01	401.19	507.99	2,525.80	99.99

[a] Small discrepancies in totals are due to rounding.
SOURCE: Basic data from Pemex.

TABLE 15

VALUE AND PHYSICAL VOLUME OF DOMESTIC SALES OF PEMEX,
BY PRODUCTS, 1947

Product	Millions of units	Millions of pesos
Asphalt.........................	98.6 kilograms	6.8
Fuel oil........................	3,556.1 liters	135.8
Gasoline.......................	1,358.2 liters	348.3
Gas oil........................	273.7 liters	26.0
Gas...........................	11.4 kilograms	5.6
Greases.......................	3.2 kilograms	2.8
Insecticides....................	a	0.4
Kerosene......................	469.8 liters	35.6
Lubricating oil.................	44.2 liters	26.2
Paraffin.......................	13.5 kilograms	21.4
Solvents.......................	a	2.5
Tractomex.....................	b	23.3
Miscellaneous..................	10.8 liters	3.4
Total......................		638.1

a Included in miscellaneous.
b Included in kerosene.
SOURCE: Basic data from Pemex.

TABLE 16
ANNUAL PHYSICAL VOLUME OF EXPORT SALES BY PEMEX, BY PRODUCTS, 1938–1946
(In millions of units)

Product	1938	1939	1940	1941	1942	1943	1944	1945	1946	Total[a]	Per cent
Asphalt (kilograms)	127.1	77.1	81.4	64.5	42.1	7.7	9.3	3.5	52.3	465.0	2.94
Fuel oil (liters)	528.5	562.3	801.0	698.8	282.2	477.2	353.5	617.1	686.1	5,006.7	31.67
Crude oil (liters)	724.3	1,363.4	1,361.1	1,202.3	490.9	218.2	104.2	386.6	524.9	6,375.9	40.33
Gasoline (liters)	373.1	255.9	134.6	177.3	62.5	1.5	0.3	b	b	1,005.5	6.36
Gas oil (liters)	425.2	334.4	560.0	332.2	125.6	211.5	316.9	286.9	252.5	2,845.2	18.00
Kerosene (liters)	23.6	7.7	32.8	30.0	0.2	0.2	0.2	0.2	b	94.9	0.60
Lubricating oil (liters)	14.0	0.3	0.1	b	b	b	b	b	b	14.6	0.09
Miscellaneous (various)	b	b	b	b	b	b	0.1	0.2	0.2	0.5	b

[a] Small discrepancies in totals are due to rounding.
b Less than one-half the unit specified.
SOURCE: Basic data from Pemex.

TABLE 17
ANNUAL GROSS VALUE OF EXPORT SALES BY PEMEX, BY PRODUCTS, 1938–1946
(In millions of pesos)

Product	1938	1939	1940	1941	1942	1943	1944	1945	1946	Total	Per cent
Asphalt	6.07	3.85	3.85	2.73	2.57	0.50	1.38	0.53	5.57	27.05	5.04
Fuel oil	11.84	13.50	20.96	17.48	9.16	14.82	11.57	18.40	27.29	145.02	27.03
Crude oil	14.50	35.02	31.76	26.57	11.01	7.70	3.43	10.86	17.44	158.29	29.51
Gasoline	16.74	10.46	6.48	7.03	2.64	0.22	0.03	0.03	a	43.63	8.13
Gas oil	16.10	15.62	29.12	16.27	7.49	14.06	20.90	17.74	16.40	153.70	28.65
Kerosene	1.16	0.61	1.93	1.75	0.04	0.06	0.01	0.02	a	5.58	1.04
Lubricating oil	2.50	0.01	0.03	0.02	0.02	a	a	a	a	2.58	0.48
Miscellaneous	0.03	0.32	0.13	0.08	0.03	0.08	0.03	0.04	0.02	0.76	0.14
Total	68.94	79.39	94.26	71.93	32.96	37.44	37.35	47.62	66.72	536.61	100.02

a Less than one-half the unit specified.
SOURCE: Basic data from Pemex.

TABLE 18

COMPONENTS OF LABOR COSTS PAID BY PEMEX, 1936–1946[a]
(In thousands of pesos)

Account	1936	1937	1938	1939	1940	1941	1942	1943	1944	1945	1946[f]
Wages and salaries	45,066	49,454	60,219	81,240	82,506	78,900	86,138	89,844	123,378	153,631	180,314
Savings fund	1,921	3,089	4,517	7,246	6,750	6,686	7,561	7,618	10,103	12,244	14,308
Housing allowance	584	1,720	2,243	5,707	5,566	6,241	5,551	5,898	7,915	12,127	14,228
Indemnities[b]	416	230	129	218	428	755	950	839	1,040	2,378	2,790
Medical service[c]	633	683	1,181	2,767	4,243	2,895	2,792	3,429	4,033	4,497	5,278
Syndicate expenses[d]	......	......	65	295	221	156	203	198	351	475	558
Other benefits[e]	517	576	326	275	249	303	329	708	927	1,317	1,546
Total[g]	49,136	55,752	68,681	97,749	99,962	95,935	103,524	108,534	147,746	186,671	219,021

[a] Figures prior to expropriation apply to the eighteen expropriated companies, with the exception of the Mexican Gulf Petroleum Company. Figures for 1938–1940, inclusive, include payments by the General Administration of National Petroleum.
[b] Includes benefits for death, accidents, and occupational sickness.
[c] Includes medicines, hospital costs, salaries of medical personnel, etc.
[d] Includes wages and salaries of syndicate officers, and travel and subsistence allowances.
[e] Includes expenses of pensions, schools, scholarships, laundry, special clothing, and various improvements for employees.
[f] Estimates. They do not include certain additional retroactive payments for equalization of wages made by agreement between labor and management.
[g] Small discrepancies in totals are due to rounding.
SOURCE: Records of Pemex.

TABLE 19

ANNUAL VALUE OF MEXICAN EXPORTS OF GASOLINE, KEROSENE, AND LUBRICANTS, 1934–1950
(In millions of pesos)

Product	1934	1935	1936	1937	1938	1939	1940	1941	1942	1943	1944	1945	1946	1947	1948	1949	1950
Gasoline	37.0	41.8	46.62	49.02	22.68	9.36	3.12	6.05	2.68	0.43	0.12	0.25	0.19	1.26	31.69	2.46	7.08
Kerosene	7.6	6.3	4.32	5.40	0.92	0.26	8.20	14.45	4.92	9.90	13.79	9.65	6.74	4.13	21.74	10.34	25.65
Lubricants	17.9	20.5	12.22	12.77	2.51	0.14	0.16	0.05	0.06	0.09	0.04	0.05	0.10	0.07	0.10	0.27	0.47
Total	62.5	68.6	63.16	67.19	26.11	9.76	11.48	20.55	7.66	10.42	13.95	9.95	7.03	5.46	53.53	13.07	33.20

SOURCE: *Anuario estadístico del comercio exterior.*

TABLE 20

VOLUME OF ANNUAL MEXICAN IMPORTS OF PETROLEUM PRODUCTS, 1936–1950

(In thousands of units[a])

Product	1936	1937	1938	1939	1940	1941	1942	1943	1944	1945	1946	1947	1948	1949	1950
Crude oil (liters)	39,096	14,159	9,485	15,398	17,784	19,893	16,311	12,866	9,982	12,277	23,925	31,242	51,878	7,135	4
Gas oil (liters)	b	b	b	b	3,992	13,142	4,718	6,672	11,839	16,264	18,616	31,151	12,315	21,738	21,397
Fuel oil (liters)	b	b	b	b	86,980	29,831	20,615	33,391	53,149	51,736	110,296	140,161	165,761	150,404	127,874
Gasoline (liters)	19,904	19,959	11,899	12,466	11,418	59,658	58,490	37,901	57,781	75,898	164,476	201,275	253,050	206,944	197,829
Kerosene (liters)	878	730	447	63	e	e	11	26	269	1,133	3,092	1,237	1,975	4,996	8,330
Natural gas[f] (liters)	c	c	c	c	3,765	7,563	10,636	18,457	23,275	33,724	51,136	51,720	50,364	50,622	81,950
Natural gas[f] (kilograms)	301	616	971	1,545	d	d	d	d	d	d	d	d	d	d	d
Kerosene (kilograms)	1,770	1,002	338	664	974	1,051	1,481	2,593	3,988	4,680	7,814	7,463	1,975	b	b
Signal oil (kilograms)	10	5	e	e	e	e	2	2	e	e	1	2	52	1	e
Lub. oil (kilograms)	10,318	14,196	7,855	8,744	13,350	19,342	17,710	26,602	29,159	40,501	38,073	46,489	42,088	50,368	59,626
Greases (kilograms)	756	1,139	710	898	1,207	1,747	1,995	1,950	2,362	2,817	3,797	3,879	3,466	4,501	4,973
Paraffin (kilograms)	4,987	12,153	9,173	11,311	10,984	15,694	3,171	3,980	8,349	4,812	12,893	12,816	16,504	23,417	31,351
Vaseline (kilograms)	319	456	223	412	329	396	302	402	955	680	1,066	578	608	525	1,206
Asphalt (kilograms)	730	873	488	192	97	166	211	795	1,479	365	3,112	6,068	6,583	9,528	6,775

[a] Kilograms are gross weight.
[b] Data not available.
[c] Imports given by weight, 1936–1939. See following item.
[d] Imports given by volume, 1940–1950. See preceding item.
[e] Less than one-half the unit specified.
[f] Liquefied gas. Does not include gas imported by pipeline.

SOURCE: *Anuario estadístico del comercio exterior.*

TABLE 21

VALUE OF ANNUAL MEXICAN IMPORTS OF PETROLEUM PRODUCTS, 1936–1948

(In thousands of pesos)

Product	1936	1937	1938	1939	1940	1941	1942	1943	1944	1945	1946	1947	1948
Crude oil........	880	537	381	706	774	840	654	458	402	496	1,056	1,997	3,547
Gas oil..........	380	646	636	297	191	481	295	518	867	1,289	1,323	2,911	1,585
Gasoline........	1,393	1,474	1,089	1,291	1,202	3,893	6,226	4,710	6,999	9,556	19,152	23,731	38,967
Fuel oil.........	1,967	3,933	4,459	925	3,394	911	706	1,179	1,960	1,968	5,226	8,211	15,024
Liquid gas.......	25	80	99	132	242	636	596	915	1,410	1,772	3,880	5,016	5,891
Kerosene........	184	133	69	43	69	80	94	164	261	295	746	581	330
Lubricating oil..	2,741	3,738	2,902	3,998	5,369	7,705	8,116	11,506	13,423	18,716	18,562	26,333	28,302
Greases.........	381	442	508	663	955	1,093	1,304	1,217	1,618	1,856	3,294	3,336	3,780
Paraffin........	1,341	3,282	2,606	3,561	5,201	6,432	1,796	2,567	4,624	2,768	8,376	9,582	12,152
Vaseline........	120	179	108	195	178	210	180	191	530	346	624	397	376
Asphalt.........	61	141	43	47	30	41	61	91	109	81	389	523	535
Natural gas.....	2,349	2,239	1,096	2,169	1,840	2,494	2,612	3,685	5,316	8,484	10,009	9,417	9,792
Total........	11,822	16,824	13,996	14,027	19,445	24,816	22,640	27,201	37,519	47,627	71,649	92,035	120,281

SOURCE: *Anuario estadístico del comercio exterior.*

TABLE 22

Labor Costs in the Various Branches of Pemex, 1938–1946

(In thousands of pesos)

Branch	1938	1939	1940	1941	1942	1943	1944	1945	1946
Production	26,390	37,426	38,415	34,258	35,208	38,409	55,065	68,418	80,275
Refining	27,896	39,808	42,154	44,740	42,555	44,402	58,669	76,814	90,124
Sales	4,841	6,933	7,121	7,321	7,628	8,308	11,424	13,489	15,826
Administration	6,700	9,444	9,638	9,616	10,328	11,592	14,414	19,362	22,721
Ship crews	b	b	b	b	7,805	5,822	8,173	8,588	10,075
AGPN[a]	2,854	4,138	2,636	c					
Total	68,681	97,749	99,964	95,935	103,524	108,533	147,745	186,671	219,021

[a] General Administration of National Petroleum.
[b] Presumably included in other categories before 1942.
[c] Absorbed by Pemex in 1940.
Source: Records of Pemex.

TABLE 23

Annual Petroleum Taxes Paid by Pemex, by Type of Levy, 1941–1947

(In thousands of pesos)

Tax	1941	1942	1943	1944	1945	1946	1947
Production	6,950	2,968	3,050	2,636	5,758	9,353	23,542
Export	2,804	1,088	806	724	1,259	1,357	2,512
Aforo[a]	1,022	532	3,317	3,891	4,937	6,957	13,883
General import	1,971	2,487	2,155	2,974	4,668	3,514	5,800
Gasoline import	314	222	527	773	1,789	16,851	26,475
Gasoline consumption	62,777	69,045	82,874	81,115	90,616	98,496	108,724
Others	323	161	155	138	174	168	250
Total	76,161	76,503	92,884	92,251	109,201	136,696	181,186

[a] A special export tax on minerals introduced in 1938.
Source: Pemex.

TABLE 24

Each Refinery Product as a Percentage of Annual Refinery Production, 1936–1950

Product	1936	1937	1938	1939	1940	1941	1942	1943	1944	1945	1946	1947	1948	1949	1950
Fuel oil	50.3	47.8	44.2	44.3	47.6	47.1	44.9	44.7	46.3	45.9	45.4	46.8	47.5	46.7	46.7
Gas oil	9.8	9.1	7.7	10.1	10.5	10.1	11.0	11.3	10.5	9.9	8.9	8.4	7.6	8.3	8.1
Crude gasoline	6.8	11.2	25.6	24.7	21.3	23.2	23.2	20.4	20.4	20.2	20.3	19.1	17.6	16.8	15.9
Refined gasoline	17.9	16.9	12.5	12.1	10.8	10.4	11.4	12.4	11.6	11.6	11.5	12.8	14.3	15.1	15.9
Crude kerosene	1.9	2.0	4.0	4.4	4.6	4.6	5.4	6.0	5.9	5.7	5.5	5.6	5.9	6.1	6.3
Refined kerosene	1.8	1.9	0.8	0.9	1.3	1.2	1.2	1.2	1.8	2.8	2.9	3.2	3.7	3.6	3.7
Oil and grease	1.5	1.2	0.9	0.6	0.9	0.4	0.6	0.7	0.8	0.7	0.6	0.5	0.6	0.6	0.5
Crude paraffin	0.1	.....	.....	.....	.....	.....	.....	0.1	0.1	0.2	0.2	0.1	0.2	0.2	0.2
Refined paraffin	0.3	0.3	0.3	0.3	0.3	0.2	0.2	0.2	0.2	0.2	0.2	0.2	0.1	0.1	0.1
Asphalt	5.8	8.1	3.1	1.9	2.1	1.6	1.4	2.3	1.7	2.1	3.9	2.5	0.6	0.6	0.6
Gas	.....	.....	.....	.....	.....	.....	.....	.....	.....	.....	.....	0.3	1.2	1.3	1.5
Miscellaneous	3.7	1.6	0.9	0.7	0.7	1.1	0.6	0.8	0.7	0.7	0.7	0.6	0.7	0.5	0.5
Total	99.9	100.1	100.1	100.0	100.1	99.9	99.9	100.1	100.0	100.0	100.1	100.1	100.0	99.9	100.0

Source: Appendix table 6.

Appendix C

PEMEX BALANCE SHEETS

1. December 31, 1945
2. August 31, 1946
3. December 31, 1947

Current assets and working capital
Cash

On hand and in banks..................................	13,308	
In domestic and foreign agencies........................	645	13,953

Notes and accounts receivable

Notes and accounts receivable, less reserve for bad debts.	19,353	
Accounts receivable for services and sundries, less reserve for bad debts.......................................	5,383	
Advances to workmen and expense funds, less reserve for bad debts...	1,638	26,373

Balances held by federal government............................			8,047

Inventories

Crude oil and refined products, net value................		65,627	
Manufactured products................................		4,955	
Other merchandise....................................		1,759	
Stocks of materials and accessories............	108,986		
Less reserve for shortages and obsolescence...	20,000	88,986	161,327

Total current assets and working capital...................		209,700

Investments and securities

Investments at nominal value............................	1,238	
Other investments and securities.........................	8,714	9,952

Guaranty deposits on contracts and sundries, net value...............		2,485
Foreign credits, less reserve for bad debts............................		21,312
Claims against insurance companies and others, less reserve...........		302

Ex-General Administration of National Petroleum

Assets to liquidate.....................................	889	
Liabilities to liquidate.................................	711	178

Fixed Assets	Orig- inal value	Depreciation and amortization	Net book value	
Properties received from the federal government in March, 1938...........	154,538	133,416	21,122	
Properties of the Ex-GANP..............	13,781	13,781		
Land of the Ex-GANP...................	15,673		15,673	
Properties acquired				
Land...............................	1,155		1,155	
Wells..............................	37,642	17,345	20,297	
Field constructions....................	11,725	11,725		
Real estate and chattels...............	251,144	37,487	213,657	
Fleet..............................	18,265	6,832	11,433	
Contracts and subsoil rights..........	131		131	
	503,924	220,587	283,468	283,468
Deferred charges, insurance, taxes, and sundries.......................				2,388
Total assets....................................				529,786

Current liabilities
  Notes payable.. 12,396
  Suppliers.. 1,730
  Guaranty deposits from contractors....................... 231
  Taxes due.. 16,002
  Wages and salaries due................................... 3,274
  Wages and salaries payable............................... 1,797
  Royalties, rent, and interest due........................ 1,217
  Sundry accounts payable.................................. 10,825   47,472

Long-term liabilities
  Bonds held by Nacional Financiera........................ 59,877
  Claims for confiscated ships............................. 6,537
  Liabilities frozen by war................................ 3,508   69,922

        Total current and long-term liabilities....................   117,394

Contingent liabilities
  Due the federal government: 10 per cent of gross
    income payable in accordance with Article 10
    of the law of December 1, 1944, for indemnification
    of the expropriated American companies......... 111,022
    Less future charges to expenses of operation... 111,022
  Liabilities arising from Article 11 of the law of
    December 1, 1944
      Royalties.................................   5,650
      Interest on capital.......................   12,598   18,248

  Provision for miscellaneous obligations....................   43,704   61,952

Special reserves
  Depreciation on confiscated ships........................ 6,881
  Fire insurance on fixed plant............................ 3,567
  Insurance on minor ships................................. 508
  Pensions... 8,000
  Exploration.. 6,434   25,390

Capital and surplus
  Capital.. 324,809
  Surplus.. 241   325,050

        Total liabilities..   529,786

ᵃ Slight discrepancies in totals and subtotals are due to rounding.
SOURCE: *El nacional*, November 26, 1946.

2. General Balance Sheet of Pemex, August 31, 1946[a]
(In thousands of pesos)

Current assets and working capital			
Cash			
On hand and in banks....................................		11,399	
In domestic and foreign agencies.........................		219	11,618
Notes and accounts receivable			
Notes and accounts receivable less reserve for bad debts..		18,569	
Accounts receivable for services and sundries, less reserve			
for bad debts..		6,471	
Advances to workmen and expense funds, less reserve for			
bad debts..		1,353	26,393
Inventories			
Crude oil and refined products...........................		75,194	
Manufactured products..................................		5,829	
Other merchandise......................................		1,362	
Stocks of materials and accessories.............	108,392		
Less reserve for shortages and obsolescence...	19,846	88,546	170,930
Total current assets and working capital....................			208,941
Investments and securities			
Investments at nominal value.............................		20,010	
Other investments and securities..........................		12,128	32,138
Guaranty deposits on contracts and sundries, net value................			2,349
Foreign credits, less reserve for bad debts............................			21,280
Claims against insurance companies and others, less reserve............			2,374
Ex-General Administration of National Petroleum			
Assets to liquidate.......................................		890	
Liabilities to liquidate...................................		711	179

Fixed Assets	Orig-inal value	Depreciation and amortization	Net book value	
Properties received from the federal				
government in March, 1938............	154,440	133,734	20,705	
Properties of the Ex-GANP..............	13,781	13,781		
Land of the Ex-GANP..................	15,673		15,673	
Properties acquired				
Land................................	1,207		1,207	
Wells................................	44,009	20,192	23,817	
Field constructions....................	13,006	13,006		
Real estate and chattels...............	318,713	46,877	271,836	
Fleet................................	20,224	8,082	12,142	
Contracts and subsoil rights...........	122		122	
	581,053	235,672	345,502	345,502
Deferred charges, insurance, taxes, and sundries......................				1,802
Total assets...				614,565

Current liabilities
    Notes payable... 34,431
    Suppliers.. 1,976
    Guaranty deposits on contracts......................... 224
    Taxes due... 21,660
    Wages and salaries due................................ 2,662
    Wages and salaries payable............................ 13,881
    Royalties, rent, and interest due...................... 393
    Sundry accounts payable.............................. 24,383
    Balance due the federal government
       (Principally the 10 per cent of gross revenues payable
        for indemnification of the expropriated companies)...... 20,688   120,298

Long-term liabilities
    Bonds held by Nacional Financiera...................... 29,100
    Claims for confiscated ships........................... 6,537
    Liabilities frozen by war.............................. 3,509   39,145

        Total current and long-term liabilities..................... 159,443
Liabilities subject to adjustment................................... 2,834
Contingent liabilities
    Due the federal government: 10 per cent of gross
      income payable in accordance with Article 10 of
      the law of December 1, 1944, for indemnification
      of the expropriated American companies......... 82,415
        Less future charges to expenses of operation... 82,415
    Liabilities arising from Article 11 of the law of
      December 1, 1944
        Royalties................................. 6,399
        Interest on capital......................... 19,094   25,493

    Provision for miscellaneous obligations.................... 58,673   84,166

Special reserves
    Depreciation on confiscated ships....................... 7,741
    Repairs on confiscated ships............................ 876
    Fire insurance on fixed plant........................... 4,133
    Insurance on minor ships............................... 748
    Pensions.. 8,172
    Exploration... 21,043   42,713

Capital and surplus
    Capital..324,726
    Surplus... 240
    Accounts of credit balance....................... 487,431
    Accounts of debit balance....................... 486,988   443   325,409

        Total liabilities... 614,565

a Slight discrepancies in totals and subtotals are due to rounding.
SOURCE: *El national*, November 29, 1946.

3. General Balance Sheet of Pemex, December 31, 1947[a]

(In thousands of pesos)

Current assets and working capital			
Cash			
On hand and in banks..................................		43,497	
In domestic and foreign agencies........................		106	43,603
Notes and accounts receivable			
Notes and accounts receivable less reserve for bad debts..		42,711	
Accounts receivable for services and sundries, less reserve for bad debts......................................		8,808	
Advances to workmen and expense funds, less reserve for bad debts...		969	52,489
Inventories			
Crude oil and refined products, net value.................		87,554	
Manufactured products................................		6,962	
Other merchandise....................................		982	
Stocks of materials and accessories.............	125,446		
Less reserve for shortages and obsolescence...	20,158	105,288	200,785
Total current assets and working capital...................			296,876
Investments and securities			
Investments at nominal value............................		10,156	
Other investments and securities.........................		654	10,810
Guaranty deposits on contracts and sundries, net value...............			1,310
Foreign credits..		23,386	
Less reserve for bad debts...............................		23,386	
Claims against insurance companies and others..............		6,178	
Less reserve for bad debts...............................		6,178	
Ex-General Administration of National Petroleum			
Assets to liquidate......................................		890	
Liabilities to liquidate..................................		711	179

Fixed Assets	Original value	Depreciation and amortization	Net book value	
Properties received from the federal government in March, 1938............	151,673	132,589	19,083	
Properties of the Ex-GANP.............	13,284	13,284		
Land of the Ex-GANP...................	15,673	15,547	126	
Properties acquired				
Land...............................	13,556		13,556	
Wells...............................	60,981	33,436	27,545	
Field constructions...................	16,038	16,038		
Real estate and chattels..............	406,211	85,630	320,580	
Fleet...............................	27,347	10,212	17,135	
Contracts and subsoil rights...........	156	82	74	
	704,919	306,819	398,100	398,101
Deferred charges, insurance, taxes, and sundries......................				290
Total assets..				707,566

Current liabilities			
Notes payable...		13,627	
Advances to customers.................................		9,572	
Commercial credits through foreign banks.................		24,231	
Suppliers...		7,759	
Freight...		5,552	
Guaranty deposits from contractors......................		271	
Taxes due..		36,014	
Wages and salaries due.................................		3,568	
Wages and salaries payable.............................		2,384	
Royalties, rent, and interest due........................		1,236	
Sundry accounts payable...............................		5,591	109,804
Balance due the federal government.......................			26,609
Total current liabilities.................................			136,412
Long-term liabilities			
Series A bonds, 3 per cent at 6 years..............	51,844		
Series B bonds, 5.14 per cent at 6 years...........	20,606	72,450	
Notes..		25,439	
Claims for confiscated ships............................		6,516	
Liabilities frozen by war...............................		3,508	107,918
Contingent liabilities			
Due the federal government: 10 per cent of gross income payable in accordance with Article 10 of the law of December 1, 1944, for indemnification[b]	796,539		
Less payments made........................	157,728		
	638,811		
Less future charges to expenses of operation...	638,811		
Liabilities arising from Article 11 of the law of December 1, 1944			
Royalties..................................	744		
Interest on capital.........................	4,868	5,612	
Provision for miscellaneous obligations....................		64,558	70,171
Special reserves			
Depreciation and repair of confiscated ships...............		13,621	
Fire insurance on fixed plant............................		4,656	
Insurance on minor ships...............................		1,215	
Pensions and indemnities...............................		14,873	
Exploration..		33,058	67,422
Capital and surplus			
Capital..		323,665	
Profit for the accounting period...................	2,073		
Less deficit from previous periods...............	91	1,982	325,647
Total liabilities..			707,566

a Slight discrepancies in totals and subtotals are due to rounding.
b This account includes payments due the Companía de Petróleo "El Aquila," S.A., and its subsidiaries for expropriation and interest, but it does not include payments due the Mexico-Texas Petrolene and Asphalt Company, Sabino Gordo Petroleum Corporation, and certain others.
SOURCE: *El nacional*, August 7, 1948.

NOTES

Notes

NOTES TO CHAPTER I

[1] "National Economy of Argentina," *Commercial Pan America*, XV (July–Aug., 1946), 27.

NOTES TO CHAPTER II

[1] Henry Bamford Parkes, *A History of Mexico* (Boston, 1938), pp. 139–141, 155.
[2] J. Fred Rippy, *Latin America in World Politics* (New York, 1938), pp. 26–27.
[3] Parkes, *op. cit.*, pp. 146–149.
[4] *Ibid.*, p. 166.
[5] F. A. Kirkpatrick, *Latin America* (New York, 1939), p. 50.
[6] Hubert Howe Bancroft, *History of Mexico* (New York, 1914), pp. 372–375.
[7] Parkes, *op. cit.*, pp. 175–181.
[8] Charles E. Chapman, *Republican Hispanic America* (New York, 1937), pp. 226–227.
[9] *Ibid.*, p. 227.
[10] Parkes, *op. cit.*, pp. 277–282.
[11] *Ibid.*, p. 285.
[12] *Ibid.*, pp. 286–287.
[13] *Ibid.*, p. 287.
[14] *Ibid.*, pp. 292–297.
[15] Harlow S. Person, *Mexican Oil* (New York, 1942), pp. 18–19.
[16] "Reales ordeñanzas para la minería de la Nueva España, 1783," México, Secretaría de Industria, Comercio y Trabajo, *Documentos relacionados can la legislación petrolera mexicana* (México, D.F., 1919), pp. 21–29.
[17] "Código de minas de los Estados Unidos Mexicanos, 22 de noviembre de 1884," *ibid.*, pp. 40–41.
[18] "Ley minera de los Estados Unidos Mexicanos, 4 de junio de 1892," *ibid.*, p. 42.
[19] "Ley del petróleo de 24 de diciembre de 1901," México, Secretaría de Industria, Comercio y Trabajo, *Legislación petrolera* (México, D.F., 1922), pp. 12–16.
[20] "Ley minera de los Estados Unidos Mexicanos, 25 de noviembre de 1909," México, Secretaría de Industria, Comercio y Trabajo, *Documentos relacionados con la legislación petrolera mexicana*, p. 43.
[21] Parkes, *op. cit.*, pp. 298–299. Also see Leopoldo Zea, *Apogeo y decadencia del positivismo en México* (México, D.F., 1944), pp. 242–246.
[22] Parkes, *op. cit.*, pp. 299–300.
[23] *Mexico's Oil* (México, D.F., 1940), p. 11.
[24] *Loc. cit.*
[25] *Loc. cit.*
[26] See appendix table 1.
[27] Kirkpatrick, *op. cit.*, p. 343.
[28] Parkes, *op. cit.*, p. 305.
[29] Charles Wilson Hackett, *The Mexican Revolution and the United States, 1910–1926*, World Peace Foundation Pamphlets, Vol. IX, no. 5 (1926), p. 339.
[30] Parkes, *op. cit.*, pp. 309–310.
[31] Ernest Gruening, *Mexico and Its Heritage* (New York, 1928), p. 104.
[32] Parkes, *op. cit.*, p. 310.
[33] Marjorie Ruth Clark, *Organized Labor in Mexico* (Chapel Hill, 1934), p. 6.
[34] Parkes, *op. cit.*, pp. 307–308.

[35] Hackett, *op. cit.*, p. 339.

[36] *Documentos de la revolución mexicana*, México, Secretaría de Educación Pública (México, D.F., 1945), pp. 7–16.

[37] Gruening, *op. cit.*, pp. 91–93.

[38] *Ibid.*, pp. 93–94.

[39] Hackett, *op. cit.*, pp. 339–342.

[40] Gruening, *op. cit.*, p. 95.

[41] "Ley de dotaciones y restituciones, 6 de enero de 1915," México, Secretaría de Educación Pública, *op. cit.*, pp. 76–83.

[42] "Pacto de la Casa del Obrero Mundial," *ibid.*, pp. 83–86.

[43] Art. 27, sec. 1.

[44] Art. 27, secs. 8–18.

[45] Art. 27, par. 2.

[46] Arts. 3, 130, and 27, sec. 2.

[47] Parkes, *op. cit.*, p. 362.

[48] Hackett, *op. cit.*, p. 350.

[49] *Ibid.*, pp. 351–353.

[50] *La verdad sobre la expropiación de los bienes de las empresas petroleras* (México, D.F., 1940), p. 47.

[51] *Ibid.*, pp. 45–47.

[52] Hackett, *op. cit.*, pp. 360–371.

[53] *La verdad sobre la expropiación de los bienes de las empresas petroleras*, pp. 47–48.

[54] *Ibid.*, p. 51.

[55] *Ibid.*, pp. 53–55.

[56] *Ibid.*, p. 59.

[57] See appendix table 1.

[58] "Current Conditions in Mexico," Association of Producers of Petroleum in Mexico (Unpublished manuscript, México, D.F., June 24, 1933).

[59] See appendix table 2.

[60] *El universal*, Apr. 10, 1932.

[61] Clark, *op. cit.*, p. 23.

[62] Moisés Poblete Troncoso, *El movimiento obrera latinoamericano* (México, D.F., 1946), pp. 216–217.

[63] Clark, *op. cit.*, p. 26.

[64] *Ibid.*, pp. 35–36.

[65] *Ibid.*, pp. 40–50.

[66] Parkes, *op. cit.*, p. 363.

[67] Clark, *op. cit.*, p. 60.

[68] *Ibid.*, pp. 70–74.

[69] *Ibid.*, p. 74.

[70] *Ibid.*, pp. 101–103.

[71] Poblete Troncoso, *op. cit.*, pp. 226–227.

[72] Parkes, *op. cit.*, p. 394.

[73] *Ibid.*, pp. 396–397.

[74] *Ibid.*, pp. 391–392, 398–399.

[75] *Ibid.*, p. 399.

[76] Gilberto Bosques, *The National Revolutionary Party of Mexico and the Six-Year Plan* (México, D.F., 1937), pp. 157–158.

[77] *Ibid.*, p. 165.

[78] *Ibid.*, p. 166.

[79] *Excélsior*, Feb. 10, 1936.

[80] *Ibid.*, Feb. 12, 1936.

[81] *Ibid.*, Sept. 1, 1936.

[82] Poblete Troncoso, *op. cit.*, pp. 229–230.

[83] *Ibid.*, p. 230.

[84] Alejandro Carrillo, *The Mexican People and the Oil Companies* (México, D.F., 1938).

[85] *El conflicto del petróleo en México, 1937–1938*, Universidad Obrera de México (México, D.F., n.d.), pp. 9–15. Information also obtained in correspondence with the general executive committee of the syndicate.

[86] Mario Sousa, "La recuperación de la economía nacional," México, Secretaría de Educación Pública, *Sobre el Petróleo de México* (México, D.F., 1938), pp. 82–83.

[87] *El conflicto del petróleo en México, 1937–1938*, pp. 11–13.

[88] *Ibid.*, p. 11.

[89] *Mexico's Oil*, p. 523. See also Mario Sousa, *op. cit.*, pp. 89–91.

[90] *Mexico's Oil*, pp. 5, 591–602.

[91] *Ibid.*, p. 795.

[92] *Ibid.*, pp. 807–843.

[93] *Ibid.*, pp. 847–873.

[94] *Diario oficial*, Mar. 19, 1938.

[95] *Mexico's Oil*, p. 84.

NOTES TO CHAPTER III

[1] Jesús Silva Herzog, *El pensamiento económico en México* (México, D.F., 1947), p. 110.

[2] President Cárdenas' Message to the Nation, Mar. 18, 1938. See *Mexico's Oil* (México, D.F., 1940), pp. 877–879.

[3] *Diplomatic Notes Exchanged between the Mexican and British Governments on Account of the Oil Industry Expropriation* (México, D.F., 1938), pp. 13–14.

[4] José López Portillo, *Exposición objectivo del plan sexenal* (México, D.F., 1938), p. 67.

[5] *Sobre el petróleo de México*, México, Secretaría de Educación Pública (México, D.F., 1938). This was a series of lectures given in the week of March 14 to 18, 1938.

[6] F. Bach and M. de la Peña, *México y su petróleo, síntesis histórica* (México, D.F., 1938), pp. 74–75.

[7] *La prensa*, May 21, 1934.

[8] *El conflicto del petróleo en México, 1937–1938* (México, D.F., n.d.), p. 78.

[9] López Portillo, *op. cit.*, p. 67.

[10] *Mexico's Oil*, p. 476.

[11] *Ibid.*, p. 592.

[12] *Ibid.*, p. 591.

[13] *Ibid.*, p. 592.

[14] Silva Herzog, *op. cit.*, p. 99.

[15] *Mexico's Oil*, p. 591.

[16] *Oil: Mexico's Position*, Mexico, Bureau of Information (Feb., 1940), pamphlet distributed by the consulate general of Mexico in New York.

[17] Joseph E. Pogue, "Oil and the Americas," address delivered June 22, 1944, before the Inter-American Institute of the University of North Carolina.

[18] *Anuario estadístico del comercio exterior de los Estados Unidos Mexicanos.*

[19] *Mexico's Oil*, pp. 591–592.

[20] *El conflicto del petróleo en México, 1937–1938*, pp. 47–50.

[21] *Diplomatic Notes Exchanged between the Mexican and British Governments on Account of the Oil Industry Expropriation*, pp. 13–14.

[22] Alejandro Carrillo, *The Mexican People and the Oil Companies* (México, D.F., 1938).

[23] *El conflicto del petróleo en México, 1937–1938.*

[24] Antonio Gómez Robelado, *The Bucareli Agreements and International Law* (México, D.F., 1940). See also *La cuestión petrolera*, Sindicato de Trabajadores Petroleros de la República Mexicana (México, D.F., n.d.), p. 30.

[25] *El plan sexenal del partido Nacional Revolucionario* (México, D.F., 1934), pp.

52–54. Also Gilberto Bosques, *The National Revolutionary Party of Mexico and the Six-Year Plan* (México, D.F., 1937), p. 166.

[26] *Mexico's Oil*, p. 94.

[27] Bach and de la Peña, *op. cit.*, p. 75.

[28] R. H. K. Marett, *An Eye-Witness of Mexico* (London, 1939), pp. 223–224.

[29] Lázaro Cárdenas, *Address Made before the First General Ordinary Congress of the Confederation of Mexican Workers, February 24, 1938* (México, D.F., 1938).

[30] *Loc. cit.*

[31] *Mexico's Oil*, p. 591.

[32] *El nacional*, June 13, 1939.

[33] Bach and de la Peña, *op. cit.*, p. 75. See also José Castillo Silva, "La expropiación de los bienes de las empresas petroleras y su justificación jurídico-económica" (Unpublished thesis for degree of Licenciado en Derecho, Universidad Nacional Autónoma de México, 1938).

NOTES TO CHAPTER IV

[1] Jesús Silva Herzog, *Petróleo mexicano* (México, D.F., 1941), p. 123.

[2] George Wythe, *Industry in Latin America* (New York, 1945), p. 288.

[3] J. H. Plenn, *Mexico Marches* (New York, 1939), p. 45.

[4] *Diario oficial*, Jan. 8, 1926.

[5] *Ibid.*, Jan. 26, 1934.

[6] *Ibid.*, Mar. 2, 1937.

[7] *El nacional*, Mar. 3, 1938.

[8] José S. Noriega, *Influencia de los hidrocarburos en la industrialización de México* (México, D.F., 1944), p. 225.

[9] *Excélsior*, Mar. 20, 1938.

[10] *Diario oficial*, Mar. 30, 1938.

[11] *Ibid.*, July 20, 1938.

[12] *Loc. cit.*

[13] Statement of Jesús Silva Herzog, general manager of the Distribuidora, quoted in *El nacional*, June 13, 1939.

[14] *Loc. cit.*

[15] *El nacional*, Dec. 4, 1946.

[16] *El popular*, July 24, 1944.

[17] *Seminario judicial de la federación*, vol. 88, pp. 1436–1443.

[18] *Anuario estadístico del comercio exterior, 1947*, p. 6.

[19] *Diario oficial*, Dec. 31, 1940.

[20] *Excélsior*, Jan. 22, 1939.

[21] *El nacional*, Feb. 19, 1939; *Excélsior*, Feb. 20, 1939.

[22] *Excélsior*, Feb. 22, 1939.

[23] I. M. Quintana, *Mexican Oil, a Statement of the Facts* (México, D.F., 1940).

[24] *Memoria, 1939–1940*, pp. 269–270.

[25] *Loc. cit.* See also *Excélsior*, Apr. 20, 1939.

[26] *Excélsior*, Nov. 25, 1939.

[27] *Diario oficial*, Aug. 9, 1940.

[28] Silva Herzog, *Petróleo mexicano*, p. 236.

[29] *Diario oficial*, Apr. 29, 1942.

[30] *Ibid.*, Dec. 31, 1946.

[31] L. J. Logan, "Mexico Looks Ahead with Pemex," *The Oil Weekly*, International Section, Nov. 5, 1945, pp. 16–20.

[32] *Diario oficial*, Nov. 9, 1940; June 18, 1941.

[33] *Ibid.*, Dec. 30, 1941.

[34] *El universal*, June 14, 1946.

[35] *El nacional*, May 11, 1947.

[36] *Ibid.*, May 6, 1941; *La prensa*, May 7, 1941.

[37] *Memoria, 1945–1946,* p. 260.

[38] *El nacional,* Mar. 1, 1947; New York *Times,* Mar. 1, 1947.

[39] *Diario oficial,* Feb. 2, 1943.

[40] *Memoria, 1939–1940; 1946–1947,* p. 145.

[41] *Excélsior,* June 18, 1945.

[42] *Diario oficial,* July 29, 1946.

[43] *Oil and Gas Journal,* Aug. 3, 1946, p. 62.

[44] *Journal of Commerce,* Sept. 8, 1947.

[45] *World Oil,* International Section, May, 1948, p. 282. See also *Oil and Gas Journal,* Apr. 22, 1948, p. 61; *Novedades,* Apr. 23, 1948.

[46] *Oil and Gas Journal,* Mar. 31, 1949, p. 60.

[47] *Ibid.,* Mar. 3, 1949, p. 46; Apr. 21, 1949, p. 124.

[48] *Ibid.,* Sept. 8, 1949; *National Petroleum News,* July 27, 1949, pp. 7, 20.

NOTES TO CHAPTER V

[1] *Mexico's Oil* (México, D.F., 1940), pp. 9–11.

[2] Robert Glass Cleland, *The Mexican Yearbook, 1920–1921* (Los Angeles, 1922), pp. 290–297.

[3] Compiled from Bureau of Mines, *Minerals Yearbook.*

[4] Ruth Sheldon, "Poza Rica Field Backbone of Oil Industry in Mexico," *Oil and Gas Journal,* May 25, 1939, p. 104.

[5] *Ibid.,* p. 26.

[6] *Loc. cit.*

[7] *World Oil,* Sec. 2, July, 1948, p. 81.

[8] Cleland, *op. cit.,* pp. 303–306.

[9] *World Oil,* Sec. 2, July, 1948, p. 81.

[10] Sheldon, *op. cit.,* p. 29.

[11] Pemex records and Miguel Manterola, *La industria del petróleo en México* (México, D.F., 1938), p. 112.

[12] *World Oil,* Sec. 2, July, 1948, p. 81.

[13] *Loc. cit.*

[14] *Excélsior,* Aug. 11, 1948.

[15] *World Oil,* July 15, 1951, p. 160.

[16] *Loc. cit.*

[17] *Boletín de minas y petróleo,* Oct., 1939–June, 1941, pp. 273–276.

[18] Sheldon, *op. cit.,* p. 104.

[19] New York *Times,* Mar. 27, 1938.

[20] Harlow S. Person, *Mexican Oil* (New York, 1942), pp. 64–65.

[21] New York *Times,* Feb. 1, July 23, 1939.

[22] *Memoria, 1939–1940.*

[23] *Anuario estadístico del comercio exterior de los Estados Unidos Mexicanos, 1937* and *1938.*

[24] *Memoria, 1941–1942,* p. 143.

[25] *Anuario estadístico del comercio exterior, 1937* and *1938.*

[26] Sheldon, *op. cit.,* p. 29.

[27] Ruth Sheldon, "Mexico Faced Many Problems in Operating Refineries," *Oil and Gas Journal,* May 18, 1939, pp. 39–41.

[28] *Ibid.,* p. 50.

[29] *Ibid.,* p. 40.

[30] *Desarrollo de la economía nacional, 1939–1947, México, Secretaría de Economía* (Mexico, D.F., 1947), pp. 54–57.

[31] *Mexico's Oil,* p. 127.

[32] *Informe anual,* Mar. 18, 1952.

[33] *World Oil,* International Section, Aug. 4, 1947, pp. 13–14.

[34] John J. Slattery, "Mexican Oil in Danger," *Mexican American Review,* Aug., 1947, p. 12.

[35] José S. Noriega, *Influencia de los hidrocarburos en la industrialización de México* (Mexico, D.F., 1944), p. 80.

[36] O. B. Irizarry and Wayne Rives, "Mexico Today, Exploration and Production," *Oil and Gas Journal*, Nov. 2, 1946, p. 44.

[37] Curtis Vinson, "Desulfurization Project Planned for Poza Rica Field," *Oil and Gas Journal*, Jan. 19, 1946, p. 54.

[38] *Informe anual*, Mar. 18, 1946.

[39] Three were reported by Pemex for 1945 and seven were reported for 1947–1950 by *World Oil*, July 15, 1949, p. 89, and July 15, 1951, p. 160.

[40] *Informe anual*, Mar. 18, 1949.

[41] Jorge D. Cumming, "El problema de las reservas petroleras de México," *Servicio de información*, Jan., 1948, pp. 82–84.

[42] *Informe anual*, Mar. 18, 1949.

[43] *Excélsior*, Aug. 21, 1947; *Journal of Commerce*, Sept. 8, 1947.

[44] *World Oil*, International Section, May, 1948, pp. 128, 282; *Novedades*, Apr. 23, 1948.

[45] *Oil and Gas Journal*, Jan. 29, 1948, p. 226.

NOTES TO CHAPTER VI

[1] Robert Glass Cleland, *The Mexican Yearbook, 1920–1921* (Los Angeles, 1922), p. 292.

[2] *Ibid.*, p. 315. Estimate from *U.S. Commerce Reports*, Nov. 7, 1921.

[3] *Mexico's Oil* (México, D.F., 1940), pp. 113–116. A study made for the Secretaría de Hacienda y Crédito Público of Mexico shows that in December, 1937, there were twenty-one refineries of all types in Mexico with a combined input capacity of about 310,000 barrels a day. (See Miguel Manterola, *La industria del petróleo en México* [México, D.F., 1938], pp. 59–61.) However, this figure is in serious error, according to other sources. (See *Boletín de minas y petróleo*, Oct., 1939–June, 1941, p. 286.) The error may be due to the inclusion of obsolete and unusable equipment.

[4] *Mexico's Oil*, pp. 113–117; *Informe anual*, Mar. 18, 1939.

[5] Jesús Silva Herzog, *Petróleo mexicano* (México, D.F., 1941), p. 191.

[6] *Memoria, 1939–1940*, p. 258.

[7] Ruth Sheldon, "Mexico Faced Many Problems in Operating Refineries," *Oil and Gas Journal*, May 18, 1939, p. 39.

[8] *Informe anual*, Mar. 18, 1939.

[9] *Ibid*, Mar. 18, 1941.

[10] *Loc. cit.*

[11] Sheldon, *op. cit.*, p. 40.

[12] *Ibid.*, p. 41.

[13] *Loc. cit.*

[14] *Memoria, 1939–1940*, p. 258.

[15] *Informe anual*, Mar. 18, 1941.

[16] *Ibid.*, Mar. 18, 1940.

[17] C. O. Wilson, "Expropriation Brings Changes in Mexican Operations and Markets," *Oil and Gas Journal*, Oct. 16, 1941, pp. 24–25.

[18] New York *Times*, Mar. 2, 1944.

[19] *Informe anual*, Mar. 18, 1947.

[20] *Another Step Forward*, Petróleos Mexicanos (México, D.F., n.d.), pp. 26, 48–49.

[21] *Ibid.*, p. 5.

[22] *Ibid.*, p. 25.

[23] Curtis Vinson, "Mexico Slated to Have One of World's Largest Refineries," *Oil and Gas Journal*, Jan. 5, 1946, pp. 42–43.

[24] *Oil and Gas Journal*, Apr. 1, 1948, p. 104; *World Oil*, Dec., 1949, p. 48.

[25] Antonio J. Bermúdez, "Dictamen relativo al estado financiero de Petróleos Mexicanos," *El economista*, Jan., 1947, pp. 42–43.

[26] *Oil and Gas Journal,* Apr. 1, 1948, p. 104; *Informe anual,* Mar. 18, 1949.

[27] Carlos Corcuera, "Organization and Operation of the Refining Division of Petróleos Mexicanos," *Oil and Gas Journal,* Dec. 28, 1946, p. 231.

[28] Pemex records.

[29] Compiled from *Anuario estadístico del comercio exterior, 1938–1948.*

[30] *Desarrollo de la economía national,* 1939–1947, México, Secretaría de Economía (México, D.F., 1947), pp. 53–55.

[31] Based on data from Pemex records.

[32] *Compendio estadístico, 1948,* p. 128.

NOTES TO CHAPTER VII

[1] Based on data from *Compendio estadístico, 1948,* pp. 155–156.

[2] *Memoria, 1939–1940,* pp. 255–256.

[3] *Memoria, 1937–1938,* p. 22; *1938–1939,* pp. 25–26.

[4] *Mexico's Oil* (México, D.F., 1940), p. 157.

[5] *Boletín de minas y petróleo,* Oct., 1939–June, 1941, p. 287.

[6] *Mexico's Oil,* pp. 162–163.

[7] *Ibid.,* p. 165.

[8] *Ibid.,* pp. 167–171.

[9] *Ibid.,* pp. 170–172.

[10] *Loc. cit.*

[11] *Informe anual,* Mar. 18, 1941.

[12] *Memoria, 1937–1940.*

[13] *Oil and Gas Journal,* Apr. 1, 1948, p. 104.

[14] *Informe anual,* Mar. 18, 1949.

[15] *Memoria, 1946–1947,* p. 127.

[16] *World Oil,* July 15, 1951, p. 162.

[17] *Loc. cit.*

[18] *Informe anual,* Mar. 18, 1939.

[19] Jesús Silva Herzog, *Petróleo mexicano* (México, D.F., 1941), p. 207.

[20] *Ibid.,* p. 191.

[21] *Informe anual,* Mar. 18, 1940.

[22] *El nacional,* June 22, 1946.

[23] Silva Herzog, *op. cit.,* pp. 207–208.

[24] *Informe anual,* Mar. 18, 1942.

[25] *El nacional,* Aug. 6, 1938.

[26] *Ibid.,* June 22, 1946.

[27] National Industrial Conference Board, *The Petroleum Almanac* (New York, 1946), p. 308.

[28] O. B. Irizarry and Wayne Rives, "Mexico Today, Exploration and Production," *Oil and Gas Journal,* Nov. 2, 1946, p. 43.

[29] *Informe anual,* Mar. 18, 1944; Mar. 18, 1952.

[30] Estimate of petroleum products moved is based on gasoline and fuel oil shipments compiled from *Revista de estadística, 1938–1945,* and estimate of general freight movements is based on data from *Memoria, 1946–1947,* p. 384, and from *Anuario estadístico, 1942,* p. 1056.

[31] *Excélsior,* May 15, 1944.

[32] *El nacional,* Feb. 3, 1945.

[33] *El popular,* Mar. 16, 1948.

[34] *Informe anual,* Mar. 18, 1949.

[35] Figures for all shipments of petroleum products for 1947 are not available. The estimate for 1947 is based on 1937–1941 experience.

[36] Estimates of total rail shipments were based on the assumption that gasoline and fuel oil constituted 55 per cent of the total traffic in petroleum products. To convert tonnage to barrels in ocean traffic, an average specific gravity for petroleum products

of 0.90 was assumed. See appendix table 9 for data concerning rail shipments. Pipeline carriage is based on Pemex data giving sources of crude oil received by each refinery.

[37] José S. Noriega, *Influencia de los hidrocarburos en la industrialización de México* (México, D.F., 1944), pp. 178–179.

[38] *Mexico's Oil*, p. 159.

[39] *Informe anual*, Mar. 18, 1941.

[40] Irizarry and Rives, *op. cit.*, p. 43; *Informe anual*, Mar. 18, 1949.

[41] *Informe anual*, Mar. 18, 1948.

[42] *Another Step Forward*, Petróleos Mexicanos (México, D.F., n.d.), p. 43.

[43] *Quinto censo de población, resumen general* (México, D.F., 1934), pp. 16–18.

NOTES TO CHAPTER VIII

[1] *Anuario estadístico del comercio exterior, 1939–1947.*

[2] Basic data from Pemex records.

[3] *Anuario estadístico del comercio exterior, 1938–1948.*

[4] Appendix tables 11 and 12.

[5] Appendix tables 13, 14, and 15; *Informe anual*, Mar. 18, 1949; Mar. 18, 1951.

[6] Pemex records.

[7] *Another Step Forward*, Petróleos Mexicanos (México, D.F., n.d.), p. 5.

[8] *Mexico's Oil* (México, D.F., 1940), p. 178.

[9] *Compendio estadístico, 1947*, pp. 434–436.

[10] Based on data in appendix tables 13, 14, and 15.

[11] Based on data in *Compendio estadístico, 1948*, p. 222.

[12] *Compendio estadístico, 1948*, p. 223.

[13] *Informe anual*, Mar. 18, 1941.

[14] *Compendio estadístico, 1948*, p. 128.

[15] *Diario oficial*, Sept. 17, 1946.

[16] Ruth Sheldon, "Marketing Harasses Mexican Oil Industry Officials," *Oil and Gas Journal*, June 1, 1939, p. 20.

[17] *Excélsior*, May 28, 1944; *El nacional*, Sept. 28, 1944.

[18] *Excélsior*, Jan. 11, 19, 22, 24, 1945.

[19] *El nacional*, July 2, 1946.

[20] *Excélsior*, July 16, 1946.

[21] *Ibid.*, July 20, 1946.

[22] *Ibid.*, Sept. 11, 1940.

[23] Pemex records.

[24] Pemex records.

[25] Appendix tables 16 and 17.

[26] Compiled from *Anuario estadístico del comercio exterior, 1946–1948.*

[27] Basic data for these comparisons are from American Petroleum Institute, *Facts and Figures, 1941*, pp. 20–23, and *1952*, p. 244, and from National Industrial Conference Board, *Petroleum Almanac* (New York, 1946), p. 342.

[28] D. M. Phelps, "Petroleum Regulation in Temperate South America," *American Economic Review*, Mar., 1939, p. 49.

NOTES TO CHAPTER IX

[1] *Anuario estadístico del comercio exterior, 1938.*

[2] New York *Times*, Mar. 27, 1938.

[3] *Ibid.*, Apr. 1, 1938.

[4] Harlow S. Person, *Mexican Oil* (New York, 1942), pp. 64–65; *Nation*, Nov. 30, 1940.

[5] Jesús Silva Herzog, *Petróleo mexicano* (México, D.F., 1941), pp. 198–204.

[6] *Excélsior*, Jan. 30, 1940.

[7] Silva Herzog, *op. cit.*, pp. 198–199.

[8] *Ibid.*, p. 199; Ruth Sheldon, "Marketing Harasses Mexican Oil Industry Officials," *Oil and Gas Journal*, June 1, 1939, pp. 18–19.

[9] Sheldon, *op. cit.*, p. 19.

[10] Silva Herzog, *op. cit.*, pp. 199–200.

[11] *Memoria, 1939–1940*, p. 275.

[12] Silva Herzog, *op. cit.*, pp. 203–204.

[13] *Ibid.*, pp. 204–205.

[14] *Revista de estadística*, June, 1940.

[15] *Anuario estadístico del comercio exterior, 1939.*

[16] *Foreign Commerce Yearbook, 1949*, U.S. Department of Commerce (Washington, 1951), p. 377.

[17] *Wall Street Journal*, Sept. 5, 1940.

[18] *Excélsior*, Feb. 27, 1940.

[19] New York *Times*, Apr. 3, 1940.

[20] *Journal of Commerce*, May 31, 1941, p. 30.

[21] *Informe anual*, Mar. 18, 1941.

[22] *Anuario estadístico del comercio exterior, 1938, 1939*, and *1940.*

[23] *Ibid., 1947.*

[24] *Compendio estadístico, 1950*, p. 287.

[25] *El nacional*, July 28, 1942.

[26] *Petroleum*, U.S. Tariff Commission, War Changes in Industry Series, no. 17 (Washington, 1946), p. 34.

[27] *Excélsior*, Aug. 13, 1948.

[28] The *Anuario estadístico del comercio exterior* shows imports of 86 million pesos and exports of only 57 million pesos in 1947. The export figure seems very low in view of the 121 million pesos given by Pemex.

[29] Basic data from *Anuario estadístico del comercio exterior*. See appendix table 19.

[30] See appendix tables 20 and 21.

[31] See *Anuario estadístico del comercio exterior* for the years 1938–1950.

[32] See table 24 and *Compendio estadístico, 1951*, pp. 215–216.

[33] Basic data from records of Pemex.

NOTES TO CHAPTER X

[1] Art. 76. See also Gilberto Bosques, *The National Revolutionary Party of Mexico and the Six-Year Plan* (México, D.F., 1937), pp. 157–158.

[2] See report of the expert commission in *Mexico's Oil* (México, D.F., 1940), pp. 189 ff.

[3] *El conflicto del petróleo en México*, Universidad Obrera de México (México, D.F., n.d.), pp. 16–18.

[4] *Mexico's Oil* (México, D.F., 1940), pp. 721–725.

[5] Data for 1936 from records of Pemex.

[6] *Mexico's Oil*, pp. 725–734.

[7] *Ibid.*, pp. 201–203, 752.

[8] *Ibid.*, p. 753.

[9] *Ibid.*, p. 203.

[10] *Ibid.*, pp. 722–734.

[11] *Ibid.*, p. 209.

[12] *Ibid.*, p. 765.

[13] *Ibid.*

[14] *Ibid.*, p. 214.

[15] *Ibid.*, pp. 768–769.

[16] *Memoria, 1937–1938*, p. 20. Records of Pemex show that in 1937 wages and salaries amounted to 49.5 million pesos, and that the companies' contribution to the savings fund was 3.2 million pesos, or slightly more than 6 per cent.

[17] Records of Pemex.

[18] *Mexico's Oil*, p. 727.

[19] *Ibid.*, p. 206.

[20] *Ibid.*, p. 772.

[21] *Ibid.*, pp. 729–731.
[22] Records of Pemex.
[23] *Mexico's Oil*, pp. 759–765.
[24] *Ibid.*, p. 767.
[25] *Ibid.*, pp. 728 ff., 769 ff.
[26] Records of Pemex.
[27] *Mexico's Oil*, pp. 722, 734.
[28] Records of Pemex.
[29] *Mexico's Oil*, pp. 475, 734.
[30] *El nacional*, July 16, 1938.
[31] *Excélsior*, Aug. 4, 1938.
[32] *Ibid.*, Oct. 16, 1938.
[33] Jesús Silva Herzog, *Petróleo mexicano* (México, D.F., 1941), p. 214.
[34] *Excélsior*, Aug. 1, 1938.
[35] Miguel Manterola, *La industria del petróleo en México* (México, D.F., 1938), pp. 68–70.
[36] Silva Herzog, *op. cit.*, pp. 242–243.
[37] *Informe anual*, Mar. 18, 1941.
[38] Silva Herzog, *op. cit.*, pp. 232, 238.
[39] *Excélsior*, Jan. 5, 1940.
[40] New York *Times*, Jan. 19, 1940.
[41] Silva Herzog, *op. cit.*, pp. 245–253; *El nacional*, Feb. 29, 1940.
[42] Silva Herzog, *op. cit.*, pp. 255–260; *Excélsior*, Apr. 5, 1940.
[43] Silva Herzog, *op. cit.*, pp. 260–261.
[44] *Ibid.*, pp. 261–264.
[45] *Excélsior*, May 21, 1950.
[46] Silva Herzog, *op. cit.*, p. 268.
[47] *Ibid.*, pp. 269–271; *Excélsior*, July 25, 1940.
[48] Silva Herzog, *op. cit.*, p. 271.
[49] *Excélsior, El universal, El nacional*, July 26, 1940.
[50] *El universal*, July 27, 1940.
[51] *El nacional*, July 28, 1940.
[52] *Excélsior*, July 27, 1940.
[53] Silva Herzog, *op. cit.*, pp. 275–276.
[54] *El universal*, Aug. 4, 1940.
[55] *Excélsior*, Aug. 2, 7, 1940.
[56] *Ibid.*, Aug. 7, 1940.
[57] *Ibid.*, Aug. 10, 1940.
[58] *Ibid.*, Aug. 13, 1940.
[59] *Ibid.*, Sept. 23, 1940.
[60] *Ibid.*, Sept. 14, 1940.
[61] *La prensa*, Sept. 14, 1940.
[62] *El nacional* and *Excélsior*, Sept. 21, 1940.
[63] *La prensa*, Sept. 22, 1940.
[64] *El universal* and *Excélsior*, Sept. 29, 1940.
[65] *Excélsior*, Oct. 4, 1940.
[66] Silva Herzog, *op. cit.*, p. 284.
[67] *Ibid.*, pp. 285–294.
[68] *Ibid.*, pp. 302–304.
[69] *Excélsior*, Dec. 4, 1940.
[70] *El universal*, Dec. 25, 1940.
[71] *El nacional*, Jan. 12, 1941.
[72] Silva Herzog, *op. cit.*, p. 304.
[73] *La prensa*, Mar. 26, Apr. 5, 1941; *Excélsior*, Mar. 27, 1941.
[74] *La prensa*, May 10, 1941.
[75] *Excélsior*, June 1, 5, 11, 1941.

[76] *La prensa*, June 18, 1941.

[77] *Excélsior*, Sept. 8, 11, 26, 1941.

[78] See the open lette rof the principal labor groups dated Sept. 17, 1941, and published in *Excélsior*, Sept. 28, 1941.

[79] *Excélsior*, Sept. 6, 1941.

[80] *El nacional*, Oct. 1, 1941.

[81] *La prensa*, Oct. 8, 1941.

[82] *El conflicto del petróleo en México*, p. 29.

[83] *Excélsior*, Mar. 6, 1942.

[84] *Novedades*, Mar. 11, 1942.

[85] *Contrato colectivo de trabajo, 1942*, capítulo i.

[86] *Ibid.*, capítulo ii.

[87] *Ibid.*, capítulo viii.

[88] *Novedades*, June 8, 1942.

[89] *Ibid.*, Aug. 27, 1942.

[90] *Ibid.*, Nov. 17, 1942; *El universal*, Dec. 12, 1942.

[91] *Excélsior*, Apr. 22, 1943.

[92] *Ibid.*, Aug. 19, 1943.

[93] *Novedades*, Aug. 23, 1943.

[94] *Compendio estadístico, 1948*, p. 223.

[95] *El popular*, Sept. 24, 1943; *El nacional*, Sept. 25, 1943.

[96] *Excélsior*, Feb. 22, 1944.

[97] *Ibid.*, Feb. 27, 1944.

[98] *El nacional*, Mar. 18, 1944.

[99] Records of Pemex.

[100] *Excélsior*, Apr. 4, 17, 1945.

[101] *Ibid.*, Oct. 27, 1945.

[102] Manuel A. Hernández, "El fracaso en México de la expropiación petrolera es un valiosa enseñanza," *El economista*, Mar.–Apr., 1946, p. 121.

[103] *Excélsior*, Mar. 2, 3, 1946.

[104] Letter from the syndicate's Secretario del Exterior y Propaganda to the author, dated July 29, 1949.

[105] *El nacional*, July 11, 1946.

[106] *Compendio estadístico, 1948*, p. 223.

[107] *Excélsior*, July 16, 20, 1946.

[108] New York *Times*, Sept. 4, 5, 1946.

[109] *El nacional*, Sept. 5, 1946.

[110] New York *Times*, Nov. 28, 1946; *Excélsior*, Nov. 27, 1946.

[111] New York *Times*, Dec. 20, 1946.

[112] *El economista*, Jan., 1947, pp. 33–38.

[113] New York *Times*, Dec. 22, 1946.

[114] *Novedades*, Dec. 22, 1946.

[115] *Loc. cit.*

[116] *Excélsior*, Dec. 22, 24, 1946; *El popular*, Dec. 24, 1946.

[117] *El popular*, Dec. 24, 1946.

[118] *Loc. cit.*

[119] *Excélsior*, Dec. 26, 28, 1946.

[120] New York *Times*, Jan. 9, 1947.

[121] *El nacional*, June 1, 1947; *El popular*, June 2, 1947; *Excélsior*, June 2, 1947.

[122] *El popular*, June 3, 1947.

[123] *El nacional*, June 16, 1947.

[124] *Informe anual*, Mar. 18, 1948; Mar. 18, 1949.

[125] *El popular*, Apr. 10, 1948.

[126] See John Coe, "Recent Labor Developments in Mexico and the Caribbean," *Inter-American Economic Affairs*, Mar., 1948, p. 64.

[127] *El popular*, Sept. 25, 1948; *Excélsior*, Sept. 22, 24, 25, 27, 1948.

[128] Coe, *op. cit.*, p. 65; *El popular,* Aug. 20, 1948.

[129] *Excélsior,* Nov. 5, 9, 1948; Jan. 9, 1949.

[130] *El popular,* May 12, 1949.

[131] *Ibid.,* May 19, 21, 1949.

[132] *Ibid.,* May 29, 31, 1949.

[133] *Excélsior,* June 2, 4, 5, 1949.

[134] *Ibid.,* June 6, 9, 10, 11, 12, 1949.

[135] *Ibid.,* Dec. 4, 6, 8, 12, 1949.

[136] Pemex records.

[137] See Manuel A. Hernández, "Observaciones adicionales al informe del gerente de Petróleos Mexicanos," *El economista,* May 1, 1943, p. 35.

[138] *Anuario estadístico, 1942,* pp. 1298, 1301–1303.

[139] *Ibid.,* pp. 1299, 1302–1303.

[140] Silva Herzog, *op. cit.,* pp. 237–238.

[141] *Excélsior,* Jan. 12, 1939.

[142] *Ibid.,* Jan. 19, 1939.

[143] *El nacional,* Jan. 25, Feb. 9, 1939.

[144] *Excélsior,* Jan. 25, 1939.

[145] *Ibid.,* Oct. 23, 28, 30, Nov. 5, 1945.

[146] Coe, *op. cit.,* pp. 59–60.

[147] *Loc. cit.*

NOTES TO CHAPTER XI

[1] Jesús Silva Herzog, *Petróleo mexicano* (México, D.F., 1941), pp. 173–186.

[2] *Memoria, 1941–1942,* pp. 145–146.

[3] *Boletín de legislación y administración,* Nov.–Dec., 1947, pp. 21–25.

[4] Silva Herzog, *op. cit.,* p. 291.

[5] Pemex records.

[6] *Informe anual,* Mar. 18, 1941.

[7] *Diario oficial,* Dec. 31, 1940.

[8] *Ibid.,* Dec. 2, 1944.

[9] Speech of General Director Antonio J. Bermúdez quoted in *Revista de economía continental,* Nov. 20, 1947, p. 603.

[10] *Loc. cit.*

[11] Antonio J. Bermúdez, "Dictamen relativo al estado financiero de Petróleos Mexicanos," *El economista,* Jan., 1947, pp. 39–46.

[12] Based on data from *Compendio estadístico, 1948,* p. 222.

[13] Pemex records.

[14] *Informe anual,* Mar. 18, 1942.

[15] *Mexico's Oil* (México, D.F., 1940), p. 245.

[16] Pemex records.

[17] Jorge D. Cumming, "El problema de las reservas petroleras de México," *Servicio de información,* Jan., 1948, pp. 83–84.

[18] Published in *El nacional,* Nov. 26, 1946; Nov. 29, 1946; Aug. 7, 1948.

[19] Antonio J. Bermúdez, *op. cit.,* p. 42.

[20] *Loc. cit.*

[21] *Journal of Commerce,* Sept. 8, 1947.

[22] *Oil and Gas Journal,* Apr. 22, 1948; Mar. 31, 1949.

NOTES TO CHAPTER XII

[1] *Compendio estadístico, 1947,* p. 533.

[2] *Mexico's Oil* (México, D.F., 1940), p. 476.

[3] *Petroleum,* U.S. Tariff Commission, War Changes in Industry Series, no. 17 (Washington, 1946), p. 86.

[4] Sanford A. Mosk, *Industrial Revolution in Mexico* (Berkeley and Los Angeles, 1950), pp. 19, 21–23, 32–35.

[5] *Anuario estadístico del comercio exterior, 1938.*

[6] See Mosk, *op. cit.,* pp. 274–275.

[7] *Anuario estadístico, 1942,* pp. 1234, 1238.

[8] *Revista de estadística,* Apr., 1937; Apr., 1938.

[9] *Anuario estadístico, 1942,* p. 960.

[10] Mosk, *op. cit.,* p. 279.

[11] *Compendio estadístico, 1948,* p. 222.

[12] *Technological Audit of Selected Mexican Industries,* Armour Research Foundation (Ann Arbor, 1946), p. 11; also speech of General Director Antonio J. Bermúdez quoted in *Oil and Gas Journal,* Mar. 17, 1949, p. 59.

[13] *Compendio estadístico, 1947,* p. 469.

[14] *Loc. cit.*

[15] *Mexico's Oil,* pp. 147–148.

[16] Appendix table 13.

[17] *Compendio estadístico, 1948,* p. 128.

[18] *Ibid.,* p. 157.

[19] Charles G. Fenwick, *International Law* (3d ed.; New York, 1948), pp. 292–293.

[20] Wendell C. Gordon, *The Economy of Latin America* (New York, 1950), p. 201.

[21] Edgar Turlington, "Foreign Investments," *Annals of the American Academy of Political and Social Sciences* (Mar., 1940), p. 106.

[22] D. M. Phelps, "Petroleum Regulation in Temperate South America," *American Economic Review,* Mar., 1939, p. 49.

[23] *Ibid.,* p. 50.

[24] *World Oil,* July 15, 1950, p. 104.

[25] *Ibid.,* p. 124.

[26] *World Oil,* July 15, 1950, p. 128; New York *Times,* Dec. 9, 1950.

[27] New York *Times,* Aug. 13, 1950; Nov. 25, 1950.

[28] *Desarrollo de la economía nacional, 1939–1947,* México, Secretaría de Economía (México, D.F., 1947), p. 50.

[29] Gordon, *op. cit.,* pp. 186 ff.

[30] Cited in Gordon, *op. cit.,* p. 195.

[31] Mosk, *op. cit.,* pp. 21 ff.

[32] Gordon, *op. cit.,* p. 196.

[33] *Mexico's Oil,* pp. 470–474, 476.

[34] See Jesús Silva Herzog, *El pensamiento económico en México* (México, D.F., 1947), pp. 99–100.

BIBLIOGRAPHY

Bibliography

BOOKS

Armour Research Foundation. *Technological Audit of Selected Mexican Industries.* Ann Arbor: Illinois Institute of Technology, 1946.

Association of Producers of Petroleum in Mexico. "Current Conditions in Mexico." Unpublished manuscript. México, D.F., June 24, 1933.

Bach, F., and M. de la Peña. *México y su petróleo, síntesis histórica.* México, D.F.: Editorial México Nuevo, 1938.

Bancroft, Hubert Howe. *History of Mexico.* New York: The Bancroft Company, 1914.

Bosques, Gilberto. *The National Revolutionary Party of Mexico and the Six-Year Plan.* México, D.F.: Bureau of Foreign Information of the National Revolutionary Party, 1937.

Callcott, Wilfred Hardy. *Liberalism in Mexico, 1857–1929.* Stanford: Stanford University Press, 1931.

Cárdenas, Lázaro. *Address Made before the First General Ordinary Congress of the Confederation of Mexican Workers, February 24, 1938.* México, D.F.: D.A.P.P., 1938.

——. *Messages to the Mexican Nation on the Oil Question.* México, D.F.: D.A.P.P., 1938.

Carrillo, Alejandro. *The Mexican People and the Oil Companies.* México, D.F.: D.A.P.P., 1938.

Castillo Silva, José. "La expropiación de los bienes de las empresas petroleras y su justificación jurídico-económica." Unpublished thesis for the degree of Licenciado en Derecho. Universidad Nacional Autónoma de México, 1938.

Chapman, Charles E. *Republican Hispanic America.* New York: Macmillan, 1937.

Clark, Marjorie Ruth. *Organized Labor in Mexico.* Chapel Hill: University of North Carolina Press, 1934.

Cleland, Robert G. *The Mexican Yearbook, 1920–1921.* Los Angeles: Mexican Yearbook Publishing Company, 1922.

Fenwick, Charles G. *International Law.* 3d ed. New York: Appleton-Century-Crofts, 1948.

García Granados, Jorge. *Los veneros del diablo.* México, D.F.: Ediciones Liberación, 1941.

Gómez Robelado, Antonio. *The Bucareli Agreements and International Law.* México, D.F.: The National University of Mexico Press, 1940.

Gordon, Wendell C. *The Economy of Latin America.* New York: Columbia University Press, 1950.

——. *The Expropriation of Foreign-Owned Property in Mexico.* Washington, D.C.: American Council on Public Affairs, 1941.

Gruening, Ernest. *Mexico and Its Heritage.* New York: Century, 1928.

Hackett, Charles Wilson. *The Mexican Revolution and the United States, 1910–1926.* World Peace Foundation Pamphlets, IX (1926). Boston: World Peace Foundation, 1926.

Hughlett, Lloyd J. *Industrialization of Latin America*. New York: McGraw-Hill, 1946.

Kirkpatrick, F. A. *Latin America, a Brief History*. New York: Macmillan, 1939.

Kluckhohn, Frank L. *The Mexican Challenge*. New York: Doubleday Doran, 1939.

López Portillo, José. *Exposición objetivo del plan sexenal*. México, D.F.: Tipográfica Sag, 1938.

Macdonald, Austin F. *Latin American Politics and Government*. New York: Crowell, 1949.

Manterola, Miguel. *La industria del petróleo en México*. México, D.F.: Secretaría de Hacienda y Crédito Público, 1938.

Marett, R. H. K. *An Eye-Witness of Mexico*. London: Oxford University Press, 1939.

Mexico. *Diplomatic Notes Exchanged between the Mexican and British Governments on Account of the Oil Industry Expropriation*. México, D.F.: D.A.P.P., 1938.

———. *Ley Federal de Trabajo*. México, D.F.: Editorial Stylo, 1948.

———. *Mexico's Oil*. México, D.F.: Mexican Government, 1940.

———. *El plan sexenal del partido Nacional Revolucionario*. México, D.F.: Partido Nacional Revolucionario, 1934.

———. *Quinto censo de población, resumen general*. México, D.F.: Talleres Gráficos, 1934.

———. *Seminario judicial de la federación*. Vol. 88, pp. 1436–1443.

———. *La verdad sobre la expropiación de los bienes de las empresas petroleras*. México, D.F.: Talleres Gráficos, 1940.

———. Bureau of Information. *Oil: Mexico's Position*. Pamphlet distributed by the consulate general of Mexico in New York. February, 1940.

———. Secretaría de Economía. *Desarrollo de la economía nacional, 1939–1947*. México, D.F.: Talleres Gráficos, 1947.

———. Secretaría de Economía Nacional. Departamento de Petróleo. *La industria petrolera mexicana, sus antecedentes y su estado actual*. México, D.F.: Talleres Gráficos, 1936.

———. Secretaría de Educación Pública. *Documentos de la revolución mexicana*. México, D.F.: Biblioteca Enciclopédica Popular, 1945.

———. ———. *Sobre el petróleo de México*. México, D.F.: D.A.P.P., 1938.

———. Secretaría de Industria, Comercio y Trabajo. *Documentos relacionados con la legislación petrolera mexicana*. México, D.F.: Talleres Gráficos, 1919.

———. ———. *Legislación petrolera*. México, D.F.: Talleres Gráficos, 1922.

Mosk, Sanford A. *Industrial Revolution in Mexico*. Berkeley and Los Angeles: University of California Press, 1950.

National Industrial Conference Board. *The Petroleum Almanac*. New York: 1946.

Noriega, José S. *Influencia de los hidrocarburos en la industrialización de México*. México, D.F.: Banco de México, 1944.

Parkes, Henry Bamford. *A History of Mexico*. Boston: Houghton Mifflin, 1938.

Person, Harlow S. *Mexican Oil*. New York: Harper, 1942.

Petróleos Mexicanos. *Another Step Forward*. México, D.F.: Talleres Gráficos, n.d.

Plenn, J. H. *Mexico Marches*. Indianapolis: Bobbs-Merrill, 1939.

Poblete Troncoso, Moisés. *El movimiento obrero latinoamericano*. México, D.F.: Fondo de Cultura Económica, 1946.

Pogue, Joseph E. "Oil and the Americas." An address by J. E. Pogue, vice-president of Chase National Bank, before the Inter-American Institute of the University of North Carolina at Chapel Hill on June 22, 1944.

Prewett, Virginia. *Reportage on Mexico*. New York: Dutton, 1941.

Puig Cadena, Fernando. *La expropiación petrolera.* México, D.F.: Universidad Nacional Autónoma de Mexico, Facultad de Derecho y Sciencias Sociales, 1939.

Quintana, I. M. *Mexican Oil, a Statement of the Facts.* Pamphlet. México, D.F.: no publisher, January, 1940.

Richberg, Donald. *The Mexican Oil Seizure.* New York: Arrow Press, n.d.

Rippy, J. Fred. *Latin America in World Politics.* New York: Crofts, 1938.

Rockwell, John A. *A Compilation of Spanish and Mexican Law.* New York: John S. Voorhies, 1851.

Silva Herzog, Jesús. *Un ensayo sobre la revolución mexicana.* México, D.F.: Ediciones Cuadernos Americanos, 1946.

————. *El pensamiento económico en México.* México, D.F.: Fondo de Cultura Económica, 1947.

————. *Petróleo mexicano.* México, D.F.: Fondo de Cultura Económica, 1941.

Sindicato de Trabajadores Petroleros de la República Mexicana. *La cuestión petrolera.* México, D.F.: Sindicato de Trabajadores Petroleros, n.d.

Standard Oil Company (New Jersey). *The Mexican Expropriations in International Law.* n.p.: Standard Oil Company (New Jersey), 1938.

Standard Oil Company of California. *Expropriation.* New York: Macben Press, 1938.

U. S. Department of Commerce. *Foreign Commerce and Navigation of the United States.* Wash.: Gov't Print. Off., 1948.

————. *United States Petroleum Refining, War and Postwar.* Wash.: Gov't Print. Off., 1947.

U. S. Tariff Commission. *Economic Controls and Commercial Policy in Mexico.* Wash.: Gov't Print. Off., 1946.

————. *Petroleum.* War Changes In Industry Series, no. 17. Wash.: Gov't Print. Off., 1946.

Universidad Obrera de México. *El conflicto del petróleo en México, 1937–1938.* México, D.F.: Universidad Obrera, n.d.

Weyl, Nathaniel and Sylvia. *The Reconquest of Mexico, The Years of Lázaro Cárdenas.* New York: Oxford University Press, 1939.

Wythe, George. *Industry in Latin America.* New York: Columbia University Press, 1945.

Zea, Leopoldo. *Apogeo y decadencia del positivismo en México.* México, D.F.: El Colegio de México, 1944.

————. *El positivismo en México.* México, D.F.: El Colegio de México, 1943.

ARTICLES

Bermúdez, Antonio J. "El conflicto de orden económico promovido por Petróleos Mexicanos," *El economista,* Jan., 1947.

————. "Dictamen relativo al estado financiero de Petróleos Mexicanos," *El economista,* Jan. 1947.

————. "Mexico's Program of Oil Expansion," *World Petroleum,* Jan., 1948.

Bullington, John P. "The Land and Petroleum Laws of Mexico," *American Journal of International Law,* XXII (1928), 50–69.

Burns, Warren W. "Mexico Making New Proposals for Return of Foreign Capital," *Oil and Gas Journal,* Mar. 25, 1948.

————. "Mexico Offers First Property for Private Development since 1938," *Oil and Gas Journal,* Aug. 3, 1946.

Coe, John. "Recent Labor Developments in Mexico and the Caribbean," *Inter-American Economic Affairs,* Mar., 1948.

Corcuera, Carlos. "Organization and Operation of Refining Division of Petróleos Mexicanos," *Oil and Gas Journal,* Dec. 28, 1946.

Cumming, Jorge D. "El problema de las reservas petroleras de México," *Servicio de información,* Jan., 1948.

Enríquez, Ernesto. "Problemas internacionales," *Cuadernos de política,* no. 3, 1942.

"Está resuelto el problema del petróleo?" *El economista,* May 1, 1942.

Hernández, Manuel A. "Discrepancias en la estadística de Petróleos Mexicanos," *El economista,* Apr.–May, 1948.

———. "El fracaso en México de la expropiación petrolera es una valiosa enseñanza," *El economista,* Mar.–Apr., 1946.

———. "La industria del petróleo en diciembre de 1941," *El economista,* Jan. 16, 1942.

———. "Observaciones adicionales al informe del gerente de Petróleos Mexicanos," *El economista,* May 1, 1943.

Irizarry, O. B., and Wayne Rives. "Mexico Today, Exploration and Production," *Oil and Gas Journal,* Nov. 2, 1946.

Logan, L. J. "Mexico Looks Ahead with Pemex," *The Oil Weekly,* International Section, Nov. 5, 1945.

———. "Pemex Plans Vigorous Exploration Program," *The Oil Weekly,* International Section, Nov. 5, 1945.

"Mas datos sobre el desastre de la industria petrolera," *El economista,* Aug., 1946.

"National Economy of Argentina," *Commercial Pan America,* XV (July–Aug., 1946).

"Ni un paso atrás en la resolución del problema petrolero," *El economista,* Nov.–Dec., 1946.

Phelps, D. M. "Petroleum Regulation in Temperate South America," *American Economic Review,* Mar., 1939.

"The Purposes and Ideals of the Mexican Revolution," *Annals of the American Academy of Political and Social Science,* Supplement, Jan., 1917.

"La reorganización de Petróleos Mexicanos," *El economista,* Jan., 1947.

Sheldon, Ruth. "Marketing Harasses Mexican Oil Industry Officials," *Oil and Gas Journal,* June 1, 1939.

———. "Mexico Faced Many Problems in Operating Refineries," *Oil and Gas Journal,* May 18, 1939.

———. "Poza Rica Field Backbone of Oil Industry in Mexico," *Oil and Gas Journal,* May 25, 1939.

Silva Herzog, Jesús. "La epopeya del petróleo en México," *La revista de economía,* Mar. 31, 1948.

Slattery, John J. "Mexican Oil in Danger," *Mexican American Review,* Aug., 1947.

Turlington, Edgar. "Foreign Investments," *Annals of the American Academy of Political and Social Science,* 1940.

Vinson, Curtis. "Desulfurization Project Planned for Poza Rica Field," *Oil and Gas Journal,* Jan. 19, 1946.

———. "Mexico Slated to Have One of World's Largest Refineries," *Oil and Gas Journal,* Jan. 5, 1946.

Wilson, C. O. "Expropriation Brings Changes in Mexican Operations and Markets," *Oil and Gas Journal,* Oct. 16, 1941.

PERIODICALS

Anuario estadístico de los Estados Unidos Mexicanos. Secretaría de Economía, Dirección General de Estadística.

Anuario estadístico del comercio exterior de los Estados Unidos Mexicanos. Secretaría de Economía, Dirección General de Estadística.

Boletín de legislación y administración. Secretaría de Hacienda y Crédito Público.

Boletín de minas y petróleo. Secretaría de Economía, Dirección General de Industrias Extractivas.

Compendio estadístico. Secretaría de Economía, Dirección General de Estadística.

Diario oficial. Mexican Government, México, D.F.

Excélsior. México, D.F.

Federal Reserve Bulletin. Federal Reserve Board, Washington, D.C.

Gráfico. México, D.F.

Informe anual. Petróleos Mexicanos.

Investigación económica. Escuela Nacional de Economía, México, D.F.

The Journal of Commerce. New York.

The Latin American News Letter. México, D.F.

Memoria. Secretaría de Economía.

El nacional. México, D.F.

National Petroleum News. Cleveland, Ohio.

New York *Times.* New York.

Novedades. México, D.F.

Oil and Gas Journal. Tulsa, Oklahoma.

El popular. México, D.F.

La prensa. México, D.F.

Review of the Economic Situation in Mexico. Banco Nacional de México, México, D.F.

Revista de economía continental. México, D.F.

Revista de estadística. Secretaría de Economía, Dirección General de Estadística.

Revista industrial. Secretaría de la Economía Nacional.

Servicio de información. Petróleos Mexicanos.

El universal. México, D.F.

The Wall Street Journal. New York.

World Oil. Houston, Texas.

INDEX

Index